AQUINO

MEL WHITE

WORD PUBLISHING
Dallas · London · Sydney · Singapore

AQUINO

Copyright © 1989 by Mel White

Library of Congress Cataloging in Publication Data

White, Mel, 1940–
    Aquino / Mel White.
        p.   cm.
    Bibliography: p.
    ISBN 0-8499-0670-9
    1. Aquino, Corazon Cojuangco. 2. Presidents—Philippines—
Biography. 3. Aquino, Benigno S. 4. Legislators—Philippines—
Biography. I. Title. II. Title: Aquino.
DS686.616.A65W45   1989
959.904'7'092—dc20
[B]   89-5776
                                        CIP

Printed in the United States of America
9801239 MP 987654321

To the courageous people of the Philippines like

Ninoy and Cory

who risk their lives daily in their nation's struggle
for peace and justice . . .

and to

good neighbors around the globe in
North America, Europe and Asia, who
understand the significance of the struggle
and have volunteered to help.

To

Lyla,
Erinn and Michael

best friends and family

With special thanks to

Ernie Owen

who had a good idea
and would not let it die.

"Salamat Po"
(Thank You!)

Doña Aurora Aquino
Senator Agapito A. Aquino
Justice Nestor B. Alampay
Jon Aranda
Myrna Arceo
Betty Go Belmonte
Feliciano "Sonny" Belmonte
Isaac Belmonte
Senator Helena Benitez
Teodoro Benigno
Bill Bussard
Bishop George Castro
Anthony Campolo
Charles Colson
George Drysdale
Dorothy Friesen
Jeff Garton
Jerry Huchel
Darrell Johnson
Arche Ligo
Archbishop Roger Mahony
Monina Mercado
Justice Cecilia Muñoz Palma
Cecil Pedilla
Stephen Perry
George Regas
Horacio Severino
Jaime Cardinal Sin
Sr. Christine Tan
Monsignor Antonio "Tony" Unson
Rolando Villacorte

Special Thanks to Nick Joaquin, Author
The Aquinos of Tarlac

The Archivists

Amelia E. Bautista
Rolando Luna
Olala Olibe
Ramona Sabalones

Michael White
Adoracion Bolos
Nancy E. Matawanan
Joseph Poyos

Mercy Servida
Edgardo J. Celis
Marqui Hood
JoAnn Ramirez
Lorna Tirol

The Archives and The Photo Sources

Benigno S. "Ninoy" Aquino, Jr. Foundation
Far Eastern Economic Review
Fookien Times Philippines Yearbook and the Star Publications
Malacañang Palace Archives, Photo Section and Press Office
Manila Bulletin, Manila Chronicle, Mr. & Ms. Publishing
National Archives of the Philippines
Office of the Presidential Press Secretary
Lopez Memorial Museum

Thy will be done! These words snatched me from the jaws of death. In Laur [Prison], I gave up my life and offered it to Him . . . picked up my cross and followed.

Senator Benigno S. Aquino, Jr.

When a bullet strikes you in the back of the head, the tendency is for the head to jerk back. So, the last thing that Ninoy saw, before his face slammed on the tarmac and the blood began to form in a pool around his head, was the sky, and the face of his Friend who had come to take him home.

President Corazon C. Aquino

The tyrant dies and his rule ends. The martyr dies and his rule begins.

Soren Kïerkegaard

The forces of repression and brutality can slay the dreamer, but not the dream. . . .

Coretta Scott King

I am sure that Ninoy is smiling at us now. We have proven him correct, that the Filipino is worth dying for. . . . Adding to Ninoy's joy is the knowledge that he pulled a fast one on me. Once again he has gone on his merry way and left me behind to pick up after him.

President Corazon C. Aquino

CONTENTS

INTRODUCTION
The Martyr and the President
(21 August 1983)

Some people suggest that I beg for mercy. But this I cannot in conscience do. I would rather die on my feet with honor, than live on bended knees in shame . . . .

Senator Benigno Aquino, Jr.

I pledged to my husband after I kissed him in his coffin that I would continue his work . . . .

President Corazon C. Aquino

At exactly 5:00 A.M., Sunday, 21 August 1983, the switchboard operator at the Grand Hotel in Taipei, Taiwan, dialed the room where Cory's husband, Benigno S. "Ninoy" Aquino, Jr., lay sleeping. The sun was just beginning to rise on the last day of Ninoy's short, productive life. He was fifty-one years old the day he died, and he was destined, or so many people thought, to be the next president of the Philippines. No Filipino, living or dead, had a more legitimate claim to that office.

In 1951, after distinguishing himself as a war correspondent in Korea for the *Manila Times*, Ninoy was awarded the Philippine Legion of Honor for Meritorious Service. He was just eighteen years old. It was the first time a local newspaperman had been so honored. Other "firsts" would follow. At twenty-two, he was the youngest mayor of Concepcion, his birthplace and hometown just fifty miles north of Manila. At twenty-eight, he became the youngest governor in the history of Tarlac Province. At thirty-four, Ninoy became the youngest senator in the Philippines and if they hadn't murdered him on that humid day in August, 1983, he probably would have become the youngest president in the history of the Philippines.

Ninoy's brother-in-law, ABC television correspondent Ken Kashi-wahara, was in a room adjacent to Ninoy's in Taipei's Grand Hotel. He was an eye-witness to everything that happened on that tragic day up until the time when khaki-clad soldiers boarded China Airline's Flight 811 and led Ninoy down the metal stairway to his death. There were dozens of newsmen and women on the plane. Hundreds of newspaper, newsmagazine, radio and television reports were filed describing the assassination and the events that followed. But only Kashiwahara's first person report in the *New York Times Magazine* tells what Ninoy Aquino did at the very beginning of his last day. Few members of the world's press thought it very important that Ninoy began the morning as he always began it, with a quite time of prayer and meditation.[1]

After the 5:00 A.M. wake-up call, Ninoy sat up on the edge of his bed and began to meditate upon the mysteries of Christ's life, death and resurrection. Ninoy would be the first to admit that there had been times in his earlier life when he had prayed ". . . more mechanically than with feeling."[2] Then Ferdinand Marcos gave Ninoy a special gift, seven years in prison. Why? Marcos and his cronies trumped up outrageous charges, including murder, to silence the courageous young senator . . . .

It would have been an election year in the Philippines and Senator Aquino was the only real opposition to President Marcos waiting in the wings. On Friday, 22 September 1972, Marcos used the greatly exaggerated threat of communist insurgency to proclaim a state of martial law, take dictatorial power over the people of the Philippines, and cancel the elections. Senator Aquino was the first man placed under arrest.

The garrison state that Ferdinand and Imelda Marcos ruled for the next thirteen and one-half years (with the uncritical support and generous military aid of the United States) was a terrible tragedy for the Philippines. But at least one good thing came from martial law. Senator Aquino "met Jesus." Without his time in prison, Ninoy might have gone on praying "mechanically" for years. But in his prison cell, something happened that revolutionized his life as much as his death revolutionized the lives of the Filipino people.

Someday reporters may tell the real story about the People Power Revolution in the Philippines and what gave Senator Ninoy Aquino and his wife Cory the strength and the courage to take the steps that began it. When they do, Ninoy himself will answer them in a letter he wrote from his prison cell at Fort Bonafacio to his friend Senator "Soc" Rodrigo:

"It was the life of Christ from birth to the Ascension. Suddenly, Jesus became a live human being. His life was to become my inspiration. Here was a God-Man who preached nothing but love and was rewarded with death. Here was a God-Man who had power over all creation but took the mockery of a crown of thorns with humility and patience. And for all his noble intentions, he was shamed, vilified, slandered and betrayed."

What happened in Ninoy's prison cell was a classic case of Christian conversion.[3] Martyrs and saints, common men, women, even children have known that moment when they experienced the presence of God in their lives in a whole new way. Ninoy was devout, a truly Christian believer, but something happened to him in Fort Bonafacio that made all the difference:

> It dawned on me how puny were my sufferings compared to him whose only purpose was to save mankind from eternal damnation.
>
> Then as if I heard a voice tell me: "Why do you cry? I have gifted you with consolations, honors and glory which have been denied to the millions of your countrymen. I made you the youngest war correspondent, presidential assistant, mayor, vice-governor, governor and Senator of the Republic, and I recall you never thanked me for all these gifts. I have given you a full life, a great wife and beautiful, lovable children. Now that I visit you with a slight desolation, you cry and whimper like a spoiled brat!"
>
> With this realization, I went down on my knees and begged his forgiveness. I know I was merely undergoing a test, maybe in preparation for another mission. I know everything that happens in this world is with his knowledge and consent. I knew he would not burden me with a load I could not carry. I therefore resigned myself to his will.
>
> To think, I have been praying the Lord's Prayer for three and a half decades without really understanding fully the words I mumbled. I repeated that prayer so mechanically that I never really knew what I was saying: Thy will be done on earth!
>
> Thy Will Be Done! These words snatched me from the jaws of death. In Laur [Prison], I gave up my life and offered it to him . . . picked up my cross and followed him.[4]

From that day, Ninoy had determined to follow in the footsteps of Jesus. In prison he "picked up his cross." He didn't know when he finished his prayers that steel gray morning in August, 1983, that he was about to carry that cross up his own Via Dolorosa, the "Way of Sadness," to the place where he would be put to death.

The world was amazed by the "bloodless" revolution in the Philippines. In fact, the "People Power" revolution was not bloodless at all. Blood was shed for all the people by one man walking in the footsteps of Jesus.

After his prayers, Ninoy made one last trans-Pacific telephone call to his wife, Maria Corazon "Cory" Aquino who was waiting anxiously in their exile home in Boston. In 1980, Ninoy had been released from prison for heart surgery in the United States. He, his wife, Cory, and their five children moved to Boston where Senator Aquino would teach at Harvard and at MIT. From his hotel room in Taipei, Ninoy was calling Cory and the children as he had promised before taking that last leg of his return trip to Manila.

The senator listened as Cory read the Bible to him. He spoke briefly with his children and then he cried. After hanging up the telephone, Ninoy sat down at his hotel desk and wrote each of his children one last letter.

For a long time I wondered what biblical passages Cory Aquino had read to her husband during the long distance call that day. Betty Go Belmonte, editor and publisher of the *Star* Newspapers in Manila, told me the answer, chapter and verse. Mrs. Belmonte had asked Cory the same question in a rare interview Mrs. Aquino granted shortly after Ninoy's death.

After saying good-bye at the airport in Boston, Cory and her family had returned to their home on Commonwealth Avenue. She sat down in the kitchen and opened their family Bible, hoping to find what she later called "a guidance," a message from God that would encourage and direct her husband. The Old Testament opened to the book of Jonah. Cory could not understand what that ancient prophet's three-day journey in the stomach of a whale could have to do with Ninoy.

Then she read St. Paul's letter to the Colossians, Chapter 4, verse 10. It says, "If Mark should meet you, welcome him with open arms." This was the passage she read to her husband over the telephone. Ninoy asked Cory what she thought God was saying to them. Cory answered that Mark could mean Marcos. [Note, in Tagalog, Cory and Ninoy's native language, the name Mark is spelled Marcos.] It could mean that President Marcos would see him. That was good news. She advised her husband "to keep cool." Then she decided that it would be best if Ninoy "read it for himself; so she gave him the chapter and the verse . . . ."[5]

After hanging up the telephone, Cory continued to struggle with the meaning of those two rather esoteric biblical passages that God had "given her for Ninoy." The first passage was the story of the prophet Jonah, who fought against God's will for him to travel on a mission to ancient Ninevah and then was shocked and saddened by what God did when he arrived. The second passage was actually just a sentence of greeting from the apostle Paul advising the reader to receive a person named Marcos "with open arms."

We don't know what Ninoy thought about the verses. But we can know for certain that on the most important day of their lives, Ninoy and Cory spent precious, expensive time connected by satellites and laser beams talking about passages from the Old and New Testament scriptures.

All his life, Ninoy had been a student of the Scriptures. But after his experience in prison, they seemed to come to life for him. From his prison cell, Ninoy wrote, "As Paul wrote to the Corinthians, 'For the sake of Christ, I am content with weaknesses, insults, hardships, persecutions and calamities; for when I am weak, then I am strong.' To this," Ninoy concluded, "I say, Amen."[6]

At 6:30 A.M. a room service waiter brought Ninoy's breakfast to his room in the Grand Hotel. Ninoy was "his usual exuberant self." The mood at breakfast was "jovial." Ninoy poured ketchup over his eggs and laughed heartily when his brother-in-law looked away in mock revulsion and said, "That's disgusting."

At that breakfast, Ninoy also talked about Cory. "One regret I have," he said, "is that Cory has had to suffer so much." He also remembered how determined his daughter, Kris, was to accompany him on this journey home. "But I had to tell her 'no.'" Apparently, Ninoy knew well the risk that he was taking.

Senator Aquino was nervous passing through customs at the Taipei International Airport. He had already delayed his arrival date by a month and two days because Marcos's defense secretary, Juan Ponce Enrile, had cabled him pleading for the delay, warning that ". . . We are convinced beyond a reasonable doubt that there are plots against your life."

But Ninoy would not postpone his trip forever as Marcos and his cronies had hoped. "I would rather die on my feet with honor than live on bended knees in shame," he had announced earlier. When reporters with him on board China Airlines Flight 811 asked Ninoy about the rumors of an assassination, Ninoy answered, "Assassination is part of public service . . . . If my fate is to die by an assassin's bullet, so be it. But I cannot be petrified by inaction or fear of assassination and therefore stay in a corner."

Before leaving on his final journey, Ninoy had met with his friend, Charles Colson, author and founder of the Prison Fellowship. Colson also had asked him about the dangers that might lie ahead. If Marcos threw him in prison, Ninoy replied, "I will be president of the Prison Fellowship." Calmly, he added with a smile, "If I'm killed, I'll be with Jesus."[7]

As the plane neared Manila, Ninoy slipped into a bulletproof vest that someone had provided him. He had received word that he might be shot at the airport and that an "assassin" would be shot in return. "That's why I'm wearing this," he said pointing at the bulletproof vest. "But if they hit me in the head," he added, "I'm a goner."

To a Japanese television crew, Ninoy warned: "You have to be very ready with your hand camera, because this action can happen very fast. In a matter of three, four minutes, it could be all over and I may not be able to talk to you again."

Although Senator Aquino was taking the death threats seriously, he thought the probable worse case scenario would be his arrest upon landing and his reimprisonment. There were at least ten thousand Ninoy fans and supporters waiting at the Manila International Airport. Television camera teams accompanied him on the China Airlines flight, and dozens of other reporters and cameramen waited for him at the airport. Few believed that Marcos or his cronies would be so arrogant or so stupid as to actually kill a Senator in that setting. Still, Ninoy knew the risk of placing himself helplessly into the hands of his enemy.

That decision to return home without guns or armies, without bodyguards or concealed weapons to protect him, was also a result of the power of the Scriptures in Ninoy's life. In 1980, the exiled Senator Aquino had attended a worship service at the North Shore Baptist Church in Chicago. At that time, many of its members were Filipino citizens who had fled the terrors of the Marcos regime. Eddie Monteclaro, a former editor of the *Manila Times* and a former president of the Philippines Press Corps, had invited Ninoy to attend worship with him at the North Shore Baptist Church.

The theme of that Sunday morning service was from the Old Testament book of Zechariah, chapter 4, verse 6: "Not by might, nor by power, but by my spirit, says the Lord of hosts." The sermon that day emphasized "that if we are to cure the world's ills, it will not be by using power or military might, but by turning to another source."[8]

In a letter he wrote shortly after attending the service, Ninoy confessed that he had been struggling to decide how he should proceed in the fight against Marcos when he returned to the Philippines. Should he lead a peaceful opposition or a violent one? Ninoy concluded the letter by saying that "the message of Zechariah 4:6 in that morning worship experience had crystallized his thinking: he would return in peace."[9]

In 1982, while Ninoy and Cory were still living in Boston, the senator had met Anthony Campolo, a well-known evangelical writer and lecturer. After hearing Campolo speak about Christ's teachings concerning the difference between power (that comes from military might) and authority (which comes from right and truth) Ninoy spoke to Campolo gratefully.

"You have given me hope," he said. "I know that when I return to my homeland I will be powerless; but you have helped me to see that

I will have authority. What I say is right, and people know it. What I believe to be true, I am willing to die for. I now believe I will have a great influence in the Philippines, even though I hold no power at all."[10]

The purser on China Airlines Flight 811 announced their arrival over Manila and asked the passengers to prepare for landing. Ken Kashiwahara remembers that while the other passengers fastened their seat belts and the reporters and cameramen looked nervously out the windows at the soldiers and policemen spread across the field, Ninoy Aquino was meditating on the life, death and resurrection of Jesus for this one last time. His head was bowed and his lips were moving in silent prayer.

As the jumbo jet moved into its gateway, a blue van pulled up, a back door opened, and a group of soldiers dressed in blue fatigues and carrying rifles and pistols jumped out, taking positions around the airplane. Inside, according to eye-witness Kashiwahara, "a ripple of nervous chatter spread through the plane as people crowded around the windows, watching the activity on the tarmac. Shutters clicked in a half-dozen cameras."

The engines were shut down. Three soldiers climbed the service stairs to the jetway. The first entered the plane and walked right past the waiting senator. The second recognized Ninoy and stopped abruptly in the aisle. He spoke quietly in Tagalog. Ninoy smiled and reached out to shake his hand. The soldiers hurried Senator Aquino down the aisle toward the exit. Ken Kashiwahara shouted above the crowd, "I'm his brother-in-law. Can I go with him?"

The third soldier turned and shouted back, "You, just take a seat!"

As Ninoy was led from the plane, plainclothes police slammed the airplane's door and blocked the view from its window with their bodies. Cameramen and reporters pushed against the door, shouting and cursing. Nine seconds after Ninoy went through that door, the first shot was heard. Four seconds later, three other shots were fired. Then there was a short burst of automatic-rifle fire.

Chaos erupted in the airplane as news crews fought for space at the windows. What they saw was chilling. Senator Ninoy Aquino lay face down on the tarmac, blood spurting from the bullet wound in his brain. Another man, the unidentified "assassin," lay on his side nearby, his body riddled with bullets. Suddenly, soldiers threw Ninoy's body into the back of a military van and drove away.

Senator Aquino had come in peace. He had smiled and shaken their hands. In trust and innocence he had gone with them down the stairway. And yet all evidence suggests that before Ninoy could even put his feet on the soil of his beloved native land, one of the military escorts cried out, "I'll do it!" A cocked pistol was raised and pointed at the back of Ninoy's head. A single shot was fired and Senator Aquino fell mortally wounded.

These assassins and their arrogant masters thought the bullet that killed Ninoy Aquino would also kill his threat against them. In fact, even as his blood spurted out on the runway, Ninoy's power over their might began to grow. They had lied. They had imprisoned. They had exiled. And now they had murdered. And with each cowardly act against him, Ninoy's authority grew in the minds and hearts of the people. Ultimately, his death was the beginning of new life for the Philippines.

Ken Kashiwahara was one of the first passengers to fight his way off the plane through the chaotic crowd "My brother-in-law has been shot," he shouted, "I must get through." The rumor of Ninoy's assassination spread to the crowd outside and through them to tens of millions of Filipinos whose lives would be revolutionized by the news. Over the next three years of struggle, they would shout his name, wave his banners and sing his song as they gathered in the streets to bring down his enemy and to propel his widow into the office many believe she was destined to occupy.

Kashiwahara finally made his way to the airport's VIP waiting room where Ninoy's special friends and family were waiting to welcome him home. At that moment Ninoy was being welcomed home by another crowd of friends. Jesus himself must have led the welcoming committee: "Well done, good and faithful servant. Enter into the rest that I have prepared for you."

Ninoy Aquino's plans for the liberation of his country had been set aside, but God's surprising, ironic, mysterious masterplan for the Philippines was already taking hold. This is the true story of Senator Benigno Aquino, Jr., who gave his life to help save the Filipino people from tyranny. And it is the true story of Corazon C. Aquino, a woman of faith and courage, who carries on her husband's struggle to bring peace and prosperity to the Philippines. It is the story of the spiritual journey they shared and of the war against evil that they began together but that Cory now fights alone.

It would be easier and more inspiring to end this book with Cory's victory over Marcos and her inauguration as the seventh President of the Philippines. But now she has served in that office for more than one thousand days and the Filipino people and the world are still waiting to see if she can truly end the tyrannies and bring her nation back to life and health again.

It won't be easy. Cory Aquino is not fighting a little, local war of no consequence to the rest of us. She is fighting in the front lines of a war against the forces of evil that threaten to undo the earth.

The storm she is facing in full fury is only beginning to move in our direction. To understand her task is to better understand our own. And to understand the source of her strength and courage is to find new strength and courage for ourselves.

"There are times when you find the work just too tiring," President Aquino said recently to a group of Christian women volunteers. "The fields we must tend seem endless. The work is never done. The difficulties never cease. But at such times, I remind myself of what Christ said when he called us to work in his vineyards. 'Take my yoke,' he said, 'for it is light.' And it is true," she assured them, "for he carries half the load."

To the members of Martha's Vineyard, an organization of Christian Filipino women, she confided her vision of the task:

"First, we must break new ground and work new life into hard, tired soil, choked with weeds that we must uproot. These weeds are the old habits of corruption that cannot seem to die.

"Second, we must cope with those who stand on the sidelines and criticize, telling us that what we dream cannot be accomplished or the hundred and one ways we could have done things better.

"Finally, just when we get the first sign of a harvest, when our first tiny plant begins to grow, a sudden storm comes up in the night and destroys our labors . . . ."

These words became especially meaningful to me during my last two visits to the Philippines. That beautiful Pacific island nation, endowed by the Creator with an abundance of human and natural resources, had just survived Typhoon Unsang and was about to suffer Typhoon Yoning, the seventeenth and eighteenth typhoons of the 1988 monsoon season. The winds of Unsang swept through those 7,107 Filipino islands leaving more than 600 people dead, more than 1.5 million homeless and billions of dollars in personal and public losses. Fourteen days later Yoning would roar across the still devastated islands leaving 49 more Filipinos dead, 400,000 more homeless and hundreds of millions of dollars in additional agricultural and property losses.

There seems to be no rest for Cory Aquino. In the Philippines, one storm follows another. As gale winds blow up high waves and tropical cloudbursts bring flooding, so a stagnating economy leads to poverty and hunger. Unemployment, low wages, and lack of opportunity for those in the countryside bring squatter squalor to the cities. Piles of garbage and waterways clogged by waste result in pollution and disease. Corruption and family nepotism in business and politics are followed by insurgencies, human rights abuses, terrorism and vigilantism. Greed, mismanagement and large scale corruption bring on demonstrations, coup attempts and a $28 billion national debt. As rumors lead to fear, so fear destroys business, trade, tourism and the nation's economy.

Cory is the president of a nation caught in the eye of a violent storm. But Cory is not alone in that storm. God is present and active there. This is the true story of God at work in the lives of Ninoy and Cory—and in the lives of the Filipino people. But especially it is the story of Cory, a woman of faith and courage who deserves our prayers, our generous support and our understanding. Her story has urgent, practical implications for each one of us.

1

The Childhood Years
(1932–1945)

Help me, dear Lord, to see through the mist, and discern the outlines of your wish . . . .

Senator Benigno C. Aquino, Jr.

In the lives of those who are committed, nothing happens by accident . . . .

President Corazon C. Aquino

Cory

Cory Aquino, the seventh President of the Philippines and the first woman to be the chief executive of an Asian nation, was born 25 January 1933. Christened Maria Corazon Cojuangco ("Cora" as she was then nicknamed), Cory was the sixth of eight children born to Jose Cojuangco and Demetria Sumulong Cojuangco. Cory's parents maintained a large house in the capital and a second family home in the town of Paniqui, a booming commercial center in the province of Tarlac, on the island of Luzon just north of Manila. Cory was born in the San Juan de Dios Hospital on Roxas Boulevard in Manila.

Cory was born into a family of wealth and political power. Her father, Don Pepe, was a congressman. His father had been a senator. Her mother's father, too, had been a senator. Among their many holdings in Tarlac, the Cojuangco family owned a 15,000-acre sugar plantation. Because it was common for Filipino politicians to maintain business or banking vocations while serving as an elected official, Cory's father continued to manage the Paniqui Sugar Mill, one of the Cojuangco properties in Tarlac, while serving as the congressman from that province.

Cory's eldest brother, Ceferino, was stillborn, and an older sister, Carmen, died of meningitis before her second birthday. Cory has five living siblings: a younger brother, Peping, a younger sister, Passy, two older sisters, Terry and Josephine, and a brother, Pedro, who is known to the family as Pete, the Kuya or older brother to them all.

The family lived in a large, two-story, Spanish-style home of stone, white-washed walls, wood trim and tile roof. It stood directly across the yard from a tin-roofed rice mill. There were servants to do most of the menial chores, so the Cojuangco family was free to listen to the shortwave radio, to read newspapers and newsmagazines and to discuss and debate the issues confronting the Philippines and the world.

It isn't hard to imagine what the Cojuangco elders were discussing during those years of Cory's birth and early childhood. The first woman president of the Philippines was born into troubled times. Less than four years before her birthday, the American stock market had crashed on "Black Tuesday," 29 October 1929, plunging the United States into the Great Depression. At that time, Cory's homeland was a colony of the United States. And just as America's original thirteen states, once colonies of Great Britain, had been subject to events in London and to the whims of King George, so what happened on Wall Street or Pennsylvania Avenue had a fairly immediate impact on the people of the Philippines.

During those nine months of Demetria Cojuangco's pregnancy with Cory, tens of thousands of American businessmen went bankrupt. Thousands of banks locked their doors. Unemployment figures skyrocketed, and President Herbert Hoover and the Congress seemed helpless to slow the economic collapse. The poor and hungry, including seventeen thousand World War I veterans, marched on Washington, D.C. to beg Hoover for immediate aid. Squatters' camps and tent cities were set up in parks, on malls and at the foot of the nation's marble monuments. Hoover finally had to use Army troops to drive the hungry protesters from the nation's capital.

The elder Cojuangcos must have talked often about the declining state of the world's economic health and the immediate and long-range implications that the growing disaster might have on their own fortunes and the fortunes of the Philippines.

During that same time, the governor of New York, Franklin D. Roosevelt, in a speech protesting Hoover's "paralysis," referred to "the forgotten man at the bottom of the economic pyramid." The Governor's speech hit an exposed American nerve and on 8 November 1932, less than two months before Cory Cojuangco's birth, Roosevelt was elected by a landslide to succeed President Hoover.

Five weeks before Roosevelt's inauguration, Maria Corazon "Cory" Cojuangco was born. During the months that followed, unemployment in the United States reached thirteen million people. Wages continued to drop. Business losses were reported at six billion dollars. Farm prices were plunging. More than five thousand banks had closed. The economy was reaching rock bottom.

As the Great Depression worked its deadly way around the globe, governments were destabilized and despots rose up with economic and military solutions that would plunge the world into war once more. In September, 1931, just sixteen months before Cory's birth, Japan, the Philippines' neighbor to the north, invaded Manchuria, a vast region of northeast China. And on 30 January 1933, just five days after Cory's birth, Adolph Hitler assumed office as Chancellor of the Republic of Germany upon the invitation of President Von Hindenburg, who regarded Hitler as the best man to stave off the economic chaos threatening the German people as it was threatening the people of the world.

Soon after Cory was born, her parents moved with their six children out of their home in quiet, rural Paniqui in the Tarlac region to Manila, the nation's busy capital. There were two obvious reasons for the move. Cory's father wanted his children to have the best possible education and he needed to be closer to the capital in order to attend the sessions of the Assembly to which he had been elected. But events in the Philippines might suggest a third reason for the move to Manila.

In Washington, D.C., just months before Cory's birth, legislation had been passed by both houses of Congress to grant the Philippines its independence from American rule. One of Hoover's last acts was to veto the bill saying: ". . . if the Philippine people are now prepared for self-government, if they can maintain order and their institutions, if they can now defend their independence, we should say so frankly on both sides. I hold that this is not the case . . . ."[1]

Senator Manuel Quezon, who was elected the first President of the Philippine Commonwealth on 15 November 1935, had countered the critics of Filipino independence with his famous war cry, "I prefer a government run like hell by Filipinos to a government run like heaven by Americans."[2]

History was being made in Manila and Cory spent her first twelve years in the heart of it. The very idea of Filipino independence charged the city with excitement. The Filipino people had tolerated colonialization longer than almost any other nation on record. For 377 years (1521–1898) they had endured the "cross and the sword" of Spain. For 37 years (1898–1935) an American Governor-General had ruled the island archipelago. Jokingly Filipinos summarize the last four and one half centuries of Philippine history under Spanish and American rule as "400 years in a convent and 40 years in Hollywood."

With rumors of independence heating to a boiling point, every politician or would-be politician in the Philippines was converging on Manila. Cory's father, Congressman Don Pepe Cojuangco, moved his family into their new home in Malate, an upper-class district of Manila just a short walk away from Manila Bay. Cory spent the first twelve years of her life living in the capital with occasional weekend and holiday visits to the family home in Paniqui.

There was a steady stream of visitors in and out of the Cojuangco home in Malate. Day and night, their living room, dining room and parlor must have echoed with conversations about business, politics, world events and especially about independence for the Philippines.

Just months after Cory and her family moved to Manila, the United States Congress passed the Tydings-McDuffie bill, a limited experiment in self-governance granting the Philippines common-wealth status and promising the Filipino people full independence in 1946. On 24 March 1934, President Roosevelt signed the bill into law. That same year, in Manila, a commission drafted a new Constitution for the Philippines and on 15 November 1935, Manuel Quezon was inaugurated first President of the Philippine Commonwealth.

The excitement over events in their homeland must have been dampened considerably for the Cojuangco family by a series of ominous events in Europe and Asia during those first years of Cory's childhood. The Italian dictator, Benito Mussolini, marched his Italian troops into Ethiopia and Albania. Civil war broke out in Spain. Hitler demanded and received the return of the Saar region from France. Nazi troops marched into Austria to "maintain order" and months later Hitler launched full-scale invasions of Czechoslovakia and Poland.

In the Soviet Union, Communist Party leader Joseph Stalin continued a ruthless purge of all his enemies. Mao tse Tung and his Communist forces began and successfully completed their long march across China and were eventually to gain control of the entire Chinese mainland. Japan sank a U.S. gunboat, the *Panay*, in China's Yangtze River and continued to expand the Japanese sphere of influence into Korea, Manchuria and Mongolia, invading China in 1937 and eventually moving its armies into Siam (Thailand) and Indo-China (Vietnam).

In the Philippines, Cory's father and his colleagues in the Congress were preparing for the inevitable invasion of their homeland by Japanese forces. With the approval of Franklin Roosevelt, President Quezon appointed General Douglas MacArthur field marshall of the Philippine army. MacArthur established his headquarters in the elegant and historic Manila Hotel on Manila Bay, not far from the Cojuangco household.

About that time, Cory was enrolled as a student at St. Scholastica's College, a private elementary school run by Filipino and German Benedictine nuns for the daughters of the well-to-do. According to teachers and to classmates who still remember her early years at St. Scholastica's, Cory was "quiet, kind, soft-spoken, and very bright . . . . Consistently, she was the valedictorian of her class."[3]

The curriculum at St. Scholastica's included the standard elementary and junior-high courses of schools in the United States; and though math and English seemed to be Cory's favorites, she excelled in every course she took and graduated at the head of her class.

Cory's childhood pictures reveal a serious but pretty little girl, her black hair worn in a straight, short bob with an occasional ribbon or barrette. Her facial features are typical of children with Chinese and Malay ancestry. In every picture she stands erect, unsmiling, gazing quizzically at the camera. Her eyes are bright, curious, timid. She wears the uniform of St. Scholastica, a white blouse with a wide collar, a dark blue jumper, white socks and dark, buckled sandals.

According to her big brother, Pete, Cory never complained about the long hours of homework required to excel at St. Scholastica's. There was just one exception that he remembers. Cory once shocked the whole family with her un-Corylike outburst, "I'm never going to learn to play the piano well!" That is the only act of rebellion anyone has remembered publicly about Cory's childhood years.[4]

Sister Gratia, Cory's kindergarten teacher, was just the first of a whole procession of nuns and Christian lay teachers in Cory's early life. In their photographs, Sister Gratia, Sister Imelda, and the others are dressed in starched white wimples with long flowing, black habits. The women stand tall and imposing in their black, open-toed sandals. They smile but their smiles seem stern, disciplined, Germanic. Along with her mother, whom Cory remembers as "a disciplinarian" and "not very forgiving,"[5] these nuns helped to shape the moral and spiritual values of the nation's future president.

At St. Scholastica's Cory learned about the Old Testament prophets who warned the kings of Israel "to do justice, to love mercy and to live humbly before the Lord." In her New Testament studies she memorized portions of the Gospels, including Jesus' warning about the last judgment when those who ignored the poor and the hungry were sentenced to be cast away and those who cared for the poor and fed the hungry were honored with life everlasting. "When you do it unto them," young Cory quoted Jesus, "you do it unto me."

In the wooden confessionals of St. Scholastica's, Cory's quiet voice first said those words, "Hear me, Father, for I have sinned." And it was there, too, after her confession, that she heard the priest's reply, "If we confess our sins, he is faithful and just to forgive us our sins and to cleanse us from all unrighteousness."

And it was in the chapel at St. Scholastica's that Cory first took Communion. There is a large, black and white photo of that central event in Cory's early life of faith. Wearing a white dress and a lacy white mantilla, Cory knelt on the padded, hand-embroidered kneelers beside seventy or eighty of her classmates. The sunlight streamed through leaded, stained-glass windows. Behind the six rows of communicants, and beneath the hand-carved wooden ceiling and the arched doors and windows, the church is packed with proud parents and grandparents, uncles and aunts, godfathers and godmothers, perfectly dressed and coiffured for the occasion.

The volunteer choir seated in the balcony beneath the rose window at the back of the church joins with the presiding priest in the introductory rites to the Mass.

"To you, my God, I lift my soul . . ."

Before the great processional, the priest calls out from the back of the sanctuary, "In the name of the Father, and of the Son, and of the Holy Spirit."

And the people, standing, echo his "Amen!"

The organ plays. The congregation joins in the opening hymn. The Mass begins with the penitential rite.

> I confess to almighty God,
> and to you, my brothers and sisters,
> that I have sinned through my own fault
> in my thoughts and in my words,
> in what I have done,
> and in what I have failed to do . . . .

From her earliest childhood, the Mass has been a weekly, sometimes daily event in President Aquino's life. Her head covered, her knees bowed, her hands folded in prayer, Cory and her classmates prayed the Collect (when the priest "collects" the needs of the people and offers them to God in prayer).

"Lord, fill our hearts with your love . . . ."

Cory and the other children followed the Epistle and Gospel readings from the New Testament in their black, leather prayer books with the dark blue ribbon attached to mark the pages.

"This is the Word of the Lord," intones the priest.

"Thanks be to God," the children reply.

Between the readings, they join their high, quiet voices in a Psalm. "Justice shall flourish in his time, and fullness of peace for ever."

They listen patiently as their priest delivers the morning homily and, relieved that it is done, join again in the priest's "Amen," make the sign of the cross, and stand to say the Apostle's Creed together:

> I believe in God, the Father almighty,
>   creator of heaven and earth.
> I believe in Jesus Christ, his only son, our Lord.
>   He was conceived by the power of the Holy Spirit
>   and born of the Virgin Mary.
>   He suffered under Pontius Pilate,
>   was crucified, died, and was buried.
>   He descended to the dead.
>   On the third day he rose again.
>   He ascended into heaven,
>   and is seated at the right hand of the Father.
>   He will come again to judge the living and the dead.
> I believe in the Holy Spirit,
>   the holy catholic Church,
>   the communion of saints,
>   the forgiveness of sins,
>   the resurrection of the body,
>   and the life everlasting. Amen.

The children are seated and lean forward in anticipation of their First Communion as the priests and altar boys prepare the bread and wine. In the one picture we have of Cory's First Communion, the little girls wait patiently in perfect rows, separated at four- or five-foot intervals with their hands folded in prayer and their eyes looking straight ahead at the carved wooden crucifix hanging on the whitewashed wall before them.

Two children selected for the occasion bring forward the bread and wine. Smiling down on them, the priest blesses their gifts, washes his hands in a symbolic gesture of purification, quotes the New Testament texts telling the story of that First Communion in an upper room when Jesus offered bread and wine and told his disciples "to eat and drink in remembrance of me."

"What is Holy Communion?" Sister Gratia had asked the children, reading from their first catechism manual in preparation for that first communion service.

"Communion is a holy meal," Cory and her friends answered in unison, "in which we receive the body and blood of Jesus Christ and recall that at the Last Supper Jesus promised to nourish us with himself so that God's life and grace would be available to us throughout our lives."

As the choir sings and the parents look on happily, the little girls file up to the altar, kneel before the priest, receive the Eucharist from his hands, and return to kneel at their pew.

To better understand Cory Aquino, president of the Philippines, one must understand Cory Cojuangco, the child in the chapel at St. Scholastica's, standing to sing the songs of faith, to confess her sins, and to receive God's forgiveness, sitting patiently through the reading of the Scriptures and the preaching of the morning's homily, and kneeling to receive the Body and the Blood of Christ—"Strength for the Journey."

Ninoy

Cory remembers meeting Benigno "Ninoy" Aquino for the first time in 1942 when both of them were just nine years old. Ninoy, born 27 November 1932, was just eight weeks older than Cory. He was born in Concepcion, Tarlac, a few miles up the road from Cory's family home in Paniqui. Like the Cojuangcos, the Aquinos were wealthy sugar plantation owners. Often, business, politics or provincial celebrations brought the two families together. The Aquinos and the Cojuangcos were neighbors with wealth, privilege and power in common. Cory and Ninoy met at a birthday party for Ninoy's father, who by his forty-eighth birthday had already served the Philippines as an assemblyman, senator and the secretary of agriculture and commerce in President Quezon's cabinet.

By the time Cory and Ninoy met as children in 1942, World War II had invaded their quiet, comfortable lives in Manila. On 7 December 1941, just four hours after their surprise attack on the American fleet anchored at Pearl Harbor, the Japanese launched a similar attack against the Philippines, destroying the greater part of the United States Air Force stationed at Clark Air Force Base and the port area of the city of Manila, just blocks from Cory's home in Malate.

And though Douglas MacArthur declared Manila an open city, the heavy Japanese bombers continued to attack the capital and on 2 January 1942, the advance elements of General Homma Masaharu's army captured Manila. For the next three years, Cory, Ninoy and their families lived under the daily trials and terrors of the Japanese occupation forces.

Ninoy's father, Benigno Aquino, Sr., decided early on that one occupation force was not much better than the other. The Philippines had been a colony of the Spanish and the Americans. Now they were a colony of the Japanese. "If they recognize our independence," Ninoy's father advised his fellow Filipinos, "we embrace them; but if not, we maintain our ideals and our loyalty to America."[6]

As early as January, 1942, Premier Tojo Hideki told the Imperial Diet: "Japan will gladly grant the Philippines its independence so long as it cooperates and recognizes Japan's program of establishing a Greater East Asia Co-prosperity Sphere."[7]

Benigno Aquino, Sr., had to make a terrible decision. Would he flee the Philippines for safety in Australia or America? Would he join the underground movement and fight the Japanese from rebel hideouts in the mountains? Or would he use his political skills to work with the Japanese with the immediate goal of mitigating the suffering of the Filipino people and with the long-range goal of full independence for the Philippines?

The decision must have been very difficult. Ninoy's father was angry with President Roosevelt for breaking his "solemn pledge" at the outbreak of World War II to the people of the Philippines "that their freedom will be redeemed and their independence established and protected . . . ."[8] After promising to use "the entire resources, in men and material to stand behind that pledge," Roosevelt changed to his "Europe first" strategy and after a bloody defense of Bataan by brave American and Filipino soldiers, Roosevelt abandoned his colony to the Japanese.

Also, Aquino and his colleagues had been commissioned by President Quezon, just before he was evacuated by MacArthur, to "Make what bargains you have to with those people [the Japanese]. Try to keep the Philippines together in one piece. Try to protect the people from Japan's brutality and avarice. You have some tough decisions to make. But the job must be done. Do it for the future of the Philippines."[9]

After struggling with his conscience, Ninoy's father volunteered to work with the Japanese. Recognizing his political and administrative skills, they first appointed him to be their commissioner of the interior. Then they asked Aquino to co-chair the committee that would draft the new constitution for the Occupation Republic of the Philippines. And on 25 September 1943, he was elected Speaker of the National Assembly.

No family in the history of the Philippines has served more faithfully than the Aquinos in the cause of Filipino independence. Ninoy's grandfather, General Servillano Aquino, had distinguished himself in the war for independence from Spanish rule at the turn of the century. Ninoy's father, Benigno Aquino, Sr., had spent much of his political life negotiating with the Americans for Filipino independence. Ninoy himself would be martyred as he, too, fought in the cause of freedom and justice for all Filipinos, bearing the mantle passed on to him by his father and grandfather.

In spite of the Aquino family's long record of service to the Philippines, during World War II, there were Filipinos and Americans alike who called Ninoy's father "Judas Aquino" for working with the Japanese. At the end of the war, along with other Filipino leaders who had continued in leadership during the Japanese occupation, Aquino was imprisoned by MacArthur. Eventually, Ninoy's father and his imprisoned colleagues were granted full pardons and honored by their countrymen for distinguished service to the cause of Filipino independence.

During the war years, life in Manila became a nightmare. The Filipino people were humiliated and terrorized by their Japanese conquerors. Hospitals and hotels, schools and churches, factories and farms, trucks, cars and buses were commandeered by the Japanese for the exclusive use of their occupation forces. The city ran short of medicine and food supplies. Even the rich had to barter furniture and clothing for what little rice was available.

The masses were starving. Emaciated beggars roamed the streets. Thousands of Filipinos were arrested, tortured and killed without reason. Those who tried to work with the Japanese were called collaborators. They were often hunted down and killed by members of the resistance; on the other hand, those who didn't cooperate were hunted down and killed by the Japanese.

But life for the Aquinos and the Cojuangcos remained fairly stable, even comfortable during most of the Japanese occupation. Ninoy's family lived on Arlequi Street near Malacañang Palace in the white-pillared mansion (formerly the German embassy) designated as the home for the Speaker of the Assembly. The Aquinos needed the large official residence to house Don Benigno and his four elder children, his wife, Doña Aurora Aquino, and his six brothers and sisters. Ninoy often played in the Palace with his boyhood friend Salvador "Doy" Laurel whose father, Jose Laurel, had been elected President of the Occupied Republic of the Philippines.

Cory

At first, Cory's family stayed in their home in the Malate area of Manila while Cory's father commuted between the capital and his sugar mill in Paniqui. Cory continued her elementary schooling at St. Scholastica's until it was closed. By the time the battle for the Pacific had turned in favor of the Allies, Cory's classes had been moved to the Assumption Convent where she began her years in Junior High School.

On 19 and 20 June 1944, one of the most decisive air-naval battles of World War II was fought in the Philippine Sea. The Japanese were roundly defeated after losing 400 planes and 3 carriers in the fighting. U.S. losses were some 50 planes in battle and another 72 that crashed while trying to land on their carriers in the darkness.

On 10 August 1944, the island of Guam was retaken by U.S. forces after some 20 days of fierce fighting and the loss of 17,000 Japanese and 1,214 Americans. On 20 October 1944, General MacArthur led the landing party on the beaches of Leyte Island in the central Philippines, fulfilling his promise of March, 1942, "I shall return."

During the last months of the war, Cory's family home in Malate was burned to the ground. The family moved into a second home on Roberts Street just off Roxas (then Dewey) Boulevard in 1945. As the American forces fought their way closer to Manila, Japanese troops became determined to hold the city at any cost. Thousands of Filipino civilians were killed by Japanese atrocities. Thousands more died in the crossfire as the Japanese were driven from the city in hand-to-hand, house-to-house combat. Even Cory and her family barely escaped death in the conflagration.

When the battle for Manila was at its hottest, when the city was in flames, when buildings and bridges were being blown apart and civilians were desperate to flee the conflict, Cory's uncle, Antonio Cojuangco, managed to call Cory's father across the war-torn city. "Come to the De La Salle side of Manila," he shouted into the telephone. "Bring your family. It is safer here."

Cory's father agreed. He rushed about trying to find transportation to get his wife and six children across Manila. But there were no cars or taxis to hire. Not even a truck or jeepney was available. Fearfully, they returned home to wait out the fierce battle for Manila. The lack of transport may have saved the life of Cory and her family; that same day, Antonio Cojuangco and his children (except for two, Ramon and his sister, Lourdes) were killed by the Japanese.

American officials pleaded with the Japanese to surrender the city. When they refused, American bombers were ordered to destroy Japan's last major strongholds in the heart of old Manila. The Walled City built by the Spanish three centuries earlier was practically leveled by the bombing and strafing runs. American troops led by Filipino guerrilla fighters used machine guns and flamethrowers to flush the city free of the remaining enemy.

On 4 July 1945, MacArthur declared the Philippines liberated from the Japanese. On August 6 an American bomber dropped an atomic bomb on Hiroshima, demolishing almost half the city, killing over one hundred thousand Japanese and burning and injuring hundreds of thousands more. On August 9, another atomic bomb was dropped on Nagasaki. On 15 August 1945, Japan accepted the Allied demands for unconditional surrender.

War in the Pacific had ended, but Manila and much of the nation were in ruins. Farms and factories were destroyed. Highways, dams, ports, railroads, bridges—the country's entire infrastructure—had been fatally wounded. Hunger and disease stalked the streets. Schools, stores and businesses were closed. Whole neighborhoods of homes were burned or boarded up. The streets were littered with the dead and dying. Once again one occupying army was replaced by another. Desperate, frightened, hungry people roamed the countryside looking for food and shelter. The city was in chaos.

Cory and Ninoy were both just twelve years old when the war ended. Cory's father became increasingly concerned for the safety and the comfort of his young family. In 1946, he made the painful decision to leave his homeland temporarily and to move his family to America. They bought a home in Philadelphia where Cory was enrolled for her freshman year in high school at Raven Hill Academy, a sister school of Assumption College, the elementary school Cory had attended in Manila.

Ninoy

Cory doesn't remember seeing Ninoy during the World War II years. Toward the end of the war, the Japanese had flown Filipino officials of the Occupied Republic, including Ninoy's father, to Tokyo. After the Japanese surrender, Ninoy's father was imprisoned by General MacArthur in Sugamo prison in Japan. Not knowing when or if she would see her husband again, Ninoy's mother, Doña Aurora, packed up their ten children and returned to the Aquino home in Concepcion, just fifty miles from Manila.

On 25 August 1946, after a year of imprisonment by the Americans, Senator Aquino was flown to Manila and imprisoned in Muntinlupa prison with other former senators, justices, cabinet members, governors and mayors who had worked with the Japanese. As Ninoy Aquino began his freshman year in San Beda High School back in Manila, his father was facing trial by a People's Court for collaboration with the Japanese. Thirteen-year-old Ninoy, who had grown up the honored child of a senator, was mocked and jeered as a traitor's son.

2

The Adolescent Years
(1945–1951)

Rizal said we can only win freedom by deserving it and that to earn it we must improve the mind and enhance the dignity of the individual, "Love what is good, what is great, to the point of dying for it . . . ."

Senator Benigno Aquino, Jr.

Transformation of nations and societies takes place first in the hearts of people.

President Corazon C. Aquino

Ninoy

"Hey, Flips," an American sergeant yelled at a small group of Filipino prisoners who were walking together in the central courtyard of Tokyo's Sugamo Prison. "Pick up the trash!"

Ninoy's father, former Speaker of the Assembly Aquino, stopped and looked for a moment in silence at the guard. With Aquino were the former president of the Occupied Philippines, Jose Laurel, Sr., the former secretary of education, Osias, and the former Filipino ambassador to Japan, Jorge Vargas. Each had served his nation during the Japanese occupation. Near the close of the war, they were flown to Japan where the Americans found them and imprisoned them on charges of "collaborating with the enemy."

"Pick up the cigarette butts around the courtyard," the young sergeant shouted once again, "and the trash near the gate!"

Ambassador Vargas remembers that Ninoy's father shouted back: "We are not convicts! We are political prisoners. We will not do anything of the sort!"

It was Don Benigno Aquino, Vargas recalls, who helped all the former Filipino leaders hold on to their dignity during their imprisonment in Japan. Ninoy's father hated the Japanese occupying forces for their cruelties against his people. Trying to prevent those cruelties was the primary reason he had cooperated with the Japanese in the first place. But to Don Benigno, in most ways one occupying force was very much like the other. Whether Spain, America or Japan, these foreign armies and the diplomats, industrialists and bankers who swarmed around them had no right to occupy and control the Philippines.

Independence for his nation was Don Benigno's lifelong passion and in 1946 when he was released on bail to return to his home in Concepcion, he began immediately to prepare his defense against the charges of collaboration and to reestablish himself as an active political force in the Philippines.

Thirteen-year-old Ninoy was just beginning his freshman year in high school in Manila. Ninoy spent Monday through Friday in his classes at San Beda soaking up the history of the Filipinos' four-and-one-half-century struggle for independence. And he spent the weekends at home in Concepcion with his father and his father's friends listening to their stories about that struggle.

To understand Ninoy and his fatal commitment to freedom in the Philippines, we have to understand at least the rudiments of Filipino history and the important roles played in that history by Ninoy's grandfather, General Servillano Aquino, and his father, Senator Benigno Aquino, Sr.

The Philippines is an Asian nation. Filipino roots are planted deep in the Asian cultures of Malaysia, Indo-China and China. Yet, for more than four centuries Filipinos have been ruled by the west. The Western domination of the Philippines began on 17 March 1521, when Ferdinand Magellan landed on the island of Samar and claimed the island archipelago for Charles and Isabella of Spain. The first European to set foot in the Philippines, Magellan sealed a blood compact with a local chief, erected a cross and concluded the first Catholic Mass to be said on Filipino soil.

Most Filipinos simply accepted the occupying forces of Spain; but you can be sure that Ninoy's father explained to his young son that from the beginning there were Filipino revolutionaries, even in the sixteenth century. In fact, Magellan was killed on the Philippine island of Cebu by a Filipino chieftain, Lapu-Lapu, the first Filipino freedom fighter.

King Charles's son, Philip, sent the next Spanish expedition under Miguel Lopez de Legazpi in 1565. Legazpi defeated the Rajah Sulayman, ruler of Manila, and set up his capitol there in the name of Philip of Spain, thus the name "Philip"pines. Even the name of Ninoy's country reflects the centuries of subjugation. Filipinos are by nature hospitable, deeply pious and pragmatic. They rushed to embrace Catholicism. Spanish became the language of the realm and with only a brief occupation by the British in 1762, Spain ruled the Philippines until 1898.

At his father's knee, Ninoy learned that there were courageous Filipinos in every century who prayed, worked and fought for freedom. Ninoy was especially moved and fascinated by the stories of his grandfather, General Servillano Aquino, a contemporary of Jose Rizal, Marcelo H. del Pilar, Andres Bonifacio, Emilio Aguinaldo and the other Filipino patriots who fought for independence from the Spanish at the turn of this century.

Ninoy's political and spiritual commitments were shaped in his teenage years by the words and the deeds of those Filipino patriots, especially Rizal, who worked and fought for freedom alongside his grandfather against the Spanish and the Americans. In a letter from his cell in a Marcos prison, Ninoy writes, "I heard the great martyr-hero [Rizal] speaking to me from his grave."

Apparently, Ninoy had been reading from Rizal's favorite Christian devotional, Thomas à Kempis's *Imitation of Christ.* Ninoy continues, "Like à Kempis, Rizal believed that God is the God of freedom who makes us love it by weighting the yoke upon our shoulders . . . Rizal said that we can only win freedom by deserving it and that to earn it we must improve the mind and enhance the dignity of the individual, 'love what is just, what is good, what is great, to the point of dying for it.'"[1]

Ninoy learned from his father that the price of freedom had come high. Tens of thousands of Filipinos had died at the turn of this century fighting for independence against Spain and the United States. Thousands of the dead had been members of the secret Katipunan Society founded in the Philippines by Bonifacio in 1892. These courageous Filipinos had pledged their lives to the cause of liberation and they had signed the pledge with drops of their own blood. On 23 August 1896, the 10,000 members of the Katipunan Society tore up their cedulas (identity cards required by the Spanish) in open defiance of Spanish rule. Thousands of Katipunan members died in the violence that followed.

Ninoy's grandfather, Servillano Aquino, was a member of the Katipunan Society. General Aguinaldo, the leader of the revolution, appointed Aquino the commander of all freedom fighters from the province of Tarlac. When the Spanish were defeated there, Colonel Aquino was appointed military governor of the province. But when another battle turned against the revolution, Grandfather Aquino was captured by the Spanish, sentenced to be hanged and then released under the provisions of a general amnesty signed with the Spanish on 20 December 1897.

In 1898, America went to war with Spain and Admiral George Dewey's American fleet sailed into Manila Harbor, destroyed the Spanish fleet, and invited the Filipino patriots under Aguinaldo to ally themselves with the Americans against the still powerful Spanish occupying forces. Filipinos thought they had found a savior in their brave new friends from America. In fact, they had found another half-century of bondage.

On 19 May 1898, Aguinaldo met Admiral Dewey on his flagship in Manila Bay. Dewey promised Aguinaldo that in exchange for Filipino help in defeating the Spanish, the United States "would recognize Philippine independence under American protection."

Aguinaldo agreed and with Admiral Dewey's blessing, on 12 June 1898, proclaimed Philippine independence from Spain. On 23 January 1899, while the war with Spain still raged, Aguinaldo was himself inaugurated the first President of the first Republic of the Philippines. President Aguinaldo called a Congress, adopted a Constitution, and formally established the first Philippine Republic while leading his troops alongside his American allies in the war against Spain.

However, the Americans broke their promises of an independent Philippines. When the United States and Spain signed the Treaty of Paris on 10 December 1898, ending the Spanish-American war, Spain was asked to formally cede the Philippines, Cuba, Guam and Puerto Rico to the United States in exchange for $20 million. Furious Filipinos argued that Spain had no right to cede the Philippines to anyone and that Admiral Dewey, representing the U.S., had promised to grant independence to the Philippines at the close of the war with Spain.

When the United States refused to honor its promise and moved to turn the Philippines into an American colony, the Filipinos had no other choice but to take up arms again, this time against the Americans. Once again, Ninoy's grandfather volunteered in the cause of independence. Aguinaldo appointed Servillano Aquino to be a general in the resistance but the Filipinos were outmanned and outgunned by vastly superior American forces.

The Americans conducted a bloody war of aggression against the Philippines. Atrocities were commonplace. In the town of Balangiga, Samar, American soldiers imprisoned men, women and children in large wooden pens where they were forced to sleep standing in the rain. To free the townspeople Filipino freedom fighters ambushed the American garrison and killed 54 American soldiers. In retaliation,

General "Howlin' Jake" Smith issued these orders: "Kill and burn, kill and burn, the more you kill and the more you burn the more you please me."[2] This scorched earth policy left at least 100,000 Filipinos dead in Batangas alone.

We know that 10,000 American soldiers died fighting to gain possession of the Philippines. What we don't know is how many Filipinos died in battle, in confinement or of war-related illness and starvation. Western journalists who covered the war estimate that between 250,000 and 1,000,000 Filipinos lost their lives in the carnage.

At the war's end, Ninoy's grandfather came down from the mountains to surrender and in September, 1900, he was imprisoned by Arthur MacArthur, America's military governor of the Philippines. Ninoy's grandfather remained in prison until 1904, when he was granted amnesty by President Theodore Roosevelt. The first Republic of the Philippines had lasted less than one year and the Philippines spent the next 42 years as an American colony.

How ironic that just 45 years later, Ninoy's father would be imprisoned for "cooperating with the Japanese" by Arthur MacArthur's son, General Douglas MacArthur, head of the American forces in the Philippines. It was not really so difficult to understand why Benigno Aquino, Sr., had "cooperated" with the Japanese. His primary political goal was independence for the Filipino people from whatever foreign nation occupied the Philippines, America or the Japanese. "I don't care who gives us independence," Ninoy's father once declared, "as long as we start independence by ourselves."[3]

Benigno Aquino, Sr., had been fighting for independence from the Americans since 1919, when he was first elected the deputy from Tarlac. He learned of Ninoy's birth by ship-to-shore radio when he was sailing to Washington, D.C., to negotiate Filipino independence. Ninoy's father was a primary force in Filipino politics, respected by his countrymen and by the Americans who ruled them. In 1935, just six years before the Japanese invasion, the United States had granted the Philippines, its only Asian colony, commonwealth status. Manuel Quezon was elected the first president of that commonwealth and Ninoy's father was chosen to proclaim Quezon's candidacy at a mass political rally in the newly built Rizal Memorial Stadium.

Don Benigno was a skilled orator and fearless debater. No issue was too small for public scrutiny. His confrontation with President Quezon over the separation of judicial and executive powers won Assemblyman Aquino the reputation for being a kind of conscience of the government. Aquino was the first man in the history of Filipino politics to be appointed the official campaign manager of his party and in the elections of 1938 he led the Partido Nacionalista to a total victory sweep.

By 1938, Ninoy's father was perhaps the most powerful man in Filipino politics. The Aquino mansion in Concepcion was built that year. The dining room table was long enough to seat twenty-four people for a formal dinner in high-back chairs. But it wasn't unusual for the room to seat sixty or seventy people for a heated political discussion or party strategy session. Ninoy Aquino spent his childhood years in a home charged with the excitement and intrigue of political power.

Then came the Japanese invasion in 1942. Ninoy was just ten years old when President Quezon and his family escaped Manila on a submarine provided by the Americans. Quezon headed a Filipino government in exile in the United States until his death in 1944. At that time, Quezon's vice-president, Sergio Osmena, became the second president of the commonwealth, a government in exile. As World War II was ending, Osmena was invited to wade ashore at Leyte with General MacArthur and in 1945 was installed formally in the Malacañang Palace where he served as president until his term ended in 1946.

During the war years, the Philippines had two governments. The first, the government in exile in the United States under Quezon and then Osmena. The second was in Japanese-occupied Manila under President Jose P. Laurel. That Occupation Republic of the Philippines (considered the Second Republic) lasted just two years, 1943–1945, and ended upon the Americans' return.

In 1946, Manuel A. Roxas was elected the last president of the commonwealth and on 4 July 1946, when the United States granted the Philippines its independence, Roxas became the first president of the third Republic of the Philippines. Ninoy was just entering his teen years as his father was facing trial for serving under President Laurel during the Japanese occupation of the Philippines.

During his early childhood years, Ninoy seldom had a chance to be close to his busy father. Don Benigno was away from home on political missions much of the time. But during World War II, Ninoy took every possible opportunity to be near his dad.

"During the Japanese times," Ninoy remembered, "I shined his shoes for him; I was his valet, his muchacho, and I loved it." Don Benigno's arrest and approaching trial only drew father and son closer. The senior Aquino was already making a political comeback. He couldn't run for office, but in 1947 he campaigned feverishly for the Liberal Party in Tarlac.

"I don't think he ever fought so hard," Ninoy said as he remembered those months in 1947 when he was fourteen years old and commuting on weekends from his school in Manila to his family home in Concepcion. "I used to go to Tarlac every Saturday just to be with him. I would go campaigning with him and I developed a very close relationship to him."[4]

During his weekend fifty-mile commutes, Ninoy would read the daily papers and prepare to take his place in the discussions and debates that would echo through his family home in Concepcion. Even as a little boy he was sent to the door to welcome his father's distinguished guests. They were amazed by Ninoy's political interests as he chatted with them in the huge living room decorated with original oil paintings, carvings, statuaries and imported chandeliers. Often on the weekends, before and after World War II, Ninoy sat with Don Benigno and his friends around that long table or under those ornate chandeliers hearing stories about the nation's past and strategies that would shape the nation's future.

Ninoy fought to spend every possible minute with his father. On Saturday night, 20 December 1947, when Ninoy was fifteen years old, he accompanied Don Benigno on a special weekend trip to Manila to attend the boxing event of the decade. The bantamweight champion of the world, Manuel Ortiz of Mexico, had accepted a challenge to his crown by Tirso del Rosario, a boxer from Tarlac, the Aquinos' home province.

Ninoy and his father sat at ringside. Ten thousand people jammed the stadium to capacity. The first three rounds were uneventful. During the fourth round, the Mexican champion knocked the Filipino challenger to the canvas and the crowd stood screaming encouragement to their fallen hero as the count against him began. Ninoy's father jumped to his feet at ringside, then suddenly sat down again. Ninoy noticed the look of anguish in his father's eyes. Apparently, Don Benigno had felt a searing pain in his chest and left arm, but he refused to leave before the fight had ended. Once again Ortiz knocked Tirso to the canvas. This time, Don Benigno could not join the screaming crowd. Suddenly, he slumped into Ninoy's arms.

Ninoy clutched at his father and tried to lift him up. Other people noticed the young man struggling to revive Senator Aquino and rushed to help. A Dr. Guillermo Rustia led the volunteers carrying Don Benigno from the stadium. There were no ambulances in the area. The doctor hailed a cab and administered assistance during the frantic drive to the Philippine General Hospital. Not long after their arrival, Ninoy's father died.

In Nick Joaquin's biography of the Aquino family, *The Aquinos of Tarlac*, one of Ninoy's older brothers, Tony Aquino, describes what happened the next day as Benigno Aquino lay in state at the Funeria Nacional. Apparently, President Roxas was among the first of the visitors. He was met by Ninoy's grandfather, General Servillano Aquino, wearing the full dress uniform of the Revolution.

The president told the general that the dead man would be given all the honors due him: necrological services and a funeral under the auspices of the State. The general looked at the president as though they were face to face on a battlefield. "Mr. President," said my grandfather, "nobody thought of giving Benigno any honors when he was alive. In fact, some people suspected him of being a traitor. I don't see how, now that he is dead, he is less of a traitor. I will take my son back to Tarlac and bury him in my own way. Thank you very much for your offer."

President Roxas approached Tony Aquino and asked the young man to speak to his grandfather. Tony still remembers that conversation. "I had talked to my father," he said. "I thought he would be bitter about all those accusations against him; but he was not. He just said: 'History will vindicate me.' But my grandfather was different; he was very hurt. So he said again: 'Thank you, Mr. Roxas. I will bury my son with the honors I think he deserves. Why should he now be a patriot because he is dead?' And he said to me, 'Tony, we are taking your father back to Concepcion. Hire a special train.' But we were able to prevail on him to accept the President's arrangements."[5]

Joaquin describes the scene on 29 December 1947, when the entire Congress of the Philippines gathered at the University of the Philippines to pay tribute to Don Benigno Aquino. Claro M. Recto, in his controversial eulogy, reminded the assembled leaders of the Philippines that the Allied powers had exonerated Emperor Hirohito but imprisoned Senator Aquino. Hirohito was a valuable pawn in the game of international politics. Aquino was not. So the Emperor remained free while Aquino was locked up in Tokyo's Sugamo Prison.

Standing by the body of his friend, Recto said:

> You were worthless to them in this game of power politics where they have always wanted to use Filipinos as lackeys, fieldhands and cannon fodder. That is why Hirohito continues on the throne of his glorious ancestors while you were thrown into a prison cell where you got the disease that would take you to the grave.
>
> Benigno Aquino! Divine Providence, in claiming jurisdiction over you, has denied human tribunals the right to judge you. The government, in paying you this homage, has cleared you of the calumny heaped upon you without due process of law. And the nation, in associating herself with this demonstration of grief, proclaims that you have served her well.
>
> Rest in peace, faithful servant of your people! When minds have recovered their serenity and intellects their discernment, when your countrymen have learned to live, work and think only for one nation and one flag, without a lackey's servility or a courtier's fawning before any foreign

power, then they will remember your splendid achievements and the noble example of your nationalism, virile and blameless, and they will call you a true patriot because you were always a true Filipino.[6]

On 31 December 1947, Benigno Aquino, Sr., was buried in his beloved Concepcion, Tarlac. Joaquin reports that the funeral procession was so mammoth that "the head of it was already in the cemetery, while the tail of it was still in the church." Four days after Ninoy's father died, the case of treason pending against him was dismissed by the People's Court. Across the nation he was praised for his immense contribution to the Filipinos' fight for independence.

Ninoy was fifteen when his father died, a senior in high school. He accompanied his mother, Doña Aurora Aquino, to the various memorial services being held for his father, but he hated them. "Ninoy thought they were being hypocritical," Doña Aurora remembers. "His father was dead, and the leaders who had condemned him while he was living had waited until his death to give him praise."

The following years were difficult financially for Senora Aquino and her six school-aged children. Before World War II, Don Benigno had mortgaged much of his farm land in Tarlac to help finance his political campaigns. To repay the loans and to feed his family during the war years, Ninoy's father sold most of the Aquino holdings. When he died, the family had what remained of their mother's land, a house in Manila and their family home in Concepcion. The total family income at Don Benigno's death was less than $5,000 a year. The Aquinos had planned to enroll Ninoy at Kellogg College in Pomona, California, where he could study animal husbandry and farming. But with the elder Aquino's death, so died Ninoy's chances to study in America.

When his father died, Ninoy thought his own world had ended. And though the young man lost all interest in his studies, Ninoy had enrolled in Manila's Ateneo University, a Catholic school steeped in the teachings and the traditions of its Jesuit founders. Apparently, he was determined to finish his university training in a hurry. He enrolled at the University of the Philippines to double his class load and commuted between the two schools. Ninoy was no longer serious about his studies. After his father's death he was bored. He escaped by going to the movies. He spent much of his time brooding and alone.

In the summer, Ninoy worked with the laborers at his brother Billy's truck-body building plant. Ninoy was determined to be self-supporting. He refused to ask his mother for money. He wanted to pay his own university bills.

In 1949, Jose Laurel, the father of Ninoy's boyhood friend, Doy Laurel, and the same man who had served as president of the Philippines during the Japanese occupation, ran for president against Elpidio Quirino. Ninoy had just graduated from high school. And though he was a freshman at Ateneo University, he skipped classes to join Laurel on the road. Ninoy became Laurel's "wonder boy." They were ambushed in Sipocot and machine-gunned in Cebu.

When Laurel lost the election, Ninoy was furious. "We were boiling mad over the worst fraud in Philippine politics," Ninoy recalled, "the darkest polls in our history." Gladly, Ninoy joined with those planning a revolution. "I was running guns," Ninoy told an interviewer. "It was up to the mountain for us, we were set for rebellion."[7] Then Laurel got word of this revolution in the making and called it off. Instead of going into the mountains to take up arms, Ninoy Aquino went back to school at the state run University of the Philippines. That same year, he became a reporter for the *Manila Times*.

Cory

At the close of World War II, while Manila still lay in ruins, Cory's family had moved temporarily to the United States. The Cojuangcos lived for one year in Philadelphia, where thirteen-year-old Cory was enrolled for her sophomore high school year at Raven Hill. At the end of that year, Cory's mother and father moved back to the Philippines; while Cory transferred to the Notre Dame Convent School, operated by the Society of St. Ursula in New York City, to finish her high school education. Cory spent her junior and senior high school years studying in the old, four-story brownstone mansion which housed her rather exclusive, religious high school in Manhattan.

In the 1949 Notre Dame Convent School yearbook, there is a photo of Corazon Aquino with a quotation from Pope Pius XII. "It is up to you," the caption reads, "to bring to the life you are entering, to the state you must help to form, an energy of true religious faith." Following the quote, the yearbook editor added, "From what we already know of Cora, this might be called a prediction of the future. Beneath her gentle manner lie a friendly disposition and a quiet charm which make her an indispensable part of our group."[8]

In May, 1949, sixteen-year-old Cory (still nicknamed "Cora") was one of just fourteen high school seniors graduating from the Notre Dame School, "Today's private Catholic secondary school for the education of tomorrow's Christian woman." During those post-World War II years in Manila, while Ninoy was learning at his father's knee about the fight for Filipino independence, Cory was in America studying in "a small school, characterized by a warm, family spirit . . . based on the Christian belief that each person is a God-related being . . . . A place where spiritual growth is fostered by religious studies, retreats, liturgies and community service . . . ."[9]

While Ninoy was defending his father's life-long struggle for Filipino independence and passing out Nacionalista Party handbills in the streets of Manila, Cory was living in New York City, studying "Introduction to the Old and New Testaments," "Faith and Justice," "Making Moral Decisions," along with the usual courses in science, social studies, French, English and math.

While Ninoy, still in his teen years, was dodging bullets to protect the ballot boxes of Tarlac and accusing the newly elected president of election fraud, Cory was walking in Central Park, meditating on the life and teachings of Jesus, staring up at European masterpieces at the nearby Metropolitan Museum of Fine Art, or squinting at the heavens in the neighboring Hayden Planetarium.

And while Ninoy was tramping about the mountains and burying guns at Peñafrancia for a would-be revolution, Cory was on vacation in Manila, celebrating her high school graduation and preparing for her festive debut at the Fiesta Pavilion of the elegant Manila Hotel.

Ninoy might have seen Cory's picture in the society page of the *Manila Bulletin* on 15 August 1949, when she appeared under the caption, "Manila Vacation." Cory, her sister, Teresita, and a young niece were photographed in a garden after arriving "recently from the States to spend the summer holidays with their parents."

Ninoy

Toward the end of that same year, Ninoy had transferred from the Ateneo University to the University of the Philippines where he would study law. School bored him. He had spent the last decade living in the heart of his nation's struggle to become a free and independent member of the community of nations. It must have been tiresome and confusing for Ninoy to sit in classes with students who were more interested in singing "Come-On-A-My House" than the new Filipino national anthem.

Ninoy was also growing tired of trying to explain and defend his father's actions on behalf of Filipino independence during the Japanese occupation. Pro-American Filipino students worked to make Ninoy's life miserable. We know that at least one of his professors joined the students in their campaign. An American-born Jesuit teacher at Ateneo, who had been imprisoned by the Japanese, had ripped up Ninoy's essays with "black looks and bad marks. . . . I don't know whether he was bitter at me because I was the son of a 'collaborator,'" Ninoy said at the time, but he suspected it. Finally, Ninoy decided to complete his university education on a part-time basis while working as a reporter for the *Manila Times*.

Ninoy's biographer, Nick Joaquin, describes Ninoy in his teen years as "a melancholy stripling, pale and shy and thin, with the smoldering good looks that could have mistaken him for a poet." In fact, in his 1948 San Beda High School graduation yearbook photo, Ninoy looks tired and unhappy at best. His shiny black hair is parted in the middle. His eyes look suspicious. He isn't smiling.

Nick Joaquin helps us understand Ninoy's unhappy graduation photo with these words: "He was grimly practical," Joaquin explains, "and worried over the finances of his family."[10]

Ninoy was seventeen when he applied at the *Manila Times*. He had no experience as a journalist but Joaquin "Chino" Roces, the distinguished columnist and publisher of the *Times*, hired him anyway, as a copy boy at approximately $7.50 a month. "I guess I was hired because I was Benigno Aquino, Jr.," Ninoy once admitted, "for old times' sake and sentimental reasons. Anyway," he added, "now I was really self-supporting."[11]

When Ninoy was still a child he worked as a kind of reporter for his father. At those large dinners at their home in Concepcion, Ninoy circulated among the guests passing out cigars and gathering important tidbits of information that he overheard along the way.

Ninoy read every newspaper or newsmagazine that he could get his hands on. "Guess what happened?" he would say running into his father's study with the latest news. "Where did you hear that?" his father would ask. "I have my sources," Ninoy, the child, would answer, grinning.

Don Benigno knew his son's sources. He even nicknamed Ninoy after them. Before World War II, Don Benigno called his son "TVT" for *Times-Vanguardia-Talibia*, the Philippines leading news-media conglomerate. When the Japanese occupied the Philippines, Don Benigno changed Ninoy's nickname to *Domei*, the leading Japanese propaganda paper.

At San Beda High School, Ninoy joined just one extracurricular organization, *The Bedan*, his high school newspaper. He covered sports events and wrote an occasional editorial. Observing Ninoy's insatiable curiosity and knowing that his son "had a way with words," Don Benigno confided in his wife, Doña Aurora that one day Ninoy could become "a good journalist."[12]

It was no surprise that late in 1949 Ninoy went to the publishers of the *Manila Times* looking for a job. He was fascinated by newspapers and newspaper people. When Joe Bautista, a *Times* editor, asked Don Benigno's seventeen-year-old son what he wanted to do, Ninoy answered, "I want to be a reporter." Ninoy was hired, but not as a reporter. "At that time," Ninoy confessed, "I couldn't even write a decent sentence." In spite of parentage and privilege, Ninoy had to work his way up the ladder just like all the others.

Ninoy's first six months at the *Manila Times* were a crash course in journalism. He practically lived in the newspaper's offices. As a copy boy, he ran pages between reporters and their editors and back again. He moved up to research, digging through the archives for background materials and double checking sources. There was a celebration when Ninoy graduated up to his own "column," the obituary page. (It didn't matter to him that nobody else wanted it.) Ninoy had served as wire service monitor, a substitute staff writer and an assistant reporter on the national defense beat when North Korean troops carrying Soviet-made weapons crossed the 38th parallel, invading South Korea on 25 June 1950.

"I'll go," Ninoy volunteered when the editors of the *Manila Times* decided to send a reporter along with the Philippine Expeditionary Force that was being sent to join the United Nations' troops in Korea. The other senior reporters had all declined. Ninoy didn't have a wife or a family. During his months at the *Times* he had paid his dues, some days spending twenty-four hours at the newspaper office, watching reporters at work, studying the way stories are edited and writing a few good stories on his own.

A young woman on the *Times* staff with the misleading name, Jim Austria, had taken Ninoy under her wing. Establishing herself as one of Manila's leading writers, she offered to train Ninoy in writing skills. By the time the United Nations' forces were ready to land at Inchon and press their way toward Seoul, *Times* editors were convinced that even though Ninoy was just seventeen years old, he could represent them well on the Korean front.

Ninoy Aquino, fledgling war correspondent, arrived in Korea in September, 1950, two months before his eighteenth birthday. He joined an international press corps of more than 300 white journalists from around the world. He was the first Asian reporter on the scene, a skinny kid whose ears stuck out and whose broad, eager smile stretched almost between them. While the tough, battle-weary news people were drinking rice wine, imported beer or cocktails, Ninoy drank only milk. The reporters liked this stripling kid in his oversized khaki uniform complete with lace-up boots and fur-collared flight jacket. Doña Aurora remembers that the reporters nicknamed Ninoy affectionately, "Aquino, the milk boy."

Just days after Ninoy's arrival in Korea, the United Nations' troops pushed back across the Thirty-eighth Parallel on their way to "reunifying the country." Seoul was liberated from the North Korean invaders. Ninoy interviewed South Korea's president, Syngman Rhee. The old man was jubilant. "The war is practically over," Ninoy wrote home, "and I expect to be back by Christmas."

On 15 October 1950, Ninoy dispatched news that General MacArthur and President Truman were meeting on Wake Island to make plans for ending the war. By October 21, United Nations' troops had advanced over the Thirty-eighth Parallel and after a two-day fight had taken Pyongyan, the North Korean capital. Ninoy had hitched rides on borrowed jeeps to report front line action. He talked his way onto a UN bomber to see the war's destruction from the air. He had connected with the Philippines' Tenth Battalion Combat Team camped in a chestnut orchard outside Pusan and wrote home that his countrymen had arrived too late for the fighting.

Then, on 6 November 1950, Chinese communist troops attacked across their border in a kind of warning maneuver. UN troops were massing on the Yalu River on the Chinese borders of Manchuria. Earlier, the Chinese had announced to the world that they "would not stand idly by" if the approaching UN troops threatened their sovereignty. MacArthur thought they were bluffing, but on 26 November 1950, one day before Ninoy's eighteenth birthday, hundreds of thousands of Chinese communist soldiers, on foot and on horseback, poured into North Korea in a massive, mid-winter counter offensive that forced UN troops to retreat in disarray.

"It was a bitter winter," Ninoy wrote the *Times*. "The winds never stopped howling."

Ninoy was on his way north to do a story on the Seventh Regiment of America's First Cavalry Division when he ran into the Americans going south in frantic retreat.

"Their tanks were useless," he wrote. "The roads were a quagmire and the American tanks couldn't maneuver. The [Chinese] horsemen were running around them swooping down on them with molotovs and knocking off the gasoline in the tanks. The horses were small, they were Mongol ponies, but they came in droves, wave upon human wave attacking."

The 140,000 American troops were in retreat and Ninoy found himself in the midst of them, staggering through the snow, struggling to survive the winter cold and the mortar fire that rained down endlessly upon them.

"One day we were told to secure a position," Ninoy remembered. "I was walking behind the Americans. All of a sudden, machine-gun fire. We all dived to the ground. I don't know how many of the Americans ahead of me got hit, but one of them staggered backwards, caught the fire of the guns, was hurled down and fell on top of me. His blood streamed down on me. I pawed myself and cried:

'Blood! I'm hit! Medic, medic!' A Filipino sergeant crawled towards me, grabbed me by the collar, dragged me out from under the dead man, and pushed me into a ditch. Then he shouted: 'Tanks! Tanks!' But the tanks couldn't move."

Ninoy couldn't write after that. "Whenever I heard a shot, I'd jump and start shaking all over again." The teenaged war correspondent spent Christmas in Manila. He tried to return to normal newspaper work in the *Times* offices, but he began to brood about the friends he had made in Korea. The Allies had regrouped and were advancing. Ninoy's depression deepened.

"Look, son," a doctor said when Ninoy confessed his growing depression, "if you run away once, you will run away again—and you can't just go on running away."

His publisher, Chino Roces, understood. Ninoy returned to the front. "The idea of death was always with me," he wrote. "The American fellow who had fallen on top of me was just a kid, a young kid. Dead so young . . . Death respected no one. You could be a millionaire or poor guy, a genius or dimwit, but neither money nor brains could help you. Here was where I became a fatalist," he added. "And this was to carry me all the way."[13]

In April, 1951 President Truman fired General Douglas MacArthur for his public statements against the president's plans to negotiate a truce in Korea. As far as MacArthur was concerned, "there is no substitute for victory." For Ninoy, the Korean war became a stalemate on 30 June 1951, when the new United Nations Supreme Commander began to negotiate a truce with the communist forces. Ninoy wired his editor for permission to come home.

"You're a worn-out soldier, kiddo," editor Boguslav replied. "Come home." Ninoy had been covering the bloody conflict for nine long months. He had watched too many people die and had even been wounded himself. Ninoy's front-line stories had made front-page news. He returned to Manila an eighteen-year-old hero, received by President Quirino at Malacañang Palace where Ninoy's mother, Doña Aurora Aquino, proudly pinned on her smiling son the Philippine Legion of Honor for Meritorious Service. Ninoy went back to his desk at the *Manila Times* and re-enrolled in his law classes at the University of the Philippines.

"What did Korea do to me?" Ninoy remembered later. "Aside from aging me ten or twenty years, it gave me the fatalism that's with me to this day. Do your job and hope tomorrow will be another day—and if tomorrow doesn't come, that's it . . . ."[14]

One of Manila's "most eligible bachelors," Ninoy dated the most beautiful and desirable women in the Philippines, including the "Muse of Manila," Imelda Romualdez, who one day would become Imelda Marcos, the nation's first lady. Ninoy also dated a debutante from his own beloved Tarlac, Corazon Cojuangco, who would become his wife.

Cory

While Ninoy was struggling to survive front-line combat in a frozen foxhole in Korea and commuting between his room at the Correspondents Club in Tokyo and his desk at the *Manila Times*, Corazon Cojuangco was in the United States, a student at Mt. Saint Vincent College, just a thirty-five minute commute by private car or train from uptown Manhattan. The serenely wooded campus on a hillside overlooking the Hudson River lies in the heart of Riverdale, then an exclusive residential suburb of New York City.

"Mt. Saint Vincent provides," in the words of its current catalogue, "a liberal arts education that can open doors for a lifetime. You will learn to think clearly and communicate confidently. You'll build a broad intellectual understanding of the world, making you adaptable to future change."

Cory majored in French and math. "She was so quiet," Sister Julia Marie Weser remembered. When Cory was elected president of the Philippines, Sister Weser seemed surprised. "She showed few signs of anything so dramatic." Her teacher in English literature, Sister Elizabeth Marian Murray, remembers Cory as "my quiet and proper student . . . very industrious, vocal and genial . . . ." Sister Murray added that she thought then as now Corazon Aquino "has deep religious conviction and great integrity of character."[15]

To other classmates Cory was a "bookish type, pleasant, a good student who always smiled but was not the kind of girl who made a big stir."[16] A school teacher from New Jersey, who remembers sitting next to Cory in her classes at Mt. Saint Vincent, claimed that Cory was ". . . quiet, intelligent, unassuming."[17]

Apparently, Cory learned her culinary skills during her college days at Mt. Saint Vincent. She and her sister, Terry, spent weekends with Tita (Auntie) Belen, their mother's sister. Cory was curious about the preparation and serving of ethnic foods and often went into a kitchen to inquire about the ingredients of a special dish, writing down on a scrap of paper exactly how those ingredients were prepared. Tita Belen was just one of Cory's many cooking teachers.

In 1953, Cory graduated from Mt. Saint Vincent with a bachelor's degree in French and mathematics. Betty Go Belmonte, one of Cory's earliest biographers, says of her four years at Mt. Saint Vincent: "In a class that produced six doctors and scores of teachers, nurses and social workers, she [Cory] went on to be what she once called herself, 'just a housewife.'"[18]

3

Ninoy, Journalist and Presidential Advisor; Cory, Student in America (1951–1954)

My single prayer has been: Let me not live to be useless. I think
God has answered my prayers . . . .

Senator Benigno Aquino, Jr.

Those not firm in the faith cannot understand the power of
prayers. Those who are [firm] never fail to be amazed at how
they are answered . . . exceeding human expectation and understanding . . . .

President Corazon C. Aquino

In 1951, Ninoy and Cory met again. She was home in Manila on
holiday from her sophomore year at Mt. Saint Vincent College in
Riverdale, New York. Apparently, Ninoy's experiences as a war correspondent in Korea had changed him considerably and Cory noticed the changes.

"I was impressed," she recalls, "because he was much more intelligent and the most articulate guy I had met. If he was not mature in
years, in outlook he was."[1]

They had met before in Tarlac in 1942 during World War II when
they were still children. "Was it love at first sight?" an interviewer
once asked her. "Heavens, no," she answered. "I was nine years old.
What does a nine-year-old girl feel about a nine-year-old boy?" Then
she added, "I remember Ninoy kept bragging he was a year ahead of
me in school; so I didn't even bother to talk to him."[2]

They met again during their mid-teen years when Ninoy was beginning his studies at the Ateneo University. "There were so many
parties," Cory recalls, "and we kept running into each other." If
Ninoy had any romantic interest in Corazon Cojuangco, she didn't

notice and she didn't care. "At that time," she explained, "my idea was to get married to someone older, at least five or six years older. My father is five years older than my mother and in school they tell you that girls mature faster than boys."

Ninoy

His experiences as a war correspondent had aged Ninoy prematurely. While other privileged Filipinos in their late teens were watching Bogart and Brando movies and dancing to Johnny Ray's "Cry," eighteen-year-old Ninoy was serving as the *Times* specialist on war and foreign news. And though he was photographed squiring various beauty queens about Manila, appearing at the nightspots and on the society page was a professional, not a personal decision.

Mrs. Joaquin Roces, the wife of Ninoy's publisher, had volunteered to produce the Miss Philippines Pageant. Because he was the nation's newest and youngest hero, Ninoy got the escort job. But the young journalist was more interested in Corazon Cojuangco than in the beauty queens he escorted about Manila. In fact, when Cory returned to the United States that summer of 1951, Ninoy began a long distance correspondence with her. His letters impressed Cory. She remembers them as being beautiful and not at all "mushy."[3]

Many people liked the way Ninoy wrote. Besides his regular stories on the Korean war, the young journalist was doing a series of field reports on the growing threat of violence and corruption in the elections scheduled for later that year. He did several feature articles on Ramon Magsaysay, President Quirino's secretary of defense, who had determined to "clean up" Filipino elections. In the past, powerful businessmen, land owners and regional warlords had been able to buy votes, stuff ballot boxes, change the final election results and scare away or even kill opposition candidates, their campaign leaders and supporters.

The National Movement for Free Elections (NAMFREL) was born that year and its observers joined ROTC officers appointed by Magsaysay in policing the polling places. The 1951 elections were not as corrupt or as violent as many had predicted. Defense Secretary Magsaysay was grateful to the gutsy young reporter whose articles had contributed to his campaign for election reform.

Just a few days after the election, Magsaysay called Ninoy. "Can you be at the airport at three o'clock?" Magsaysay asked. "We are leaving for Bacolod." Briefly, he explained to the young reporter that an opposition candidate named Moises Padilla had been murdered.

The corrupt and powerful governor of Negros Occidental was the chief suspect. He and his "special police" and "civilian guards" had conducted a reign of terror against their enemies in the province. Magsaysay was angry. He was determined to put an end to the triumph of bullets over ballots. He invited Ninoy to accompany him on the dangerous journey.

Ninoy's headline story on the death of Moises Padilla, who was shot in the back by the forces of the governor, made Magsaysay a hero. "Democracy in the Philippines is dying," the people cried, "and Magsaysay is its only savior." Magsaysay made the most of Ninoy's dramatic description of Padilla's death. In 1954, Magsaysay would seek and win the presidency of the Philippines. On the campaign trail audiences cheered and wept when Magsaysay remembered that night, "When I held in my arms the bleeding symbol of democracy: the body of Moises Padilla."[4]

Ninoy was a great story teller. In 1952, the owners of LVN Studios in Manila asked him to write a screenplay for a film dramatizing his experiences as a war correspondent. Ninoy not only wrote the script, but he scouted locations, coached actors and served as technical consultant to the shooting and editing of "Korea."

Show business was only a sideline to Ninoy. His real interest was journalism. Actually, at nineteen years old, Ninoy was working long hours every day as a reporter for the *Manila Times* and finishing his studies in law at the University of the Philippines in a round-the-clock frenzy of stories to investigate and write, deadlines to meet, law libraries to visit, legal briefs and case studies to read, lectures to attend and exams to pass.

At the close of the 1952 school year, Ninoy accepted a roving reporter assignment for the *Times*. Philippines President Quirino had suggested a "Pacific Pact" of Southeast Asian nations against communism and it was Ninoy's job to discover the general attitude toward such a pact from the leaders of Taiwan, Hong Kong, Thailand, Vietnam, Burma, Malaya, Singapore and Indonesia.

Those three months visiting the capitals of Southeast Asia revolutionized Ninoy's thinking about democracy and the western democratic states. He began the tour convinced that communism was a terrible threat to Asian freedom and that it was crucial for the South East Asian nations to be allied with the west. He ended the tour shocked and saddened by the terrible reputation that France, England, Holland, Australia and even America had earned while they were colonizing the Asian peoples:

To the Asian, [Ninoy wrote] the Western argument that "if communism wins, Asians stand to lose their civil liberties" is meaningless.

To the Asian now jailed by the French in the numerous prisons of Vietnam for being "too nationalistic," civil liberties have no meaning. To the Asian jailed [by the British] on St. John's Island in Singapore for possessing intelligence and nationalistic spirit above the average, civil liberties are likewise meaningless. The Filipino is aware of and has enjoyed America's benevolence; but to the rest of Asia, the American looks like the Frenchman, the Britisher and the Dutchman. To Asians, these people are the symbols of oppression. And many Asians would prefer communism to Western oppression.[5]

Ninoy discovered that Asians were fearful of being drawn into the cold war between the superpowers. They were afraid that Quirino's proposed organization of Southeast Asian nations was just one more American trick to get them aligned with the West against their Eastern neighbors.

Those same Asian nations had been colonized, often brutally, by the Western democratic states. Democracy was another name for oppression in that part of the world. "Asia for the Asians" was the cry that Ninoy heard in country after country. He began the journey believing in the Western theory that if communism were allowed to take hold in even one East Asian nation, the rest would fall like dominoes. Ninoy returned to Manila with the awful reality that "To the Asian, democracy and oppression are synonymous."[6]

Ninoy's articles helped lead to the formation of SEATO, the South East Asian Treaty Organization. But Ninoy himself returned to Manila convinced that the Philippines needed a president who was more sensitive to the problems of the poor and more open to the cries for justice that were arising from the peasant and workers unions and even from the Filipino revolutionaries, the Huks, who were fighting the government from their strongholds in the mountains.

Ninoy came home believing that Ramon Magsaysay should replace Quirino as the next president of the Philippines and the young journalist spent much of his extra time in 1952 and 1953 convincing Magsaysay to run for president and then helping him get elected. The "neutral" reporter was finding himself more and more a political activist.

Ninoy began his career as a journalist when he was just seventeen. It was easier to remain neutral and uncritical of his elders when he was still underage. But in 1953, Ninoy turned twenty-one. He had come of age and his experiences at home and abroad were making it more and more difficult for Ninoy to remain neutral in the various issues that were confronting and confounding the Filipino people and the people of Southeast Asia.

Cory

While Ninoy's views and values were being permanently revolutionized by his travels in the Philippines and throughout Southeast Asia, Cory was completing her education at Mt. Saint Vincent College just a thirty-minute commute from uptown Manhattan.

While Ninoy was discussing democracy, communism and the future of Asia with the leaders of eight Asian nations, Cory and her three fellow Filipino students were delighting the 106 classmates of their all-girl school with their preparation of traditional Filipino foods and their performances of traditional Filipino songs and dances.

While Ninoy was battling the corrupt governor of Negros Occidental and working behind the scenes to get Magsaysay elected president of the Philippines, Cory and her three Filipino classmates were dancing the quick steps of the Tinikling back and forth over the bamboo sticks to the eager applause of the Sisters of Charity and their young women classmates.

It is important to remember that although Cory Cojuangco was distant from the front lines and political battles that were shaping Ninoy, she was also being shaped by another kind of struggle in the comforts of her college campus in Riverdale, New York. By her late teenage years, Cory's spiritual training as a child had taken hold. Often during her high school and college years, Cory went to church every day. And in her room and on long walks through her heavily wooded campus above the Hudson River, she would meditate on the life of Jesus. Cory read widely. She was not unaware of the problems in her homeland. She prayed daily for her friends and family in the Philippines and she diligently sought God's wisdom and direction for her life and for theirs.

Even as a student, Cory Cojuangco's rosary was one of her most prized possessions. Everywhere she went, Cory carried that simple, silver crucifix hanging from a delicate strand of 59 crystal beads. Devout Catholic believers understand how helpful the rosary can be in bringing to mind the most important events in the life of Jesus. But there are Protestant believers who still find the practice strange, even offensive.

For Cory the rosary was a simple and helpful way to organize her meditation. At the beginning and the end of the day she would hold the cross in her hand and repeat silently the Apostle's Creed. Then Cory's fingers would move to the first large bead on the chain of beads attached to the cross. That bead, larger than the rest, would remind her to pray the Lord's Prayer. Whether she was walking on the path above the scenic Hudson River or kneeling in her room or in the college chapel, Cory would use the beads, one by one, to organize her meditations on the life of Jesus.

Her rosary beads were divided into five groups with ten crystal beads per group. On Mondays and Thursdays, Cory would use the beads to recall the five Joyful Mysteries surrounding Jesus' birth and childhood: the annunciation, the angel's visitation to Mary, the birth of Jesus, the dedication of the infant Jesus and the discovery of the twelve-year-old Jesus in the Temple with the teachers. On Tuesdays and Fridays Cory would recall the Sorrowful Mysteries surrounding Jesus' death: the agony in the garden, the scourging at the pillar, the crowning with thorns, carrying the cross on the Via Dolorosa and His crucifixion on Golgatha. And on Wednesdays and Saturdays, Cory would use her rosary to meditate on the five Glorious Mysteries: the resurrection, the Ascension into heaven, the descent of the Holy Spirit and the honoring of Jesus' mother, Mary.

The long-time feud between Protestant and Catholic believers concerning Mary was not an issue to Cory. Repeating the Ave Maria as she meditated on Christ's life, death and resurrection was as simple and as beautiful as a musician strumming a guitar to accompany a beautiful melody. Daily, throughout her life, Cory would use the rosary to think about Jesus. Ninoy, too, used the rosary to meditate upon these central New Testament teachings. In fact, after thinking about his Lord and praying one last time for strength and guidance, Ninoy got off the airplane that carried him home. He was shot and killed with his rosary still clutched in his hand.

While Ninoy was being shaped as a political activist, Cory was practicing the presence of Christ in her life and seeking God's will for the future. It is easy to praise Ninoy the activist while discounting the spiritual disciplines of Cory the pietist. But looking back over the years one cannot help but wonder if Cory's prayers were being answered for both of them.

Cory graduated with her bachelor's degree in French and mathematics in 1953 and returned to the Philippines immediately. She enrolled at the Far Eastern University for a three-semester course in law. She remarked later that she was not interested in becoming a lawyer, but that she was interested in understanding law as a discipline. Cory may have had another, more personal motive in choosing to study law.

During her last year at Mt. Saint Vincent, Cory and Ninoy had been writing each other regularly. That correspondence has not yet been made public. In fact, Cory has consistently refused every request to reveal the letters' contents. "That much of myself I would still want to keep private," she said. "When I am dead, then perhaps, the rest of the world can read them."[7]

Still, it isn't difficult to imagine at least the political content of those letters that Ninoy wrote Cory from his tour of Southeast Asia or from his desk at the *Manila Times*. Ninoy's letters must have challenged her thinking as his articles in the *Times* were challenging the thinking of a nation. He must have shared with her his own dreams about using his legal skills to help shape the future of the Philippines. Perhaps his letters helped to make Cory curious enough about the law to study it on her own. We can be certain that their letters were also romantic. When Cory returned home, Ninoy proposed marriage.

"Let's just be friends," Cory responded to Ninoy's first marriage proposals.[8] ". . . I thought it wiser," Cory explained years later, "since we had not really been together all that much, to see first if we really liked each other. So all that year after I graduated, when he was asking me to marry him, I thought it best for us to wait."[9]

Ninoy

Dating Ninoy Aquino must have been an exhausting and exasperating experience. He was still shuttling between his law classes and his reporting duties, but Ninoy's life had been complicated further by his growing friendship with Ramon Magsaysay who in December, 1953, had been inaugurated the third president of the third Republic of the Philippines.

Ninoy was offered a position in Magsaysay's government. He gratefully declined. Nevertheless, the new president continued to cultivate Ninoy's friendship, to seek the young journalist's advice and even to use him on an occasional secret mission. On Valentine's Day, 14 February, 1954, Ninoy began one such mission that would risk his life, help end his career as a "neutral" journalist and launch his life-long fight for justice in the Philippines.

Early the morning of February 15, Ninoy, his driver, a *Times* photographer and Manuel Manahan, chairman of Magsaysay's Presidential Complaints and Action Committee (PCAC) set out in an army jeep toward the foothills beyond and above Clark Air Force Base just north of Manila. As they sped around a hairpin curve in the bumpy, unpaved road above the little town of Angeles, a military checkpoint appeared directly ahead. A heavy steel barrier blocked their way.

"Stop!"

A young sergeant in the Armed Forces of the Philippines (AFP) carrying a machine gun with a pistol strapped to his waist stood in the road in front of them. Ninoy showed his presidential papers. An officer was summoned.

"You know that this is an unsecured area?" a lieutenant warned as Ninoy explained that they had presidential permission to drive into the steep, wooded hills and jungled plateaus of the no-man's-land above the American Air Force base.

Ninoy nodded and smiled. He knew well the dangers that they might face on the road ahead. Hidden in the rocky, heavily wooded hills were members of the notorious Huks, a guerrilla army of peasants, laborers, students, intellectuals, socialists, communists and even ex-priests and nuns who had combined "to form a political and military force to overthrow the pro-American capitalists and their political cronies who ruled the Philippines."

Ninoy had heard it rumored that the Huks' supreme commander, Luis Taruc, had grown disenchanted with the increasing influence of communist ideology on the Huk movement. Apparently, Taruc wanted to meet with Magsaysay in hopes of winning concessions from the government before the communist hardliners who opposed compromise and sought all-out war took complete control of the Huk rank and file. The president secretly commissioned Ninoy to go into the hills to find Taruc and to bring him down.

"Raise the barrier!"

The young lieutenant signaled Ninoy and his three companions to proceed into the mountains. The jeep jerked forward. Just one day earlier, Ninoy had met secretly with Taruc's personal representative. Even meeting with Taruc, the Huk "Supremo," would be a journalistic and political coup.

Ninoy first heard about the Huks from his father during World War II. The Hukbalahap (a Tagalog acronym for the People's Anti-Japanese Army) or Huks had been formed by Filipino patriots during World War II to fight the occupying forces of Japan. The Huks fought the Japanese invaders, but refused to ally themselves with the Americans or with the American-supplied Filipino freedom fighters. They condemned Ninoy's father, Benigno Aquino, Sr., and all other Filipinos who "collaborated" with the Japanese.

When the post-war elections were held in 1946, Huk leader Luis Taruc was one of six Democratic Alliance candidates who won a seat in the National Assembly. Taruc was a committed nationalist who opposed America's continuing presence in the Philippines after independence was granted that same year.

When the American Congress asked the Philippines to approve a bill to grant American corporations "the right to dispose, exploit, develop, and utilize all agricultural, timber, and mineral lands in the Philippines,"[10] Taruc became a leader of the opposition. Unfortunately, the Americans had limited the amount of war reparations they would pay if the trade bill wasn't passed. Taruc's opposition threatened the disbursement of $620 million in funds promised the Philippines by the Rehabilitation Act.

The majority parties combined to unseat Taruc. His life was threatened. Eventually he fled back into the mountains where he was elected supreme commander of the new Huk guerrillas, a nationalist movement with pro-communist leanings.

"Stop!"

Suddenly, Ninoy's driver slammed his foot on the brake and swerved to avoid hitting another young man carrying a machine gun in the road ahead. This time the checkpoint was manned by Huk guerrilla fighters. Ninoy and his party quickly climbed down from the jeep. Following their Huk guides into the dense jungle on a secret trail, they passed under the noses of soldiers who were searching for the Huks and especially for their leader, Luis Taruc, the Huks' Supremo, whom Ninoy had come to interview.

At sunset Ninoy and his guerrilla escorts climbed down a rugged cliff to a beachlike dry river bed. Stretched out on the still warm sand they waited until dark for Taruc. Suddenly, heavily armed soldiers in khaki uniforms emerged from the dense foliage. Taruc walked briskly out of the shadows to greet them.

Taruc impressed Ninoy during their frank and friendly discussion. "I am a Filipino first and last," the Supremo said plainly. And though he had opposed Magsaysay in the elections, Taruc was convinced that the new president was the people's choice. "It is for us to accept their verdict," he added. That night, Luis Taruc, the Huk guerrilla leader with a price on his head, promised Ninoy Aquino, the son of his former enemy, his "unequivocal loyalty" to the nation and to its president.[11]

During the long, silent trek back through the jungle to their jeep, Ninoy had plenty of time to think about Taruc and the cause for which he fought. There were at least thirty-five million peasants in the Philippines. Poor and hungry, they owned no land and worked at slave wages for the rich absentee families who owned the farms and plantations. The landowners were supposed to share 50 percent of the harvest, but every season it seemed that the tenant farmers were left with almost nothing. To house and feed their families between the harvests, peasant workers had to borrow money from their landlords at 100 or even 200 percent interest! If a typhoon or a drought damaged just one crop, the tenant farmers plunged hopelessly into debt. As a result, millions of Filipino farmers and their families found themselves in an endless cycle of poverty and despair.

Taruc and his Huk guerrillas represented the peasant farmers. Immediately following World War II when America granted independence to the Philippines, hope for land reform and the eventual end of the unjust and dehumanizing tenant system surged in the hearts of the Filipino masses, but the same rich families who had controlled the nation's economy before the war, reestablished power under the Republic.

Because members of the same wealthy families held key political and military positions, they could use the armed forces of the Philippines to put down dissent and to maintain their hold on the economy. In 1946, when President Roxas launched an all-out war on Huk strongholds, Taruc had written, "Mr. President, extremists may want you to order the bombing and cannonading of the poor—to kill them by the thousands . . . . But they should know that they can never bomb out the people's new-found hopes and convictions."[12]

Ninoy went down from the mountains with a growing respect for Taruc and his Huk compatriots—and for their commitment to the poor.

"Where is he?" President Magsaysay asked Ninoy eagerly upon his return.

Ninoy knew that Magsaysay's generals were anxious to capture and imprison Taruc. To reveal his hiding place would be a betrayal. Ninoy still trusted Magsaysay, but he didn't trust the generals—and he wasn't sure what the president might do to pacify them.

"Will he negotiate?" Magsaysay asked. "Will he come down and talk to us?"

Ninoy didn't know for certain what Taruc might do. Their first meeting had been simply an exchange of ideas. The president asked Ninoy to find Taruc again and to bring him down. Magsaysay guaranteed Taruc's safety; so three days later, Ninoy repeated his dangerous journey into the mountains. This time he noticed that every step he took was under surveillance by military forces on foot and in helicopters. It was more and more apparent that Ninoy was being used by the military to capture the guerrilla leader. Ninoy met with Taruc and found that the Huk Supremo was indeed willing to negotiate face to face with President Magsaysay. Ninoy arranged a third secret meeting with Taruc.

Ninoy was again impressed by the Huk leader. His enemies called Taruc an atheist, but the old man talked openly of his faith in God. His enemies called Taruc a card-carrying communist, but Taruc denied the charges saying he was a socialist who had never been nor ever would be a communist. His enemies called Taruc an agent of Moscow. But Taruc shared with Ninoy his love for the Filipino people and his undying commitment to them and to their nation.

On May 15, Ninoy rushed to Malacañang Palace to tell the president that Taruc had agreed to come down from the mountains. As they talked, the room filled with military personnel. Magsaysay promised Ninoy that Taruc would be left in the journalist's care and safekeeping. The president promised to wait alone in a neutral spot

Ninoy the war correspondent

Ninoy in Boston

Cory and Ninoy
in Happier Times

(left)
Ninoy, the
candidate in prison

(below)
Ninoy's hunger strike

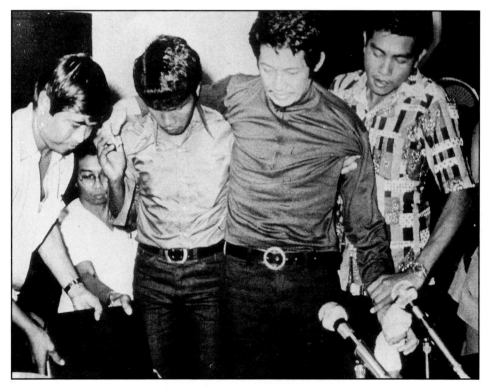

(right)
Aquino and a
well-wisher inside
CAL Flight 811

(below)
Aquino identified by
military escorts

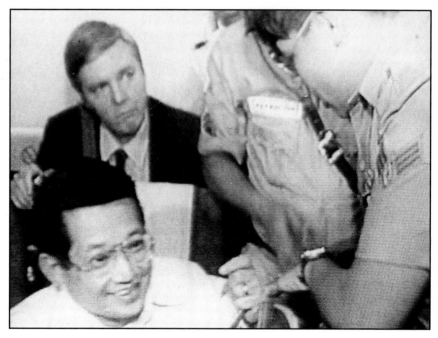

Aquino leaving plane

Scenes on the tarmac

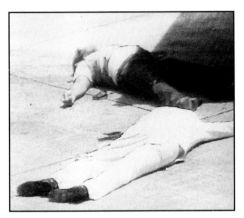

Aquino's body
on view for
the people

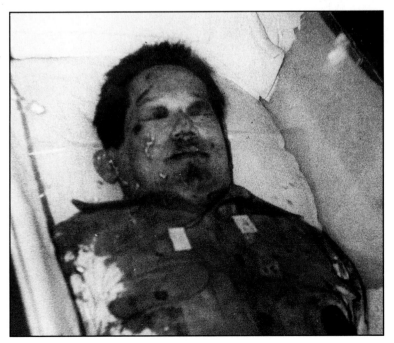

Cory for President rally

Cory at Carmelites' Convent in Cebu

(the presidential yacht) to receive the Huk Supremo in good faith. But Magsaysay broke his promises. Shortly after Taruc surrendered himself to Ninoy, they were stopped by a military unit and Taruc was removed from Ninoy's care and taken to prison where he remained for the next thirteen years.

Ninoy was furious, feeling he had been betrayed by the president of his country. He had been used by the military to destroy the work of a man whose goal was simple—to help his impoverished neighbors to a better life. Years later, Ninoy described Taruc's important influence on his Christian faith and on his decision to enter politics:

> He [Taruc] was one of the few men who impressed me early in my life. How many men have thought of doing, but didn't do, what he did? This guy was tempted with wealth; he refused it. He could have compromised with the Establishment; instead he went to the hills. He was soft-spoken, but he fought hard. He never talked to me of communism; he talked of the lot of the poor in this country. He opened my eyes to the inequities in my own hometown: how the peasants there would borrow ten pesos from the landlords and come back to find that a zero had been slipped in to make their debt a hundred pesos. And they had nowhere to take their grievances. The courts? The landlords, said Taruc, hired the best lawyers to fight simple folk who seldom went more than ten kilometers from where they were born and would die.
>
> Taruc said he had never asked for anything but an improvement in the lot of the peasants. "If I had wanted wealth," he said, "there were a lot of offers; I could have gotten a million just to stop this revolution." He said to me: "I say this to you, Mr. Aquino, who were born rich, whose family is landed, in the hope that you will be enlightened about these things." A man had to do something and he said he had felt he simply had to fight for those poor peasants. And I thought to myself: "This is the first Christian I have met."[13]

Ninoy Aquino often visited Taruc in prison. The young journalist apologized to the Huk leader for the president's betrayal of them both. Ninoy did manage to keep one promise that he had made to Taruc. The Huk leader's son, Romeo, was living in Manila. He had dropped out of school. Ninoy promised Taruc that he would help his son get back into college. In fact, Ninoy and Cory put Romeo through medical school and in 1963, Romeo became a doctor.

For a few months after Magsaysay betrayed him, Ninoy refused to answer the president's telephone calls or invitations to Malacañang Palace. But Magsaysay was persuasive. He explained the political "necessities" of his actions. He promised Ninoy that no harm would come to Taruc in prison. Somehow, after two months of trying, he managed to reestablish his relationship with the angry young journalist.

Ninoy was just twenty-one years old. Already, he had suffered the wounds of war as a correspondent on the front lines of Korea and in the hills above Manila as a secret agent of the president. Ninoy was tired of the conflict. Chino Roces, his publisher at the *Times*, suggested that Ninoy take time off to travel and to write abroad. President Magsaysay asked Ninoy to study the American intelligence agencies. Ninoy was ready for rest and relaxation. He was willing to travel and work abroad, but first he wanted to marry Cory so that she could make the journey with him.

Cory

Apparently Cory had decided to accept Ninoy's proposal, but not right away. She refused to date other men and told her friends that one day she would marry Ninoy and until that day she wouldn't even look closely at the prospects of another suitor. One of her girlfriends remembers telling Cory, "You led such a dull existence."[14]

Still, Cory wasn't ready. Everyone else seemed to be. Ninoy had been courting Cory for more than a year. He was certainly ready for the marriage. Both their families were ready. In fact, in their home province of Tarlac, an Aquino-Cojuangco marriage would be the social event of the decade. Their two families had been close for generations. Between the two of them they owned some of the largest sugar-growing plantation areas in the province. Cory's father, Don Pepe, was the godfather of Ninoy's sister, Lupita. The marriage seemed made in heaven, but Cory still resisted.

It must have been a dramatic moment in Ninoy's life. Both President Magsaysay and Ninoy's editor, Chino Roces, were encouraging him to get away from Manila, to travel abroad. The surface reasons were obvious. Ninoy needed a rest. But below the surface another more ominous reason could be detected. Ninoy's life was in danger.

He had made several powerful enemies during his last few years reporting for the *Times* and negotiating for the president. The army didn't like him for his interference in their attempts to capture Taruc. The Huks didn't like him for his apparent "betrayal" of their Supremo. With Ninoy's series of controversial articles on the Southeast Asian nations and on politics in the Philippines, he had offended communists and capitalists alike. Even the American Embassy officials must have been confused by Ninoy's openness to truth wherever he found it. Innocently, Ninoy had angered almost everyone. And though the circumstances are still confusing, on 1 October, 1954, it appears that one of Ninoy's enemies tried to kill him. Fortunately, this first assassination attempt on Ninoy's life had a happy ending. After the incident, Cory finally said, "Yes!"

Ninoy and Cory were together when the would-be assassin struck. Because it was still customary for two single people to be accompanied on a date, Cory's elder sister, Josephine, had gone with them to lunch and to a movie in Manila. After the film, the three young people drove onto Highway 54 in Ninoy's white Buick convertible, the same car he used to pick up Taruc, the Huks' Supremo. Apparently, the assassin followed Ninoy's car as he drove Cory and Josephine to their parents' home in Pasay City, a large district of Metro Manila. No one noticed the jeep that tailed them.

Suddenly, on a nearly deserted stretch of highway, the assassin rammed Ninoy's Buick from behind. Apparently, the jeep hit the convertible with such force that both front doors flew open. As Ninoy struggled to control it, the car lurched from side to side. Josephine was thrown out on the jeep's first impact. Cory followed almost immediately. Because Cory's sister was wearing a full skirt and long-sleeved top, she wasn't seriously injured as she rolled to the side of the road. But when Cory was tossed out the open door, the car must have been closer to the edge of the highway and she fell flat into the gravel with tremendous force. Fortunately for both young women, there were no other cars passing along the highway and the jeep that struck the Buick had already sped away.

Nobody ever identified the hit-and-run vehicle or its driver. Ninoy Aquino, the assassin's target, wasn't even scratched in the incident, but Cory was badly scratched and bruised. It was an American golfer returning from a late round at a nearby country club who saw Ninoy's desperate waves and drove the three young people to the Lourdes Hospital. Amazingly, there were no serious injuries, but the attending doctor asked Cory to stay at the hospital overnight.

Cory's parents were at Baguio City, a famous resort in the mountains north of Manila. Cory knew that her parents would suspect the worst if they were called from a hospital in Manila. In spite of her black and blue bruises, Cory and her sister returned to Baguio. Ninoy followed after them. When the elder Cojuangcos heard the hit-and-run story, they told Cory never to ride in Ninoy's car again. They were afraid for their daughter's safety.

But Ninoy had his own version of the story. "You fell from that car on purpose," he told Cory jokingly, "to force me to marry you."

In fact, even the elder Cojuangcos knew it was the perfect time for Cory and Ninoy to marry and to leave the country until the dust had settled and the truth were known about Ninoy's role in the capture and imprisonment of Taruc.

Ten days later, on 11 October, 1954, Cory and Ninoy stood side by side making their wedding vows at the altar of Our Lady of Sorrows, Cory's home church in Pasay City. Standing next to Ninoy at the altar was the president of the Philippines, Ramon Magsaysay, the principal sponsor of their wedding. Days later, Cory and Ninoy Aquino left Manila for an extended honeymoon-working vacation. They would begin their life together as they ended it, by living and traveling in the United States.

4

Ninoy, the Farmer and Politician; Cory, the Housewife (1955–1966)

Beyond the greed, the pride, the insolence and the pretensions of those who rule us through force and fear and fraud, there is a living, Almighty God who knows the dark mysteries of evil in the hearts of men. I know his justice, truth and righteousness will reign and endure forever . . . .

Senator Benigno Aquino, Jr.

Pray that we may not forget the witness of the past years, when in our need we sought God's kingdom and righteousness, and in answer all these blessings were added unto us . . . .

President Corazon C. Aquino

The newly married Mr. and Mrs. Benigno Aquino, Jr., spent four months on their working honeymoon in America. Cory took Ninoy on a tour of Notre Dame, her high school alma mater in Manhattan. They visited Mt. Saint Vincent College and talked to Cory's old friends and teachers there. For three wintry months they lived with Ninoy's sister and brother-in-law, Mila and Charlie Albert, in Maryland. Charlie Albert was the military-attaché of the Philippine Embassy in Washington, D.C.

When they weren't touring East Coast villages, seeing films and plays in Manhattan or climbing the monuments in Washington, D.C., Ninoy was hard at work on "a little assignment" for President Magsaysay: to write a report on the recruiting and training of agents by America's Central Intelligence Agency. Ninoy's report on the CIA must still be buried somewhere in the musty files of the Malacañang Palace. Exactly why President Magsaysay asked Ninoy to study the CIA during this particular time in history isn't known, but it isn't hard to guess.

In 1954, in the United States, Dwight D. Eisenhower was half way through his first term as president. The cold war between the U.S. and the U.S.S.R. superpower states was intensifying. The leaders of the democratic nations of Europe and North America were alarmed by the communists stated goal of world domination. Television, rapidly becoming the number one source of information and entertainment in America, found the "international communist conspiracy" a perfect subject to exploit in dramatic fiction and on the news. Waving his long list of names of government employees who were "communists or communist sympathizers," Senator Joseph McCarthy soon dominated the medium and cast his long shadow over the American political landscape.

In Asia, the Southeast Asia Treaty Organization (SEATO) was formed (including Australia, Great Britain, New Zealand, Pakistan, Thailand, the United States and the Philippines) as a direct response to reports of communist aggression in that area. And in the Philippines, "communist fighter" Ramon Magsaysay, Defense Secretary and then president of the Philippines, was being praised by his Asian neighbors for his success at rooting out communist influence in his nation.

Filipino communists who had been active in Huk leadership believed that a total overthrow of the elected government of the Philippines was the only solution to poverty and injustice, but during Ramon Magsaysay's term as Secretary of Defense (1950–1953) and then as president of the Philippines (1953–1957) this communist threat was practically eliminated.

As secretary of defense, Magsaysay made surprise inspections of army and constabulatory field units, fired corrupt and incompetent military officials, and promoted men who shared his vision and his integrity. He tripled the military budget and in 1950 managed to capture and imprison most of the leaders of the Filipino Communist Party Politburo.

There was a simple reason that neither China nor the Soviet Union rushed reinforcements to the Philippines. The Filipino peasant rebellion was homegrown. The communist powers, large or small, had virtually no contact with the guerrilla fighters in the Philippines. These farmers, students, workers, a handful of intellectuals—and the communists among them—were Filipinos. Most of them had left their homes and families and taken to the hills with one goal: to help the poor in their struggle against the rich.

Tens of millions of landless Filipino farmers were victims of a tenant farming system that kept them in bondage to a handful of wealthy Filipino families. Millions of Filipinos were ill-housed, ill-clothed and ill-fed. Fighting communists was one thing. Really working to eliminate the problems that gave communism its excuse for being was another.

Ninoy respected Ramon Magsaysay because he worked to improve the plight of the poor, suffering, landless Filipinos. During Magsaysay's seven years in government service, the Huk peasant rebellion (like the Filipino Communist Party) went into decline.

President Magsaysay placed strong controls on the army and civil guard units who had harassed, tortured and murdered the peasants in the name of anticommunist warfare. Magsaysay had produced one of the nation's first nearly honest, almost violence-free elections. And he had instigated various projects to improve the terrible plight of the poor Filipino farmer, including agricultural extension services, cash credit for peasants, barrio health clinics, agrarian courts to hear disputes between tenants and landlords, new bridges and roads, several hundred "liberty wells," and irrigation canals.

According to Benedict J. Kerkvliet, the chronicler of the Huk rebellion, during Magsaysay's brief presidency the government "devoted far more attention and money to rural public works and agrarian reform than it had during the previous six years."[1] Magsaysay's enlightened reform of the military and his increased aid to the poor brought hope to the Filipino people. That hope led to the temporary decline of the peasant revolutionary movement and to the decline of the communist threat.

After Magsaysay's success as secretary of defense, an American postage stamp was released bearing Magsaysay's picture and under it the caption, "Freedom Fighter." Magsaysay was praised in the U.S. by the media, including a cover story in *Time* magazine and a front page biography in the *New York Times*. He was the conservative's darling yet he was praised as well by such liberal leaders as Adlai Stevenson, the democratic candidate for president, and Supreme Court Justice William Douglas. As Magsaysay's friend, advisor and personal envoy, Ninoy was granted red carpet treatment on his honeymoon and easy access to the headquarters of the CIA.

But all was not work on that four-month honeymoon. Cory remembers that during their time in the United States, both Aquinos began to put on weight. Ninoy became "addicted" to fresh-squeezed orange juice and to white chocolate. Years later Cory estimated that Ninoy put on at least twenty pounds during their honeymoon.

"I was getting a little round myself," Cory recalls, "because I was already expecting our first child."[2]

When Cory and Ninoy returned from their honeymoon in February, 1955, it was too late for Ninoy to enroll for his final year in law school. He had already finished the first semester of his fourth year. Only the review courses remained. And though Ninoy planned to complete his law degree upon their return to Manila, another, more interesting option presented itself—and Ninoy dropped out of law school forever.

During those first months back home, Ninoy returned to his beat-up typewriter and metal desk at the *Manila Times*. But his career in journalism, like his study of law, was coming to an end.

"I was writing," Ninoy told his biographer, "but my heart was no longer in it. The traumatic experience with Taruc had shattered some more illusions, had increased cynicism—about words and covenants and government and the presidency."[3]

Cory's father, Don Pepe Cojuangco, was a governor of the Development Bank of the Philippines. He told Ninoy about a piece of Huk-infested jungle property near Concepcion, Ninoy's hometown in Tarlac Province. The property was undeveloped, but the soil was rich. With hard work and patience that little piece of land could become productive. The Development Bank was about to auction the land to the highest bidder and Don Pepe encouraged Ninoy to consider buying it himself.

Ninoy was tired of the intrigues of Manila and fascinated by the possibilities of returning to the land. He sold his white Buick convertible and almost everything else of value that he owned. He borrowed another 40,000 pesos for a down payment on the property. For the next few months Ninoy commuted between Manila and Concepcion. He spent the week farming and the weekends visiting his pregnant wife in the city.

In August, 1955, Ninoy was visiting Cory in Manila when her labor pains began. Cory remembered that he wasn't much help during the crisis.

"I was rushed to the hospital at two in the morning," Cory recalled, "by Ninoy and my parents. In the car, my mother was timing my labor pains, while my father held my hand. It was the first time I saw Ninoy at a loss on what to do. It was my mother who kept me company in the labor room. My father later told me that Ninoy was so nervous he kept going up and down the stairs."[4]

Ninoy knew as little about farming as he did about caring for his new born baby daughter. Fortunately he had a mother and a mother-in-law to help Cory during those first few months after giving birth. And to help him transform his little piece of jungle into a working rice farm, he hired his mother's overseer to assist him. He also went to his grandfather, General Servillano Aquino, for counsel and advice.

Ninoy's grandfather was eighty-one years old in 1955. He had fought for Filipino independence against Spain, against America and against the Japanese. In 1946, when the general was 72, he fell in love with Belen Sanchez and eloped with her. When he was 75, his wife gave birth to a baby boy whom the general named Herminio. And at 81 he was still able to help his grandson, Ninoy, to farm the land.

The jungle was thick. There were vines to root out, trees to cut down and stumps to pull up or blast away. General Servillano taught Ninoy how to shape rice paddies in the wet delta soil. The old man helped his grandson design an irrigation system that would keep the paddies watered during the dry seasons between the annual floods. And the general showed Ninoy how to plant and harvest the rice. But most of all, General Servillano taught his city bred, law-student, journalist grandson how to work with the peasant farmers who tilled the land.

"Grandfather was teaching me the ropes: how to handle the country folk; I was staying with them. I ate with them," Ninoy said years later. "At night we barricaded ourselves in. I had a machine gun and my brother's automatic rifle."[5]

The Huk rebellion was in decline, but it wasn't dead. Ninoy's farm was in the central plains of the island of Luzon. The Huk peasant rebellion against their rich land-owning masters began in this very region. In their violent protests against the peasants' plight, the Huks raided farms, burning the outbuildings, stealing the animals and terrorizing farmers and their families. When the alarm was sounded, the army or the local constabulatory forces would arrive and do nearly as much damage in their search for the guerrillas as the Huks themselves would do. Ninoy armed himself and his workers against attack from whatever source, but there is no record of an attack against him or his workers.

"I had terrific credentials among the Huk," Ninoy explained, "[as] the boy who befriended Taruc."[6] And of course Ninoy's friendship with President Magsaysay didn't hurt his reputation with the army or the constabulatory forces either. In fact, it was President Magsaysay who called Ninoy just months after he planted his first crop to suggest that the twenty-two-year-old farmer run for mayor of Concepcion.

The Huks had controlled Concepcion during World War II. A Huk mayor ran the city. After liberation, the wealthy and powerful Feliciano family overwhelmed the Huks and muscled their way to political prominence. In 1955, the farmer families around Concepcion were tired of Huks and of the Felicianos. They appealed to Ninoy to mount a mayoral race against both candidates.

"I told them they must be off their rockers," he said. "I wasn't interested in running. It was a grudge fight between them and the Felicianos and they were trying to get me into it."[7] When Ninoy refused to run for mayor, the wealthy farmers called the president. The president called Ninoy.

"You're asking me to put my life on the line," Ninoy argued.

It wasn't an exaggeration. Ninoy's fears were prophetic. Politics in Concepcion were as corrupt and as dangerous as politics in Manila. The candidate from the far right, the town's mayor, Nicolas Feliciano, had his civilian guards to intimidate the voters. Gorgonio Narciso, the former Huk mayor representing the far left, had his own Huk warriors to back him. Ninoy would be Magsaysay's candidate, the man caught in the middle.

"Run as my candidate," Magsaysay suggested. "If you want, I'll go to Concepcion and campaign for you."[8]

At the heart of Ninoy's difficult decision was a moral issue as important to him as it was to Magsaysay. The president was trying to enforce the Land Reform Code, which called for a 70–30, tenant-landowner sharing of the crops. If the peasants could get what they deserved from the harvest and end the cycle of poverty and despair, the communist threat and the Huk peasant rebellion would end forever.

The Felicianos represented the wealthy and powerful tenant farmers. Narciso represented the radical peasant movement. Ninoy walked the middle ground. He could understand both positions and seek a healthy compromise. So, President Magsaysay would not take Ninoy's "No" for an answer.

"In Concepcion," Ninoy argued, "to get involved in politics is to get into the eye of the storm. I don't think I'm your man for it."[9]

The president prevailed. Ninoy announced his candidacy and began to plan his first election campaign. Shortly after his first posters went up on the whitewashed walls of Concepcion, a long parade of Huk guerrilla fighters and their supporters rode into town on bullcarts. They were carrying ropes and torches, shouting threats. Just twenty-two years old, Ninoy stood in the flickering shadows. He was in debt for a farm that had not seen its first harvest, with a wife and infant child to care for. All week he struggled to clear and plant his farm and then drove the long, lonely road between Concepcion and Manila every weekend to see his wife and daughter. His new private life was just beginning. He had already been burned once by public intrigue. He didn't want to be burned again.

That night, Ninoy drove back through the darkness to Manila. He entered his mother's home and slumped into a chair beside her.

Ninoy told his mother that he was giving up. He was frightened, and he wanted to quit. Beginning a farm and a family were enough responsibilities. He didn't want to get caught in between Feliciano's "goons, gold and guns" and Narciso's Huk fighters. Anyone caught in the crossfire between those two violent factions would end up the loser, he was convinced.

"If you don't go back," Doña Aurora told her son, "I will—and I'll run for mayor."

When Ninoy asked his mother how she planned to do it, she answered, "I'll run somehow, because someone has to run—or the family will never live this down."

"'All right.'" Ninoy finally replied. "'I'll go back.' And I did," he recalled later, "But this time I was running scared."[10]

Cory still remembers Ninoy's first campaign.

"From the first day Ninoy entered politics," she wrote, "I kissed all hope of a private life good-bye."[11]

Ninoy moved Cory and their daughter, Ballsy, into an old, wood-framed, five-bedroom house in Concepcion. From early morning until late at night the people streamed through the house getting acquainted with "Magsaysay's boy." At first Ninoy was shocked that almost no one knew of his reputation as a prize-winning war correspondent or a special advisor to the president. Only a handful of people in Concepcion read the *Manila Times*. The countryfolk had to see Ninoy up close as they had seen his father when he was their candidate.

Doña Aurora joined the family on the campaign trail. She had campaigned for her husband, Senator Benigno Aquino, Sr. Now, she was campaigning for her son.

Cory's father was also a politician, but she had never really campaigned for anyone before Ninoy's mayoral race. She was a very private person. And the stream of countryfolk, politicians, their workers and advisors, ended that privacy forever. Cory was rather timid and reserved. On one election swing through Tarlac she whispered to her husband that she needed a toilet rather urgently. Ninoy handed her an old tin can. She prided herself on her homemaking and cooking skills, but in Concepcion she had to learn to cook on a clay stove while neighbor women who dropped by watched with giggles and unsolicited advice. Above all, Cory needed time to be by herself, to meditate and to pray. With a newborn child and a husband in the midst of a political whirlwind, it was a struggle to find any time or any place to be alone.

"I had to learn to adjust," she said years later. "I told myself that since I was in it I might as well make the most of it."[12]

In the towns and villages of Tarlac Ninoy developed his own unique style of campaigning. He learned how to talk to voters, how to influence and impress a crowd. Ninoy loved to watch the local candidates in action, and was amazed by their public speaking skills. Often, village officials had no schooling, no high school or college degrees, but they could hold an audience spellbound for hours. They were story tellers. In their own way and in their own words, they made their points by retelling stories from the Bible, from local folklore and even from ancient mythology. Those local candidates were following Jesus' example. They were teaching in parables and Ninoy decided that he, too, would learn that ancient technique.

Ninoy learned his lessons well. When the votes were counted, he had won by a rather healthy margin. In the city, he took 50 percent of the votes from Feliciano. In the countryside, he took 50 percent of the votes from the Huk candidate. But though Ninoy was elected, his victory was soon challenged.

Hoping for a chance to unseat the young "carpetbagger" from Manila, Feliciano's men stole Ninoy's birth certificate from the archives in the town's old cathedral. A mayor in the Philippines had to be twenty-three years old by the day of his election. Ninoy turned twenty-three several weeks after the election. When Feliciano filed a protest, the local court decided against Ninoy. Ninoy's supporters appealed to the Supreme Court and while they waited for its verdict, Ninoy took the oath of office in January, 1956, and became the youngest mayor in the history of Tarlac Province.

That same month Ninoy worked alongside his laborers in the rice paddies as his grandfather, the general, stood nearby offering advice about the harvest. They say that Ninoy was a lucky farmer. His rice paddies yielded a bumper crop. In fact, Ninoy's luck was due in good part to his diligence. In farming as in politics, Ninoy planned carefully and worked endless hours to see his plans realized.

"Ninoy never left anything to chance," Cory remembered, "as far as his political campaigns went. Everything had to bear the mark of his careful planning. He learned to do with very little sleep and hardly any food at the height of the campaigns. For him, getting as many votes as time and energy permitted was the preeminent consideration."[13]

Ninoy had run for office promising "to be a bridge between the haves and the have-nots." He was from a wealthy family, but he knew that the nation would be divided and destroyed by civil war if the rich refused to hear the cries of the Filipino poor. Knowing the terrible plight of the peasants, he called for the tenant farmers to give the workers their fair share of the crop, to provide them access to education and health care and to give the peasant workers a piece of land they could call their own. Ninoy went even further by insisting that his own family set the first example.

Doña Aurora Aquino, Ninoy's mother, remembers those first weeks that her twenty-three-year-old son was mayor of Concepcion.

"Because I went to communion every day," she said, "he would tease me and say: 'What do you do for the poor of Christ, Mommy? Your piety is only between God and you. There's no transversal in it as on the cross. Where does your neighbor come in?' I would tell him: 'That is your work. You are in the foreground; I, in the background. You are the activist in this family and I am the contemplative.'"

Doña Aurora still remembers her son's reply:

> "Mommy, if you really care for your tenants as you say, those who have been with you for years and years, you would give them a piece of land—at least the land on which their houses stand." At first I was apprehensive, [Doña Aurora recalls] because of the other landlords: what would they say? And their tenants might demand the same thing. Ninoy said: "Don't think about that. You begin. Somebody has to begin." So we did it. We gave each of our tenants the lot on which he lived; they can use it for collateral; and now they have this barrio where they themselves are the landowners. This was done at Ninoy's instigation and it was done when he was mayor.[14]

In 1956, not long after he was elected mayor of Concepcion, Ninoy was called to Manila by President Magsaysay. The president missed Ninoy's wise counsel. He wanted the young man back at his side, and he promised funding for schools, roads, bridges, clinics, whatever Ninoy needed if he would just come back to Manila.

At first Ninoy was stricken by his conscience. He had been elected mayor. He must not compromise that responsibility. It didn't take long to realize that the best way he could serve his people was to accept Magsaysay's offer. By serving the president, Ninoy would win for his people exactly what they needed.

So he made a pact with President Magsaysay to work in Concepcion in the daytime and then drive to Manila at night. Somehow Ninoy managed to keep his promises both to the president and to the people of Concepcion. He worked as mayor from early morning until his offices closed at 5:00 P.M. Then he drove to the Malacañang Palace and worked for President Magsaysay from 7:00 P.M. until 1:00 A.M. Ninoy called those days in Concepcion and those nights in Manila his "salt mines." And though he served the president until March, 1957, Ninoy refused any payment for his services. "Although I was on his [the president's] staff," Ninoy explained, "I was not on his payroll. I was the mayor of Concepcion."[15]

On 17 March, 1957, President Magsaysay was killed when his airplane crashed into Mount Manunggal on the Island of Cebu. Ninoy was shocked and saddened by the nation's loss and by his own personal loss of a friend and political mentor. He remembers feeling Magsaysay's death in the same way he had felt his father's, and though Vice-President Carlos Garcia called Ninoy and asked him to continue as a presidential advisor, Ninoy refused. "I'm going back to Concepcion," he said, "to be a farmer and a full-time mayor once again."

Late in 1957, the Supreme Court decided that Ninoy's election as mayor of Concepcion had been illegal. The Administrative Code was clear. A mayor must be twenty-three years old on the day he is elected. On election night, Ninoy was nineteen days short of his twenty-third birthday. He had served effectively as mayor for almost two years when he found himself a farmer once again.

That same year, Cory's father, Don Pepe Cojuangco, purchased Hacienda Luisita, the last of the great Spanish-owned haciendas, 7,000 hectares (more than 17,000 acres) of farm land and a sugar refinery in the village of San Miguel not far from Concepcion. Because Ninoy was familiar with farming and labor problems he was hired to manage the huge estate.

Ninoy spent the next two years proving himself an able, determined farmer. Dressed in blue jeans, leather boots and a loose cotton shirt with sleeves rolled up to his elbows, Ninoy worked from sunrise until late at night transforming the rundown sugar plantation into an efficient and profitable operation. People still remember how he traveled across the huge plantation at a dizzying pace by horseback, jeep and helicopter. Machinery was imported to assist the workers in planting, harvesting and refining the sugar cane. He diversified the plantation's primary source of income with broccoli and onion farms, citrus orchards and cattle ranches. Villages, parks and bird sanctuaries were built by his workers.

Ninoy seemed determined to transform Hacienda Luisita, once the symbol of Spanish imperialism, into a model Filipino farm. He worked hard to end the cycle of misery that plagued the lives of the Filipino peasants who worked the land. He was convinced that generosity would lead to productivity. According to his biographer, Nick Joaquin, Ninoy raised salaries and devised profit-sharing schemes. He started a high school on Luisita and offered classes at nights and on the weekend. He ran a computer profile on his workers' income and hired social workers to assist his employees in money management.

Ninoy began a company hospital. He sent doctors and nurses in well-equipped vans to circulate among the barrios where the thousands of workers lived. After putting Taruc's son through medical school, he hired the young doctor to work on the estate. He offered free medical and dental care, free housing, free education and free utilities to his workers.

"I didn't know," Ninoy said later, "that a managerial post would mean my becoming father, mother, uncle, doctor, nurse to a population of from twelve to fourteen thousand people!"[16]

Ninoy hated the old class system. Workers lived in squalor while owners lived on great estates. He refused to live in the Hacienda's casa grande but commuted instead from the Aquino home in Concepcion where he lived alone.

In December, 1957, about the same time Ninoy agreed to manage Hacienda Luisita for his father-in-law, he and Cory had their second daughter, Aurora. Cory and their two children lived in Manila. Ninoy managed the estate and drove back and forth between Concepcion and Manila to be with his growing family.

"Just a year after we got married," Cory recalls, "we both agreed that since Ninoy would be in public life, I would be primarily a mother. He discouraged me from having a career, and I didn't fight him, since staying at home was commonly accepted once you had a family."[17]

In fact, Ninoy's political career was about to begin its incredible ascent. In 1959, Ninoy ran for vice-governor of Tarlac. He was just twenty-seven years old and about to run for governor when President Garcia urged him to run for vice-governor instead: "I knew your father, Ninoy, and I know you. You will be president one of these days. I don't want you to begin by making too many enemies. There is such a thing as pacing. You are still young. You may win, but you will win the hard way."[18]

Ninoy took the president's advice. Elected the youngest vice-governor in the history of Tarlac, he commuted between his managerial chores at Hacienda Luisita, his vice-governor's office and the presidential palace in Malacañang. There, after President Garcia suffered a serious heart attack, Ninoy consented to serve as a presidential advisor once again.

In February, 1960, Ninoy and Cory had their third child, a son, Benigno Aquino III (Noynoy). Their third daughter, Victoria Elena (Viel), was born that next year, in October, 1961. With Ninoy so committed to his political career, Cory was pretty much left alone to care for their four young children.

"As his political career progressed," Cory recalled, "I became equally convinced of how essential it was for me to be with my children. If both parents had been busy doing their own thing, I'm afraid my children would not have grown up to be the responsible persons they are now."[19]

Just before the elections in 1961, President Garcia appointed Tarlac's governor to a cabinet position making Ninoy, at twenty-eight, the youngest governor in the history of the Province.

"Ninoy was lucky in his political career," Cory recalls. "He fought hard, indeed, for his victories; but they seemed to come, one after the other, like a destiny . . . . Everything seemed to be going Ninoy's way and people began talking about him as presidential timber."[20]

Cory supported her husband's political ambitions and was proud of his public accomplishments, but she insisted on remaining in the background. She didn't enjoy or seek publicity. Ninoy and his friends and supporters might drop by any time of the day or night. She would see that food and drink were provided but when the men got down to their serious discussions, she would excuse herself and retire to the family quarters to be with her children.

Some of Ninoy's associates remember that Cory could seem distant, even cold. She didn't like to accompany Ninoy on his endless rounds of necessary social events. She liked to stay at home with the children. When they were young she read to them and played games with them. She took them to movies and for walks in the countryside. As they grew older, when she was free to become a more public person, she still chose to read at home alone or to watch a movie with her family.

Cory made almost no impression on the growing number of strangers who entered and departed the Aquino household in growing numbers. She was obviously bright and capable and caring, but she didn't play the traditional role of the political wife who worked to win friends and influence people on her husband's behalf. When introduced, Cory would manage a smile and a friendly nod, but she seldom entered into conversation and turned away as quickly as she could to return to her own private world. She was wife and mother above all things and she wasn't interested in the social games that people wanted her to play.

Through it all, Cory did maintain her own private spiritual life. She went to church regularly and attended retreats. Daily she meditated on the life of Jesus. She read the Gospels and prayed faithfully for God's will to be done in her life, in Ninoy's life and in the life of her family. And she taught her children to do the same.

As Ninoy's political star ascended, Cory must have had to struggle to maintain her spiritual disciplines. Her husband's days in public office began early and ended late. Ninoy would commute by car to the Malacañang Palace to serve President Garcia as a personal advisor or by helicopter to his governor's office in Tarlac. And when Ninoy was at home, he was often accompanied by large numbers of friends and political supporters.

When Ninoy became governor of Tarlac, he and Cory bought a rather unimposing home in Quezon City, one of the large cities in the greater Manila area called Metro Manila. The house that became the Aquino family home in Manila looks today much as it did more than twenty-five years ago. It is a ranch-style bungalow with eight rooms, a cement roof carport, a small back yard and a heavy steel fence mounted in concrete between the house and the sidewalk on Times Street. Though the house was undistinguished in appearance, through its doors passed a growing stream of the nation's most powerful and impressive people.

As Ninoy plunged deeper and deeper into his own political destiny, Cory seemed to pull farther and farther back from it. But if Cory appeared to be unsupportive of her husband or her husband's goals for the Philippines, in fact she was supporting him in the best way she knew, by keeping the family intact and by maintaining the spiritual disciplines that would see them all through those rather dark and dangerous days.

Becoming governor of Tarlac didn't end Ninoy's problems. Almost immediately after his appointment, President Garcia was defeated in the 1961 presidential election by Diosdado Macapagal. Ninoy lost his political patron and the province of Tarlac lost its presidential favor. To political writers, it appeared Ninoy's career was on the decline.

Governor Aquino had campaigned against Macapagal. The president wasn't about to release funds to the opposition, and for eighteen months Tarlac suffered. Ninoy couldn't get aid to build or even repair needed roads and bridges, schools and hospitals, power or water systems. Governors and mayors were switching to Macapagal's Liberal Party, but Ninoy believed in a two-party system and he had campaigned against placing so much power in the hands of the president. Still, Macapagal liked Ninoy and promised Tarlac five million pesos in urgently needed aid if Governor Aquino would switch. Finally, after one and one-half years of holding out, Ninoy gave in.

From that day, Ninoy saw himself as a "political turncoat." He claimed that "no amount of tears or honest sweat can ever remove the stain of that abominable act . . . . Let's face it," he added, "a governor is measured, not by the high standards of political morality he upholds . . . but by the actual, physical, material benefits he has brought home to his people."[21]

Governor Ninoy Aquino was reelected by a landslide in the 1963 elections. President Macapagal kept his word and between 1963 and 1969 Tarlac prospered under presidential patronage and under Ninoy's administrative and political skills.

In 1965, Ninoy offered his own farm in Concepcion in an experiment that President Macapagal was conducting to end the tenant farmer system and to divide up the old estates into family farms. Ninoy gladly joined in the president's land reforms. He divided up his land among the peasants and taught them how to make profitable their family-sized farms. Eventually, he sold his entire farm in Concepcion to the men who once farmed it for him.

In the 1965 presidential elections, Ninoy delivered his Province to Macapagal, but the president was defeated and Ferdinand E. Marcos was elected the sixth president of the Third Republic of the Philippines. This time, Ninoy refused to switch party loyalties. His last two years as Governor of Tarlac were a misery. President Marcos was in the mood to get even and once again presidential funds were withheld from Ninoy's province. But Ferdinand Marcos wasn't willing to limit himself to pressuring Ninoy by drying up the funds for Tarlac. He also began a personal attack on the young governor, suggesting that Ninoy was a communist.

In 1966, in the countryside near Concepcion, Ninoy's hometown, five poor tenant farmers were murdered by soldiers of the Armed Forces of the Philippines. President Marcos, their commander-in-chief, promoted the soldiers, saying their victims had been Huk guerrillas. It would become a common Marcos ploy to use soldiers or hired assassins to pose as Huks and to terrorize local towns and barrios. It was the beginning of a twenty-year reign of terror that Marcos used to keep his people in check and to keep the anticommunist monies from America pouring into the Philippines.

When Ninoy heard about the "Huk murders" in Concepcion, he launched his own private investigation of the tragedy. It didn't take him long to discover that the five men were not Huk guerrillas, but simple peasant farmers who had been murdered by the military. Ninoy confronted President Marcos in the press.

"Naturally, Aquino would do that," Marcos replied. "He's a communist himself, a Huk-coddler."

It was the beginning of a long, stormy confrontation between Ferdinand Marcos and Ninoy Aquino that would eventually lead to Ninoy's assassination and to Marcos's fall from power, twenty-one years later.

Ninoy, the Senator;
Cory, the Housewife
(1967–1972)

All things mortal have an end, even the longest, darkest night, a dawn! Have faith, have patience, hang on, tomorrow may just be the day . . . .

Senator Benigno Aquino, Jr.

During those times when the problems of our country seem beyond solution, I am strengthened by Christ's promise: "Seek and you shall find, knock and doors will be opened, ask and you shall receive . . . ."

President Corazon C. Aquino

President Ferdinand Marcos was a corrupt and corrupting influence on the Philippines for almost forty years. In 1939, when he was just twenty-two years old, Marcos was found guilty "beyond reasonable doubt" of the murder of Congressman Julio Nalundasan. Ferdinand's father, Mariano Marcos, had been defeated for his third term in Congress by Nalundasan. Seeking revenge for his family, Marcos, a law student and member of his college pistol team, allegedly shot his father's enemy through the heart.

Marcos passed his bar examination while in prison and at the outbreak of World War II, through the political influence of his family, a higher court overturned Ferdinand's conviction on a technicality. Young Ferdinand was released to fight the Japanese. Years later when Marcos was elected president of the Philippines he claimed to have been wounded five times while serving as a guerrilla officer and to have won 22 American and Philippine war medals and citations.

On his first state visit to America, President Marcos was cheered by the joint houses of Congress when he claimed to have received scars trying to save an American soldier. "My American comrade died in my arms," Marcos proclaimed, "Filipino and American blood commingling in Philippine soil."

Marcos so impressed President Lyndon Johnson and key members of the American Congress that he and Imelda returned to Manila with an economic aid package of $195.4 million. Years later, when someone actually took time to examine the facts, President Marcos's war record and his war stories turned out to be lies, carefully manufactured to move and to deceive Americans and Filipinos alike.

Marcos's political career began in 1949 when he was elected to the Congress of the Philippines. The new congressman learned quickly that he could use his place in government to accumulate both money and power. In 1953 he spotted Imelda Romualdez, that year's "Muse of Manila," sitting with her family in the congressional visitors' gallery. He wooed and won her. In 1954, Ferdinand and Imelda were married.

Ferdinand and Imelda Marcos were bright, attractive, and charismatic. In the beginning, they were symbols of hope. The nation needed a strong leader. Marcos seemed the perfect candidate. And the first few years of his administration were filled with promise.

What Ferdinand and Imelda did to the Philippines is a tragedy almost beyond comprehension; but an even greater loss is what the Philippines might have been under a legitimate Marcos presidency. Ferdinand Marcos had the power and the resources to transform the Philippines into a prosperous Asian nation. Instead, he bled his country dry. Ferdinand and Imelda's greed for power and money triumphed over any altruistic dreams they might have shared. Together they would lie, extort, terrorize and murder to get and keep power over the people; until one day in 1986, the people would take their power back.

At each step along the way, there were courageous Filipinos and even a few prophetic Americans who tried to warn our two nations of the Marcos menace. In spite of the warnings five American presidents—Johnson, Nixon, Ford, Carter and Reagan—backed the Marcoses with billions of dollars of aid while those who told the truth about the conjugal dictatorship were ignored, harassed or intimidated. Often, the names and reputations of those who opposed them were smeared by Marcos and his cronies. Many were bankrupted or lost their positions in business or in government. Some were held as political prisoners, questioned and tortured in military camps in downtown Manila—and even in the presidential palace. Many others were murdered, their bodies mutilated and dumped on city streets or buried in shallow, unmarked graves.

Ferdinand and Imelda Marcos would tolerate no opposition. It is
no small miracle that Ninoy Aquino survived as long as he did.

Marcos had been president of the Philippines for less than three
years when Ninoy took his Senate seat in 1968. He was the only
opposition candidate who managed to survive the bloody and corrupt campaign that Marcos fought to get his slate of candidates
elected. According to one historian, the U.S.-trained paramilitary
and police agents under Marcos control were responsible for 117
"politically motivated killings" during the 1967 election and in the
last thirty-six hours before the polls opened, thirty-seven people
were murdered in an attempt to terrorize the electorate.[1]

President Marcos wanted to run the nation unopposed, but he
had to bribe, terrorize and murder the voters to achieve his ambitions. Ninoy Aquino and his friends and co-workers stood directly
in Marcos's path.

Marcos's hatred for the Aquino family went back at least one gener-
ation. Ferdinand hated Ninoy's father, Senator Benigno Aquino, Sr.,
for being a part of the government that prosecuted him for the murder of Congressman Nalundasan. Even before he was elected to the
Senate, Ninoy had earned Ferdinand's wrath on several occasions. But
Marcos especially disliked Ninoy for revealing to the press that the
five farmers in Tarlac had not been murdered by communist guerrillas
but by soldiers in disguise and for suggesting that the commander-in-
chief of those same soldiers bore some responsibility for their act of
terror. The president's hatred for Senator Aquino grew white hot
during Ninoy's term in the Senate.

On 5 February 1968, in Ninoy's first speech to his colleagues, he
began a relentless and prophetic attack on the Marcos administration that would not end until Ninoy's murder by the military at the
Manila International Airport fifteen years later.

"May I rise on a question that disturbs all thinking men?" Senator
Aquino began, standing at his desk in the Senate chamber. "May I
call your attention to a danger which creeps upon us: the insidious
development in our midst of a garrison state?"

To consolidate his power and to eliminate the influence of his
enemies, President Marcos was uniting the army, the air force, the
navy, the Philippine Constabulary, a national police agency, and
even local police forces under one central command (his own)
and was granting power to those same forces that belonged in
civilian hands.

"Marcos justifies this policy reorientation," Ninoy claimed, "in
the name of efficiency." But the young senator went on to warn that
"Efficiency is not an end in itself. Admittedly, dictatorship is more
efficient than democracy."

After describing the dangers of turning civilian tasks into military hands and after illustrating carefully exactly how Marcos was putting his people into place for an eventual dictatorship, Ninoy concluded his speech to his fellow senators with this challenge: "Let us act by our mandate and check—today, not tomorrow—this dark, this bold, this insidious scheme to transform our democratic society clandestinely into a garrison state."[2]

Ninoy's speech made headlines. Just thirty-five years old, a freshman in the Senate, he was taking on the president. A courageous new voice was being heard on the national political scene and people liked the sound of it, but few would listen carefully to Ninoy's prophetic warnings and even fewer would heed them.

Marcos had the trump card and he played it. "The communist threat" made it easy to overlook the basic ideals of democracy and Ferdinand Marcos used "the communist threat" to get what he wanted from Filipinos and Americans alike.

President Lyndon Johnson was glad to authorize Marcos's request for a secret, multimillion-dollar plan "to reorganize, retrain, and re-equip the entire Philippine police establishment from top to bottom as a computerized paramilitary force under the control of President Marcos, to suppress any form of protest against his continued rule."[3]

It is fairly clear why not many people in the Philippines or in America took seriously Ninoy's warnings about the Marcos threat. At that very minute the communists were flexing their muscles throughout Asia. If Marcos needed to compromise democracy in order to take a stand "against communism," few people seemed to care.

On 23 January 1968, just twelve days before Ninoy's first senate speech, a North Korean patrol boat seized the *Pueblo*, a United States intelligence vessel on patrol in the Sea of Japan. Seven days later, on January 30, the communists in Vietnam launched their powerful Tet offensive just when a brief holiday truce was about to take place. It is no wonder that Ninoy was largely ignored when on 5 February 1968, he warned the senate that "Our democratic political system is slowly but systematically being strangled by a creeping militarism."

Because the American military bases in the Philippines seemed crucial to America's worldwide struggle against communist expansion, nobody in America listened. And the future of those bases were in the hands of President Marcos. As a result the staunchly "anti-communist" President of the Philippines could get almost anything he wanted from a grateful American president.

Nobody in the Philippines listened because Marcos was using "the communist threat" to get what he wanted from his own congress as well. In his speeches on radio and television, President Marcos painted a frightening picture of the "rapid growth" of the Communist Party in the Philippines and of its military forces, the New People's Army.

In fact, that same year a handful of Filipino farmers, students and intellectuals had met in Pangasinan Province to reorganize the Filipino Communist Party to oppose the excesses of the Marcos administration. Between 1968 and 1972, when Marcos proclaimed martial law and ended what was left of democracy in the Philippines, there had been less than 350 Filipinos recruited to serve as guerrillas in the New People's Army.

The NPA "was a joke" said a U.S. intelligence official at the time of martial law in 1972.[4] Marcos was simply using "the communist threat" to create a police state in the Philippines. Only Marcos seemed troubled by Ninoy's speech. For three weeks the president used every available opportunity to attack Senator Aquino's words as "the ravings of an irresponsible imagination." Then, when Ninoy's warnings in the senate seemed to be ignored by press and public alike, Marcos backed off.

The president's overreaction was Ninoy's first proof that he had stumbled on to something bigger than even he knew. Instead of retreating from Marcos's scathing attack, Ninoy began his own undercover investigation of the Marcos military and discovered to his horror that the president had been training his own private army in a sinister project code-named Jabidah.

On 28 March 1968, Senator Aquino walked to the microphone in the Senate chamber to denounce Jabidah! In his "Special Forces of Evil?" speech Ninoy exposed the president's "super-secret, twin-goaled operation to wipe out the opposition—literally, if need be—in [the presidential elections of] 1969 and to set this country on a high foreign adventure."

The senator had flown undercover to a secret training base where he saw with his own eyes that the president was "building a secret strike force under his personal command—to form the shock troops of his cherished garrison state."

Ninoy discovered, too, that dozens of the young recruits who complained of their bizarre mission and of the camp's primitive conditions had disappeared. He interviewed worried and grieving friends, parents and wives of the missing men. Ninoy checked out their stories against the stories of their commanders. In his senate speech Senator Aquino said, "If the Army cannot produce these men . . . they will have to stand the accusation of murder and—maybe—even mass slaughter."[5]

At least twenty-six recruits were missing and considered murdered when on Easter week, President Marcos's public relations office took out full-page ads to defend the military and to denounce Ninoy and the Senate's inquiry. "We feel truly hounded," the ad read, by "the seemingly endless congressional investigations encircling us."

Ninoy was incensed. On 15 April 1968, he stood before his senate colleagues to condemn Marcos for his Holy Week campaign to discredit Congress and to silence the opposition. He charged the president with reducing politics in the Philippines "to a dirty, no-holds-barred, no-honors-staked guerrilla political warfare."

When Marcos claimed that he and his military were not guilty of shedding blood, Ninoy, in his speech titled "Mr. M—and Pilate, too," named the cold-blooded murders and the massacres that he traced directly to the Marcos military, " . . . all weaving," charged Ninoy, "a pattern of cresting violence in the rule of a man whose big boast to fame are the men he killed in his wartime exploits and who fancies himself as the Warrior-President."

Ninoy ended his speech with another prophetic warning that Marcos's full page ads during Holy Week were meant to "make the Senate look like a collective nuisance, a fly in his pie, when what it is doing is exactly what the founding fathers meant it to do—a Chamber of the People, not his echo and not his stamp."[6]

After Ninoy's dramatic revelations in the Senate chambers, Jabidah was junked. And though his speeches were headlined and applauded, no one really took seriously Ninoy's warnings that President Marcos wanted to become another Asian strongman dictator without democratic restraints. Though Ninoy was the lonely, often ignored and severely criticized voice of the opposition, he continued his attacks on Ferdinand Marcos and the Marcos government throughout his first year in the Senate.

Cory

Frankly, there is very little known about Cory during her husband's four years in the Senate. Cory shunned publicity. And, somehow, the wife of the controversial freshman senator was able to keep her life and the life of her young children almost hidden from the media and the public. Even after becoming president herself, she has revealed almost nothing of those difficult days when her husband was Enemy Number One of Ferdinand and Imelda Marcos. During Ninoy's campaign for the Senate in 1967, Cory went door to door on her husband's behalf. But once Ninoy was elected, she returned to her home on Time Street and worked full time behind closed doors as mother and wife.

During these years Cory did take time to maintain her own

spiritual disciplines. She attended church regularly; she studied the Gospels herself and read Gospel stories and the stories of early Christian saints and martyrs to her children. Even during times of political crisis, Cory insisted that Ninoy and the children accompany her to church. But with her busy husband and growing family Cory had little time to take on political causes of her own.

Cory's children were still very young. When Ninoy was elected to the Senate, the Aquinos' eldest daughter, Ballsy, was just twelve years old. Their second daughter, Pinky, was ten. Their son, Noynoy, was seven and their daughter, Viel, was six. Their fourth daughter (and last child, Kristine—Kris) was not born until Ninoy's third year in the Senate.

It isn't difficult to understand why Senator Aquino had little time to spend with his family. He was hard at work trying to rescue his country from chaos. And though she understood and supported his cause, Cory was determined that their young children have at least one full-time parent. In her only substantial interview about those senatorial years, Cory admitted that she took some pride in her parenting role and even felt a little miffed on those rare occasions when Ninoy didn't acknowledge it.

"Whenever the children received an award for academic excellence," she wrote, "Ninoy would be careful to point out that they took after him. I think these were the only times he took full credit for what were not entirely his efforts.

"I think," she added, "I had something to do with how our children finally turned out, because when they misbehaved, he would never reprimand them himself but asked me to do it. 'Be sure to talk to your child,' he would tell me, 'and tell her (or him) to do better next time, or else . . . .'"

"I think it was because his politics took him so much away from his children that he always wanted to be popular with them. I guess we, no, he, had decided on a division of labor. He would be the indulgent parent and I would be the disciplinarian."[7]

During Ninoy's brief term in the Senate, Cory parented four young children, was nine months pregnant, brought their fifth child into the world, and nursed and changed their new infant daughter. There was little time to do anything else.

"With each baby," Cory remembered, "Ninoy became less nervous and we no longer needed kin to keep us company. Ninoy was thrilled at being a father, but he was always a nervous one. He was always afraid to carry our babies during their first months. He could be helpful only as far as removing wet diapers. But, when it was messier than that, he would call me . . . shouting in a loud voice that he couldn't handle it."[8]

Ninoy

If Ninoy had fears in the nursery, he was fearless on the Senate floor. When a popular Filipino journalist, Rafael Yabut, was almost fatally wounded by assassins after exposing graft and corruption in the offices of the national lottery, Ninoy took up the cause himself. In his Senate speech "Shenanigans, Syndicates, Stinks in the Sweepstakes" Ninoy revealed that the Sweepstakes offices were "saddled by mismanagement, ridden with irregularities, peculiarities, even downright anomalies."

When President Marcos presented his 1969 budget for scrutiny and approval Ninoy called it "one big presidential pork barrel." "This budget is cluttered and littered with unitemized lump-sum appropriations," Ninoy charged, "275 million pesos in all . . . with this 275 million pesos in his hands—to dispose and dispense as he pleases—President Marcos can seduce, subvert and force our provincial, municipal and barrio leaders to turncoat in droves. This is not good for our political stability," Ninoy claimed. "This will be tragic for our democracy."

At the end of his fiery budget address, "A Carrot and a Stick for Mr. Marcos," Ninoy concluded with another prophetic warning. "In effect," he said, "we are asked to transform this people of ours into a nation in craven dependence upon one man, Mr. Ferdinand Marcos."[9]

When President Marcos gave Imelda a bridge for a birthday gift (to span the provinces of her birth and childhood) at a cost to the nation of at least 60 million pesos, Ninoy stood in the Senate chambers and with his own unique mixture of humor and disdain accused the president of monumental misuse of the people's monies.

"In another time, in some other better circumstances," Ninoy said, "I will not be standing here tonight, but instead will be applauding on the sidelines. In us, after all, is melted the Latin and the Oriental, wide awake bloods that divine and pamper their women . . . . But we are a people struggling . . . in fact, in a desperate climb out of poverty and want . . . a government almost financially bankrupt."

After laying out what that bridge would cost the people, Ninoy addressed Imelda Marcos:

> Please talk the president out of it. Tell him there are other needs, other demands, other priorities . . . . Tell him that 60 percent of his people die without ever getting to see a doctor or a nurse . . . . Tell him that 480,000 Filipino boys and girls remain out of the classrooms, that they need 12,000 new classrooms and an even greater number of teachers

. . . . Tell him that the roads [leading from both sides of her bridge] are in a nightmarish state . . . . Tell him that the mass of his people live in squalor in city slums and in abject poverty and want in the barrios. Tell him that our country's farms are plagued with rats, that a massive rat extermination drive cannot get going for lack of funds. Tell him—for us—to be candid and to tell the people exactly in what bad shape are our finances, in what runaway state criminality is in our land, and in how pitiful situation the government is in trying to cope with all these . . . . And yes, tell him too, dear Imelda, that he does not have to keep on giving proof of his love for you.[10]

Ninoy returned to his desk in silence. It was not the first time he had attacked Ferdinand and Imelda together for their personal misuse of the nation's funds. It would not be the last. In a Senate speech late in the summer of 1968, Ninoy condemned "the Malacañang and presidential yacht shing-a-loos that he and his wife [Ferdinand and Imelda] have been throwing for the current 'In Crowd,' lavish socials—revelries, almost—that go into the morning while the nation writhes, grovels and groans in poverty, in misery and want."

Ninoy described the Marcos-perpetuated system of "privilege," "fringe benefit," "tong," or the infamous "ten percent." Ninoy denounced the government's on-going demands for bribes and kickbacks from businessmen. "They call it 'kil-kil,'" Ninoy claimed, "because the squeeze play keeps on recurring and the businessman gets it coming and going."

"How they do it," Ninoy wondered, "I can't exactly say." But he was sure that Ferdinand and Imelda, their family and cronies were behind the "squeeze play." He ended his speech with another accusation against them. Their pile, he claimed:

. . . has risen in the form of a spanking new apartment building at the end of Roxas Boulevard, a fabulous summer house in Baguio City, a holding company in Nassau, a hotel in Taipei, and, I am told, a collection of fabulous jewels.

It is time [Ninoy went on] that we give our antigraft law real honest-to-goodness teeth, teeth to protect the citizen against dishonesty, thievery, and knavery in public office. It is time we think of country and people first, of self and kin last. It is time we yield to duty, not succumb to personal booty.

It is time that we give our Filipino businessmen a break. For as our businessmen, industrialists, and other entrepreneurs increase their profits, so will the government increase its tax intake . . . . Or dare we risk the people's wrath with our greed? Or worse, the wrath of our Maker . . . . Or dare we really taunt the Maker? I dare not. For I fear that He may not even write on the wall as He did at Babylon, and simply let us perish in our wickedness.[11]

Ninoy wasn't accusing Ferdinand and Imelda Marcos simply as a matter of opposition politics. The young senator foresaw in 1968 that the president and his wife were on their way to bankrupting the nation. Already, they were opening bank accounts at the Credit Suisse in Zurich and in banks in the Bahamas, the Cayman Islands, Hong Kong, the Netherlands Antilles and in the Chase Manhattan Bank of New York City. It was becoming more and more apparent over the years billions of dollars, much of it loaned or granted to the Philippines as economic aid to help the suffering Filipino people, were stuffed into the Marcoses' private accounts or used to buy real estate, expensive art or jewelry for Imelda's growing collection.

Early in that same summer of 1968, Imelda and her eldest daughter Imee went shopping in the United States and spent 3.3 million dollars in only eight weeks, almost $100,000 for each of their shopping days.[12] The American president, the American Congress and the American ambassador to the Philippines were all well aware of the Marcos family and "their excesses." A few low-grade officials raised questions when tens of millions of dollars of American aid was sent in personal checks or cash to Marcos or deposited directly into bank accounts or banks that Ferdinand and Imelda owned or controlled. Now and then a ranking official would wonder aloud if something wasn't rotten in the Philippines, but in fact as long as America had the military bases, no one seemed to care about Marcos's greed or political ambition.

But Ninoy Aquino cared desperately. In speech after Senate speech he documented the crimes of Ferdinand and Imelda against the poor, suffering people of the Philippines and against the generous but uninformed people of America who wanted to help them. Ninoy begged public officials from both countries to help him stop the first family of the Philippines before they destroyed the nation. Ninoy's courageous words went largely unheard and unheeded.

But the Marcos family heard Ninoy loud and clear. By the end of his first year in office, Senator Aquino had so enraged Ferdinand and Imelda that they had become determined to stop him. At first, they tried to use the law to get Ninoy removed from his Senate seat. They accused him of being a Huk-coddler, a communist and a communist sympathizer. They threatened him with criminal suits, but the only charge they could make stick against Ninoy was the same charge that had cost him his mayor's job in Concepcion, nearly fifteen years before.

The Constitution of the Philippines states that a senator must be thirty-five years old at "the time of his election." On 14 November 1967, when the voters elected Ninoy to the Senate, there were still thirteen days until his thirty-fifth birthday. But on 15 December

1967, when he was sworn into office Senator Aquino was thirty-five years and seventeen days old.

A Senate Electoral Tribunal was convened to determine whether an election is over when the voters cast their ballots or weeks later when the winning candidate is sworn into office. Marcos was certain that his people on that blue ribbon panel would find that Ninoy's election had been illegal. That ruling would silence the president's most powerful critic.

Until the final votes were counted, everyone, including Ninoy, was certain of his defeat. At the very last moment, one brave senator on the panel surprised the nation and its president by swinging his vote to Ninoy. Finally, after a year of uncertainty, Ninoy was cleared by the Marcos tribunal. He would continue leading the opposition to the Marcos regime until martial law was declared just three years later.

In his year-end report to the people, Senator Aquino reviewed the accomplishments of his first year in office. He concluded with another prophetic warning, this time regarding his own future. "I have angered the man with the cosmic forces behind him—the President, Mr. Marcos—to a rage and a wrath that mark me as his mortal political enemy. It is a fury that, as events are testimony, has known no bound."[13]

In spite of Ferdinand and Imelda's growing hatred, Ninoy did not retreat. He ended his end-of-the-year report with this promise for 1969, "I pledge to give President Marcos twice of what I gave him this past year, a double-dosage of fiscalization where fiscalization is needed and a double amount of aid and help where public needs may warrant them."

"Fiscalization" was one of Ninoy's favorite words. He saw himself as a watchdog over the nation's treasury. Every peso was intended for the public good. Although Ninoy grew up in a wealthy family, early in his life he had seen and felt the suffering of the Filipino masses. When millions of pesos that should have been used to help end the suffering were stolen or misspent, Ninoy was enraged.

In 1969 Ninoy's full wrath fell on the president's wife, who had been squandering more and more of the nation's funds. And though she claimed to be using the government grants and private donations on her own pet projects "for the people," most of the monies were ending up in Imelda's personal treasury. She called herself a Filipino Robin Hood, picking the pockets of the rich to help the poor. In fact, she was picking the pockets of rich and poor alike to help Imelda.

During their first year in office, she headed a Christmas drive for the needy. Past presidents' wives had also handled the task, but Imelda changed the rules. All checks contributed to the fund were to be made out in her name and even a quick "fiscalization" showed that most of the money contributed to aid the poor ended up aiding Imelda.[14]

By 1969, after four years in office, the president's wife had graduated to the big time. When she discovered that a Philippine-American Cultural Foundation had collected contributions of 90,000 pesos to create a modest cultural center in Manila, she volunteered to take up the cause in her own name. After all, she, too, wanted to help build a place where new Filipino talent could be discovered and the art, music and dance of the Philippines could be celebrated.

As always, the president's wife dreamed big dreams for her new cultural center. She had architects draw up plans for a huge marble structure with dancing fountains overlooking Manila Bay, a building that Ninoy Aquino would call "A Pantheon for Imelda." At a press conference Imelda claimed that the stage would rival the size of the New York Metropolitan Opera. Imelda's cultural complex would include glass and marble lobbies and a theater with crystal chandeliers, 2,500 upholstered seats, and red and gold carpets and curtains. The landfill on Manila Bay not far from the American Embassy on Roxas Boulevard on which the "Pantheon" would stand required hundreds of tons of rocks and earth to be hauled, dumped, levelled and landscaped.

No one even dared to guess how much Imelda's cultural center would eventually cost. She promised to raise it all from private donations. "There will be no public monies used," she promised. But Imelda's plan would eventually cost the public upwards of 100 million pesos and early in the project's history Senator Aquino mounted his own personal "fiscalization" war against it.

In his "A Pantheon for Imelda" speech before the Senate early in 1969 Ninoy warned that "These are times of deepening crises in our life as a people."

In fact, "the showcase of democracy in Asia" that the United States "liberated" from its colonial rule at the end of World War II had become a massive slum. Per capita income in the Philippines was less than $250 a year. And though a handful of rich and powerful families lived in mansions and drove Mercedes cars, the poor lived in dirt-floor shanties, struggled for food and employment, suffered without adequate medicines or medical care, and lived and died with ever-decreasing hope for the future.

More than half the country's children under the age of ten suffered from serious malnutrition. Because they were starved in the womb and weaned on salt, rice and an occasional morsel of dried fish, tens of millions of children suffered in varying degrees from physical or mental retardation.

"A growing number [of citizens]," Ninoy continued, "no longer repose hope in the government to give them justice and relief by the normal administrative, judicial and legislative processes. Many have taken to justice by the gun. And many more have joined the 'Parliament of the Streets.'"

In fact, Filipino students, like their counterparts in Europe and North America, had taken to the streets to protest their government's inaction on issues of their vital concern. In America, students were risking their lives to register black voters and to march in the streets on behalf of civil rights and against the war in Vietnam. In the Philippines, students were taking to the streets to protest the excesses of President and Mrs. Marcos and the continuing rule of the masses by the old and still powerful Filipino families.

"At a time when the impoverished mass groans in its want," Ninoy went on, "Mr. Marcos and his lady have responded with a display of ostentatious living . . . by callously having a continuing ball at the people's expense, by pursuing single-mindedly the construction of monuments to their rule, like the 50 million peso Imelda Cultural Center on Roxas Boulevard."

To the president's defense that the first lady's "civic project" was "not a government venture, funded by contributions, not a government expenditure . . . ." Ninoy answered, "This is a deception and a distortion that makes all the other deceits and lies of the Marcos administration pale in comparison."

In the speech that followed, Ninoy proved step by step that the president and his wife were breaking the law to build the cultural center, that they had already squandered millions of dollars with the building still half finished, and he made the listener wonder how much of those monies had already been deposited in the private foreign bank accounts of Imelda and her cronies.

Using the cultural center as an excuse, Mrs. Marcos was raising funds from at least three different sources. Some of the tens of millions of pesos came from abroad. For example, on a visit to the White House, Imelda had convinced President Lyndon Johnson to give $3.8 million that had been appropriated to aid Filipino soldiers who had fought alongside the Allies in World War II. According to Ninoy she had drawn at least another $5 million from world banks involved in financing the economy of the Philippines.

Bankers and businessmen in the Philippines were also asked to "contribute" their share. According to journalist/author Raymond Bonner, Imelda wrote letters to Filipino executives telling them exactly what they should "donate" to the project and then she sent her couriers to pick up the amount in cash.

Various government agencies and their public accounts were plundered directly by the first lady in her Cultural Center scheme. Again, it is Raymond Bonner who tells the story of a courier from the Filipino tax commissioner who was seen hurrying into Imelda's private rooms in the palace with suitcases loaded down with five million pesos in cash. When he hurried out again he explained to an eye witness that he was "shaking and perspiring" because "She's not satisfied."[15]

Ninoy closed his speech by telling the story of Evita Peron, "a fascinating life's story—of absolute power and absolute corruption."

And though he denied suggesting any "equation" or "identification" with Evita and Imelda, Ninoy admitted that he had ". . . risen at the risk of Mrs. Marcos' scorn and wrath, because a voice must be raised to try and put a stop to the First Family's wasteful misuse of public money . . . ."

> I have risen at the risk of her rage, [Ninoy repeated] because out there, barely 200 meters away from the fabulous Imelda Cultural Center, a ghetto sprawls, where thousands of Filipinos are kept captives by misery and poverty. Father Veneracion, the reformer-priest of Leveriza, will tell anyone who dares have his conscience stricken, of the cases of malnutrition and starvation in his parish-ghetto. He will tell you, Mr. President, of how poverty makes of men social outcasts and antisocial criminals.
>
> I have risen at the risk of her ire, because barely two kilometers from the Imelda Center, in Manila's North Harbor area, are jammed cardboard houses where two or more Filipino families share rooms no bigger than two meters by two meters.
>
> I have risen at the risk of her vengeance, because not far from her fabulous center are government hospitals where our Filipino poor fail to get proper care for lack of adequate equipment and medicines. Corridors are jammed with the sick, and the stench in the toilets would be enough to incapacitate a healthy man.
>
> I have risen at the risk of her spite, because I am plainly revolted by this will to immortality while the nation suffers and lies on the razor's edge . . . .
>
> The social needs, the forgotten Philippines' needs, cry out for attention, Mr. President.
>
> With 50 million pesos this nation can go a long way to improving the sorry situation in which our underprivileged mass now live . . . .
>
> With 50 million pesos low-cost, high-rise apartment dwellings can be built where Tondo's cardboard jungle now lies . . . .
>
> With 50 million pesos a national hospital can rise alongside the Tondo apartments and signal a step towards lifting the mass out of the rut . . . .

But no, Mr. President, a 50-million-peso cultural center must first be constructed—so the bejeweled elite, the nation's first 100 families, can enjoy the Bernsteins and the Bolshoi, so they can live it up!

This center will go down in history. And by it, Imelda and her husband will be remembered . . . but it will be a monument to her extravagance and her insatiable craving for high living . . . .

It will stand there—by the bay—as a monument to shame . . . to betrayal of public trust . . . to the nation's elite, bereft of social conscience . . . . It will stand there, Mr. President, as a monument to perfidious infamy![16]

To this day no one knows for certain how much money Imelda raised to create the cultural center or what percentage of those monies were kept by the first lady and her cronies. The building cost far more than 50 million pesos and it is estimated that tens of millions were squirreled away in private bank accounts from Manila to Zurich. President Nixon asked then California Governor Ronald Reagan and his wife Nancy to represent him at the gala opening of the cultural center. At the lavish event, the Reagans were treated like visiting royalty. Ferdinand Marcos revealed that Ronald Reagan had been his very favorite movie star. It was the beginning of a lasting friendship.

The year 1969 called for a presidential election in the Philippines. Senator Aquino warned his Senate colleagues that Marcos had determined to be the first president to succeed himself in office. To guarantee "a landslide victory," Ninoy was afraid that Marcos might bankrupt the national treasury and plunge the Philippines into another siege of election violence and bloodshed.

In his speeches that year, Ninoy warned prophetically that the nation was teetering on disaster. The great majority of the people were hungry, ill-housed and unemployed. Prices were rising. The economy was faltering. The foreign exchange reserves were depleted. And because the peso was losing its value, the poor were becoming poorer still. Graft and corruption continued unchecked in business and in government. Crime in the streets was mounting. There were more murders per capita in the Philippines than in any other Asian nation. No longer willing to sit idly by while the president and his first lady presided over the destruction of the Philippines, students were taking to the streets to protest the human rights and economic abuses of the Marcos administration.

At the beginning of the year, Ninoy had suggested that if Marcos would agree "to subordinate self and party to the national consensus" and "serve as a sort of national manager to administer the agenda of the nation," Congress and the political parties would agree to a moratorium on partisan politics, cancel the elections and grant the president his second term by simple acclaim.

"Unhappily," Ninoy admitted later, "I can't blame the many who will refuse [this plan] . . ." because, of "the unacceptability of the main personality involved in my proposal: Ferdinand Marcos . . . . A review of his record reads like a list of dirty laundry."[17]

And though Ninoy's suggestion was misunderstood and roundly defeated, it would be seen later as an inspired warning for what those elections would cost the nation and her people. Years after that bloody and costly 1969 presidential election, Ernesto Maceda, Marcos's campaign manager, would admit in an interview: "We were prepared to cheat all the way." Two weeks before the election, Maceda withdrew 100 million pesos from the Central Bank to buy Marcos his "landslide victory." Maceda and his election team used an air force plane and presidential security to travel to cities, towns and barrios across the island nation leaving envelopes stuffed with thousands of pesos in their workers' hands to trade for votes.[18]

Once again Marcos triumphed through the election-winning formula of "guns, goons and gold." But this time, the president and his first lady had gone too far. The rumors were spreading that Ferdinand and Imelda had looted the national treasury to buy votes and to stuff their secret bank accounts. Members of the Congress threatened to begin impeachment proceedings against Marcos on charges of corruption and election fraud.

Threatened by impeachment, Marcos told the world that he was giving away everything he owned. No one believed him. And on 30 December 1969, when Ferdinand was sworn into office, students took to the streets to protest his election. By 26 January 1970, when Marcos visited the joint sessions of Congress to deliver his state of the nation address, thousands of students had organized to protest. At the close of the address, as the Marcos family left the Legislative Building, the peaceful protestors surged forward. Presidential security forces overreacted, and a scuffle followed. Ferdinand dragged Imelda through the crowd after being hit on the head by a cardboard crocodile whose mouth was stuffed with money, a caricature of the president himself.

Seconds after the president and his party were safely away, riot troops stormed into the mass of students breaking heads with their clubs in a violent counter protest.

". . . the police, tasting blood and wanting more, chased the students," Ninoy said on the floor of the Senate that next day. "They clubbed any who came on their way, collared those who fell," he said after quoting from the pamphlet the students had distributed citing their reasons for the protest. "We have come to appeal for the safe and sound conduct of the Constitutional Convention of 1971," the pamphlet read, ". . . our last hope, our last chance, for the ordering of our society according to democratic processes."

". . . I was there last night and I saw them brutalized," the young senator added. After thanking God that no student was killed by the vicious police attack, Ninoy warned, "God may not be kind again if one of the demonstrating students, armed only with their idealism, should fall before a hail of police bullets."

Four days later, when Marcos broke off negotiations with four of the student leaders, 4,000 protestors converged on Malacañang, the presidential palace. As they crashed through the gates, the students were met by a cloud of tear gas and a hail of bullets fired by Marcos's guards. Four students were killed.

"These were young students," Ninoy announced on the Senate floor two days later. "Not grizzled rebels—innocent, unarmed, defenseless . . . . They were killed in cold blood . . . and they were fleeing, not locked in combat with the guards of Mr. Marcos!"

The president had claimed to the army of reporters who converged on the Palace that the whole demonstration was communist inspired. "I will not allow communists to take over," the president warned ominously to the world's press. "The Republic will defend itself with all the force at its command until your armed elements are annihilated. And I shall lead them."

Once again, Ninoy was incensed. He knew the leaders of that student protest. He had investigated and found no communists and few communist sympathizers involved in the movement. Once again, Marcos was wrapping himself in the cloak of "the communist threat" to defend his regime.

"Ominous words, Mr. President!" Ninoy warned, ". . . this brings to mind a repression worse than what characterized the Red witch-hunts, the Red herrings and the Red bogeymen of the early fifties . . . . Sinister designs can be read here, Mr. President, which only fascist minds can suggest.

"Worse yet, I fear," he added, "if the country continues to crack up in his hands, Mr. Marcos may conveniently pursue this and force the Republic into a real life-and-death crisis, impose martial law and put the government and the country in his iron hand."

Ninoy admitted that the students had been wrong to break down the palace gate. Newspapers had estimated the losses at 250,000 pesos and Marcos said the nation "was revulsed" by the students' actions.

"But this same nation," Ninoy replied, "was not revulsed by public officials who have rigged the stockbrokers, taken multimillion-peso kickbacks and conspired among themselves against the country in Election '69.

"The students destroyed 250,000 pesos worth of property Friday night," he continued in his Senate speech, "Black Friday, January 30," "but these leaders have pillaged and ravaged the Republic down to its last dollar!

"Yes, the students broke some Malacañang gates. But is this reason to break student legs and student arms? And what about the leaders who forced open the gates of the Philippine National Bank and the Central Bank for their private looting?"

As he stood before his colleagues of the Senate, Ninoy Aquino explained the students' discontent:

> They are not so much against their elders [Ninoy said], as they are against the viciousness of the system, not so much against government as they are against duplicities, not so much against democracy as they are against the travesties in our democracy.
>
> They find the blessings of democracy a hypocrisy in the face of so much poverty, of shameless corruption and shameful stolen elections, of dubiety in justice, of so many disadvantaged and a very few privileged. Given this, they find empty meaning in the equal opportunity guarantees of the Constitution!
>
> In their homes and their schools, they hear complaints against corrupt politicians and rapacious employers only to find their own parents and teachers get all excited when the same politician and the same boss honor them with a visit. This has revulsed them!
>
> . . . Yes, Mr. President [Ninoy concluded], we are gripped by crisis, a crisis fraught with danger and peril to us all. But not the crisis born of the imagined conspiracies and conspirators of Mr. Marcos. Our crisis, sir, is a crisis of aspiration—among our young—and a crisis of conscience— among their elders, among us, their leaders. How shall we respond?

The student protest movement had one last hope for the future of democracy and justice in the Philippines. The old Constitution of 1935, drafted while the Philippines were still under American colonial rule, needed to be replaced by a constitution that described democracy in uniquely Filipino terms. In 1970, 320 delegates had been elected to form a Constitutional Convention, nicknamed Con-Con, that would draft the new document. Student protest leaders were depending on Con-Con to open the doors on a new era for democracy in the Philippines.

But those same protest leaders were afraid that Ferdinand and Imelda Marcos would try to undermine the integrity of the delegates to Con-Con. They were afraid that Marcos might get a constitution that would place him and his family in power forever and soon enough, the student's fears were justified.

From the beginning, Ferdinand and Imelda had planned to use the

Constitutional Convention as an extension of their own ambitions. Members of the president's staff had been assigned "to identify the 'needs' of delegates and then to provide them with government loans, civil service appointments for friends and relatives, special clearance through customs, and so forth."[20] When a convention resolution was introduced that would prohibit Ferdinand or Imelda from another presidential term, the first family set out to undermine the integrity of the convention altogether.

Even before the convention, President Marcos had warned that the only person in the nation strong enough to succeed him against "the communist threat" was his wife, Imelda. The controversial Con-Con resolution would end the Marcos dream of a political family dynasty. The first family decided to intervene quickly and forcefully to get the resolution defeated.

At first they tried to bribe and flatter the delegates. They invited Con-Con officials, their wives and families, to parties, teas and fancy dinners at the palace or at expensive restaurants around Manila. At these gala and elaborate affairs, Marcos and his staff passed out envelopes filled with pesos in a blatant attempt to bribe Con-Con delegates to take their side against the controversial resolution.

He would try to intimidate those delegates he couldn't flatter or bribe into submission. On 16 August 1971, a bomb exploded in the men's room of the constitutional convention hall. It was a deafening but rather harmless warning of the tragedy that would follow.

On 21 August 1971, during a preelection political rally at the Plaza Miranda in Manila, fragment grenades were tossed onto a platform where the opposition party candidates sat waiting. Spectators and members of the press were killed. And when the smoke cleared, many of Ninoy's closest friends and political co-workers were mangled and left near death by the blast. Ninoy spent the night rushing from hospital to hospital, comforting the wounded candidates and party workers.

Marcos blamed the attack on the communists. In fact, presidential staffers eventually confessed that the bombing plot had been planned and carried out by soldiers in disguise working directly with Marcos's top military advisor, General Fabian Ver.

Using this new "evidence" of "the communist threat," Marcos jailed opposition leaders and suspended the writ of habeas corpus. "That writ," Ninoy answered in his senate speech, "is the cornerstone of our liberty in this Republic." Without it, President Marcos could put away his enemies indefinitely without hearing or trial.

"In one single maneuver," Ninoy explained before the Senate, "Mr. Marcos has felled his two most consistent critics: the opposition Liberals in the hospitals, [and] the student activists in jail."

Once again Marcos accused Ninoy of being a communist himself and though Ninoy's closest friends and supporters had been seriously injured in the blast, Marcos accused Ninoy of supplying the Plaza Miranda bombers with money and materials.

To the president's ridiculous charges, Ninoy answered as he had always answered, "I am not, never was, and will never be a communist. I am not, never was, or ever will be a member of the New People's Army, and I categorically deny, flatly deny, all the charges of the president."

For almost four years, Senator Ninoy Aquino had been rising in the Senate to warn the nation of the Marcos conspiracy. Few people took him seriously. They knew that Ferdinand and Imelda were ambitious, but they never dreamed that the president and his wife were plotting a conjugal dictatorship that would rule the Philippines for more than twenty years. The people knew that the Marcoses were greedy, but no one imagined that they would end up stealing billions of dollars in public and private funds and eventually bankrupt the nation. The people knew that the president and his wife loved power, but few even suspected that Ferdinand and Imelda would imprison, torture and murder tens of thousands of their own people to get power and to keep it.

On 1 June 1972, Ninoy closed a senate speech with these words:

> I discussed all this in the hope that our citizenry, led by the members of this august assembly, be alerted and be more vigilant in safeguarding our liberties. In closing may I recall these plaintive words written by an anonymous German poet at the beginning of the Second World War:
>
> "They persecuted the workers and the farmers, and I did not protest. They persecuted the students and the young, and I held my tongue. They persecuted the Jews, and I kept my peace. Now they persecute me . . . Who is left to protest?"[21]

When reporters rushed to the palace for Marcos's reply to Senator Aquino's latest speech, the president spoke these ominous words:

"I think we should disregard this politically obsessed upstart," Marcos said, "whose notoriety has called attention to his subversive and other questionable activities. We will attend to him later."

In the following months, President Marcos would keep his word. And just as Ninoy had warned, suddenly there was no one left to protest.

6

Ninoy and Cory:
The Prison Years
(23 September 1972–May, 1980)

There is something providential in the persecution of tyrants. If only for my conversion, I should owe the tyrant my eternal gratitude!

Senator Benigno Aquino, Jr.

Ninoy liked to quote St. Paul's letter to the Corinthians: "For the sake of Christ, I am content with weakness, insults, hardships, persecutions and calamities, for when I am weak, then I am strong!"

President Corazon C. Aquino

On 13 September 1972, black clouds boiled up over Manila. The mood inside and outside the Senate Office Building was dark and foreboding. All summer long monsoon rains had fallen. In July alone the capital was deluged with almost seventy inches. Flood waters swept away the houses of the poor. Even the palace grounds were flooded.

But political storm clouds had also boiled up over the capital throughout that long, miserable summer. Another kind of unnatural storm threatened the city. Senator Ninoy Aquino waited at his desk in the senate chambers to deliver the warning. Aides scurried about. Ninoy checked and cross-checked his references as lightning flashed and thunder rattled the windows of the senate chambers.

During the last two weeks of August and the first two weeks of September, the natural terrors of thunder and lightning had to compete for attention with the sounds of terrorist bombs exploding across Manila. Cory, at home with her children, heard the daily news with a growing sense of dread. On August 15, explosives went off almost simultaneously at the Telephone Exchange and the Sugar Institute Offices. Forty-eight hours later, the Department of Social Welfare was bombed and two days after that, explosives ripped open the water mains of Quezon City.

At midnight, on August 30, the Phil-Am Life Building was rocked by an explosion and minutes later an armored car was blown apart on its nightly rounds to the Philippine Banking Corporation. On September 5, Joe's Department Store was bombed. One young woman was killed. Forty-one clerks and shoppers suffered injuries. In all, nineteen terrorist bombs exploded and at least six other bombs were discovered armed and ready to explode in the Greater Manila area during those last stormy days of summer.

In the speech he was about to deliver, Senator Aquino would suggest that the president himself was responsible for the acts of terrorism. President Marcos blamed the New People's Army for the rash of bombings. In fact, in 1972 the NPA was still a struggling band of insurgents with armed supporters numbering only in the hundreds. Ninoy had good reasons to suspect that the bombs were just another Marcos plot to create hysteria. Once again the ruthless and amoral president was using "the communist threat" to get his way with the Filipino people and with his friends and supporters in the White House.

President Marcos's second and final term in office would soon end. His attempts to bribe or threaten the constitutional convention into allowing him to succeed himself had failed. The Con-Con delegates had also managed to block Imelda's plan to follow her husband into office. Desperate measures were required and Ferdinand Marcos had just the plan.

The president of the Senate gavelled the meeting to order. As Ninoy awaited his turn to speak, he must have known what it would cost him to reveal Marcos's plan to his senate colleagues and to the nation. "Operation Sagittarius" was the code name for President Marcos's secret directive to prepare for the declaration of martial law and to end democracy in the Philippines. Ninoy Aquino had uncovered that plan.

"I have just received information from confidential sources in the Armed Forces of the Philippines," Ninoy began that day, "regarding a top-secret military plan, ordered by President Marcos . . . as a prelude, maybe, to clamping martial law."

Ninoy described the secret presidential orders to mobilize police and military forces under his command.

"What is surprising," Ninoy added, ". . . is that the so-called increased sabotage activities and liquidation plans by urban guerrillas operating in the Greater Manila area is the main excuse for the plan—and yet, the plan was conceived even before the bombings!"

The season of Sagittarius, the ninth sign of the Zodiac—denoted by the symbol of the arrow or dart—begins in November, the month elections were to be held in the Philippines.

"I wonder," Ninoy continued, "if this plan is intended to shoot down our cherished civil liberties with the arrow or the dart of a Marcos military rule. Or could this be an arrowhead or the spearhead of a more devilish plot to transform our Republic into a garrison state?"[1]

The senate chambers were silent when Ninoy finished his prophetic speech. The young senator sat down at his desk and buried his face in his hands. He knew that a few courageous newspaper editors would headline the story. There would be a handful of brave Filipinos who would protest, but most people inside and outside the government would ignore his warnings. Nine days later, just as Ninoy had predicted, President Marcos declared martial law. And with his public proclamation numbered 1081, democracy died in the Philippines.

On that day, Friday, 22 September 1972, Ninoy was attending a senate-house conference committee meeting in a suite at the Hilton Hotel in Manila. Just after midnight, policemen knocked on the door. "Martial law has been declared," a colonel announced to the stunned senators and congressmen gathered around the conference table. Senator Ninoy Aquino was the first to be arrested.

On a car telephone, Ninoy managed to contact Cory. "Listen carefully," he said. "Martial law has been declared. I have been arrested. I'm being taken to Camp Crame."[2]

Apparently, Cory told the children. Then she rushed to Camp Crame where she was escorted into a large gymnasium. The families, friends and co-workers of other political prisoners were gathering there. Like Cory, they had come hoping to see loved ones who had been taken from them by police and soldiers pounding on their doors in the night.

While Cory waited, Senator Aquino had been booked and fingerprinted by his arresting officers like a common criminal. Marcos's men allowed Cory and Ninoy just a few minutes together before Ninoy was transported to his cell at Fort Bonifacio.

"It's okay," he told her. "I'll be okay."[3]

Eyewitnesses remember that he whispered instructions for Cory to relay to his political friends and co-workers. They remember, too, that he smiled faintly as he was taken from her. No one in that gymnasium would have believed that Senator Aquino would spend the next seven years in a Marcos prison. But most of the friends who would have defended Ninoy and urged his release were silenced by their imprisonment as well. And the newspapers, radio and television stations whose reporters would have rushed to his defense were closed down by presidential order.

More than 30,000 people were arrested in those first few days following the declaration of martial law. Few if any of those arrested were communists or even communist sympathizers. For example, the men jailed with Ninoy in the maximum security cells at Fort Bonifacio, the Philippine Army headquarters in Makati, a Manila suburb, included Senators Jose "Pepe" W. Diokno and Ramon V. Mitra, Jr.; ex-Senator Francisco "Soc" Rodrigo; Joaquin "Chino" Roces, the publisher of the *Manila Times* (Ninoy's old friend and former employer); Teodoro Locsin, the publisher of the *Manila Press*; Nap Rama, a leader in the constitutional convention; Jose Mari Velez, a popular television newsman in Manila; the distinguished *Manila Times* columnist, Maximo V. Soliven and even Justice Vicente Rafael, a former member of the Supreme Court.

In the opening lines of his proclamation of martial law, President Marcos claimed that "lawless elements" and "ruthless groups of men" were "waging an armed insurrection and rebellion against the Government of the Republic of the Philippines in order to forcibly seize political and state power in this country . . . ."

Once again the wily Marcos was stirring up the threat of communist insurrection as an excuse to silence anyone who threatened his ambition to rule the Philippines with absolute and unquestioned power. Unfortunately, Filipinos and Americans alike believed the Marcos lie.

Those who supported President Marcos's grab for power had their reasons to believe that democracy should be disregarded temporarily. Marcos promised the people of the Philippines "a new society." And there were plenty of reasons to be tired of the old. The peasant farmers, the workers, the students and their families had been victims of violence all too long. As he declared martial law, the president promised to control the nation's military and police forces. He also promised to seek out and destroy the guerrilla units of the NPA and to disarm the private security armies of the rich.

At the time of martial law, violent crimes were on the increase, especially in the Greater Manila area. In all of Asia, there was no per capita murder rate higher than in the Philippines. Marcos promised to use his new powers to stop the violence. He would also promise to execute drug dealers and to imprison crime bosses and their gangs.

In declaring martial law, President Marcos even promised to promote land reform in the Philippines. Some 95 percent of the country's wealth was controlled by just a handful of powerful Filipino families and corporations. President Marcos promised to break up the monopoly of power that the old families held. He promised to collect more taxes from the rich and to give land to the landless peasants. And in the beginning he delivered on some of his promises.

But as time passed, too many promises proved to be lies. President Marcos was using his old rhetoric about "the communist threat" and his empty promises of peace and prosperity to end democracy in the Philippines. His storm troops silenced his critics in the Philippines while the American president, Richard Nixon, the American Congress and the American press stood by in approving silence. Ferdinand and Imelda had charmed and bullied their way to power. Now, for the next thirteen years, billions of dollars in loans, grants and gifts, in American and other foreign currency, would continue to flow into Manila to help prop up their conjugal dictatorship and to help enlarge their secret bank accounts and their real estate and stock portfolios.

While Ferdinand and Imelda were imprisoning, torturing and murdering their enemies, Cory Aquino was hard at work trying to keep her family together and her husband and her husband's cause alive. It wasn't easy. Suddenly, Cory was the single parent of five young children. The two oldest Aquino daughters, Ballsy and Pinky, were seventeen and fifteen. The only son, Noynoy, was twelve. Viel was eleven and the youngest daughter, Kris, had not yet reached her first birthday.

As always, Cory was committed to her family. Even in this new crisis she insisted on being a full-time mother. Still, she managed to visit Ninoy at Fort Bonifacio on every possible occasion. She also made endless phone calls and wrote dozens of letters to President Marcos, to military officers and to government officials on his behalf. She also wrote, telephoned and visited Ninoy's friends and supporters who had not been jailed in an attempt to free her husband and to mobilize opposition to martial law.

After almost four months in prison, Ninoy managed to slip into Cory's hands the first of many articles and letters of protest that he would compose for the world's press. He addressed his long memo on Marcos to his "Co-workers in the Journalistic Profession." He told them that on Saturday, 23 September 1972, that the people of the Philippines work up "to no newspaper, no radio and no TV."[4]

"And like all other dictators," Ninoy continued, "Marcos has invoked the people as rationale for his act." Then he quoted Marcos. "I am utilizing this power vested in me by the Constitution to save the Republic and reform our society." Ninoy answered Marcos's claims with a sneer. "Noble purpose? This is smaltz!"

Ninoy and Cory smuggled other longer, carefully documented articles to the world's press. From his prison cell, Senator Aquino continued his bold attacks on the Marcos regime. Ninoy wrote long position papers detailing the president's destruction of the Filipino economy and the death of democracy in that land. His articles appeared in *The New Yorker*, *The Baltimore Sun*, the *Far Eastern Economic Review*, the *Honolulu Star-Advertiser* and the *Bangkok Post*. As word of Ninoy's attacks filtered back to Malacañang, Ferdinand and Imelda began to rage.

On 12 March 1973, guards entered Ninoy's cell. They blindfolded him and led him to a presidential helicopter. He and another senator, Pepe Diokno, were transported to a prison about thirty-five minutes flying time from Fort Bonifacio in Metro Manila. Ninoy remembered counting the seconds and trying to figure the distance of that flight.

When Ninoy's blindfold was removed he found himself in a tiny dungeon with barred windows boarded with plywood panels. There was no ventilation. The room was bare except for a metal bed with no mattress and a bright neon tube that burned day and night.

Guards stripped the senator naked. They removed his wedding ring, his watch and his eyeglasses. His shoes and clothes were taken away. He was given one set of underwear and a T-shirt. He was ordered to use a bedpan for his toilet and every morning he had to ask his guards for his toothbrush and toothpaste.

After Senators Aquino and Diokno disappeared from Fort Bonifacio, Cory Aquino and Nena Diokno worked desperately to find their husbands and to win their release. Once again, Cory wrote letters and made phone calls. Once again, she appealed to military and government officials and even to the palace. No one even bothered to respond. And Ferdinand and Imelda Marcos refused to consider Cory's plea for clemency on Ninoy's behalf. She visited the offices of various military commanders trying to find out exactly where her husband had been taken. Finally, she petitioned the Supreme Court and won an order to visit Ninoy on Easter Sunday, 22 April 1973.

In a letter to "Soc" Rodrigo, Senator Aquino described those "30 harrowing days in a sweat-box and in complete solitary confinement." At first, Ninoy thought they planned to kill him. He suspected that his guards "were the dreaded 'monkeys,' Marcos's secret terrorists who were trained in torture and licensed to kill." He thought they might be putting drugs in his meager rations so he refused to eat. He lived on six crackers a day. His weight dropped from 190 to 148 lbs.

In that letter to his friend and confidant, Ninoy described the spiritual transformation that he had experienced during his month of solitary confinement in the prison at Laur. From childhood, Ninoy had considered himself a Christian. He had attended church regularly. Prayer and meditation were a part of his daily routine; but in his letter to "Soc" Rodrigo, Ninoy confessed that often during his years in government he had prayed and meditated "more mechanically than with feeling." There had been little opportunity for spiritual growth during those busy years in government. Time for prayer, meditation or the study of the Gospels had been sacrificed to the daily demands of his responsibility as mayor, governor and senator. As a result, his spiritual muscles turned flabby. He discovered that he wasn't spiritually prepared for his arrest and imprisonment. During those first weeks after being thrown in jail, he admitted, he had faced a spiritual crisis.

"At this point of my desperation and desolation," he wrote, "I questioned the justice of God." What kind of God is there, Ninoy wondered, who would allow a dictator to triumph while "I who tried to walk the narrow path of public service with integrity am now about to meet an uncertain fate. Is this justice?" he asked.

He had even doubted God's existence. If there were a God, Ninoy feared that "he was having a very good sound siesta. And I was afraid when he finally woke up, I would have been gone!" Ninoy also wondered how a loving God would allow him to die without even giving him one last chance to see his children whom he feared he was "soon going to leave at the mercy of a fatherless world. And my poor wife Cory," he added "will have to carry my responsibilities on her frail shoulders." Those questions, Ninoy confessed, "assailed and kept me sleepless."[5]

But Ninoy's cellmate during those first long weeks at Fort Bonifacio, "Soc" Rodrigo, was a devout Christian believer. In their cell, Ninoy and "Soc" had long, animated discussions about the life, death and resurrection of Jesus. Ninoy remembered those conversations when he was transferred to solitary confinement at Laur. And in the midst of his loneliness, his doubting and his fear, Ninoy began to meditate and to pray in earnest.

"Suddenly, Jesus became a live human being," Ninoy wrote. "His life was to become my inspiration. Here was a God-Man who preached nothing but love and was rewarded with death. Here was a God-Man who had power over all creation but took the mockery of a crown of thorns with humility and patience. And for all his noble intentions, he was shamed, vilified, slandered and betrayed."

"Then," Ninoy confessed, "it dawned on me how puny were my sufferings compared to him whose only purpose was to save mankind from eternal damnation."

What happened next to Senator Aquino in his hot, miserable cell in Laur is a classic kind of Christian conversion:

> Then [he wrote] as if I heard a voice tell me: "Why do you cry? I have gifted you with consolations, honors and glory which have been denied to

the millions of your countrymen. I made you the youngest war correspondent, presidential assistant, mayor, vice-governor, governor and senator of the Republic, and I recall you never thanked me for all these gifts.
I have given you a full life, a great wife and beautiful, lovable children.
Now that I visit you with a slight desolation, you cry and whimper like a
spoiled brat!"

With this realization I went down on my knees and begged his forgiveness. I know I was merely undergoing a test, maybe in preparation
for another mission . . . I therefore resigned myself to his will.

To think, I have been praying the Lord's Prayer for three and a half
decades without really understanding fully the words I mumbled. I
repeated that prayer so mechanically that I never really knew what I was
saying: Thy will be done, on earth!

Thy Will Be Done! These words snatched me from the jaws of death.
In Laur, I gave up my life and offered it to him . . . picked up my cross
and followed him.[6]

Ninoy's suffering had just begun, but in that lonely cell in Laur,
God was preparing him to triumph over the suffering.

Late in August, 1973, after eleven months in prison, Ninoy was
brought before a military tribunal in Moran Hall at Fort Bonifacio.
Cory sat with the spectators praying silently for her husband's release. The army lawyers leveled six trumped-up charges against him,
ranging from illegal possession of firearms to subversion and even
murder.

There were hundreds of reporters in the crowd. They whispered
excitedly when the senator was charged with murder, but they grew
silent again when Ninoy rose to speak. They remembered his speeches
in the Senate. He was robust then, pudgy, almost fat. His face had
been round and deeply tanned. His eyes had sparkled and he wore a
ready grin. But the reporters hardly recognized Ninoy as he stood
before that military tribunal in his tan pants and dark polo shirt. He
had lost forty-five pounds in prison. As he stood pale and gaunt, his
eyes didn't sparkle. There was no sign of the old Aquino grin. But
once again Ninoy's courageous voice was heard denouncing President
Marcos and his "grab for unlimited power."

Ninoy refused to answer the charges against him. He refused to
participate in a hearing he considered illegal and unconstitutional.
Instead, he used his words to condemn martial law and the man who
had proclaimed it.

"Mr. Marcos has grabbed almost unlimited power because he
claims the democratic methods bequeathed to us by our heroes and
founding fathers have become ineffective. He has embarked on the
ambitious program of fashioning a New Society where the people
must be held together with military discipline and led as if they were

a bunch of sheep, too stupid and too blind to be allowed to proceed in the direction of their own choice.

"It is my belief," Ninoy warned, "that martial rule can only cripple the Filipino—his lofty spirit, his initiative and originality, his moral courage and mental energy, his genius and industry, all the forces that make a nation great and strong . . . ."

Ninoy made an impassioned speech against martial law and the Marcoses' tyranny. And though the military court had leveled charges against him that could lead to the death penalty, Ninoy refused to defend himself or even to discuss the charges.

"You have your duties to perform," he told the military panel. "And I have my sad fate to meet. I have chosen to follow my conscience and to accept the tyrant's verdict. I would rather die on my feet with honor than live on bended knees in shame."[7]

When Senator Aquino finished his speech, reporters and spectators cheered. Ninoy was returned to his cell. But in the weeks and months that followed, he was forced to appear before the tribunal to hear the witnesses Marcos had assembled against him. Ninoy refused to cooperate in the proceedings. He refused to answer the phony charges against him and he continued to level his own charges against the court and the dictator who had convened it.

When Cory wasn't in the courtroom trying to support Ninoy by her presence, she was caring for her family and continuing her campaign to win her husband's release. She continued to telephone, to write and to visit everyone in the military or in the government who would hear her.

Cory, the five Aquino children and members of their wider family were allowed into Fort Bonifacio on Wednesday afternoons from 3:00 until 5:00 P.M. Ninoy presided over these sessions, amazing all who attended with his grasp of current events in the Philippines and around the globe. These were planning sessions in the family's ongoing campaign against Marcos and martial law. Ninoy's messages, articles, interviews and instructions were memorized or smuggled out in the children's clothing.

On Saturdays, Cory visited Ninoy alone. Allowed to spend the weekends on conjugal visits with her husband, she was strip-searched by a female "custodian" before and after each visit. She carried extra blankets to drape over the television camera that threatened their intimacy and they whispered to avoid the hidden microphones taping their conversations day and night.

During the week Cory acted as Ninoy's representative to the press, to his political co-workers and to the general public. She didn't like handling press conferences or making speeches, but she determined to do her best to represent Ninoy even if she didn't enjoy the public spotlight. On weekends Ninoy coached her in the questions that people would ask and exactly how she should answer them. Cory organized a small army of volunteers, including courageous nuns, to help distribute Ninoy's statements and to appear in his support when he was brought before the Military Commission.

On 4 April 1975, after the military tribunal had dragged on for more than a year, Ninoy went on a hunger strike.

"A time comes in a man's life," he said, "when he must prefer a meaningful death to a meaningless life."

Ninoy had studied the history of nonviolent protest. He was an admirer of Gandhi and Martin Luther King. Ninoy knew that a hunger strike might mean his death, but he had no other way to oppose the corruption of the Marcos regime. So, against the protest of his family and friends, Ninoy Aquino began a hunger strike that would last for 40 days.

On May 6, after Ninoy had gone 34 days without food, Cory announced to the nation that her husband had been forcibly transferred from his cell in the prison at Fort Bonifacio to an intensive care ward at the Veterans Memorial Hospital. In a sworn affidavit, Cory reported that during Ninoy's fast he had become seriously dehydrated. There was a growing possibility that his liver and kidneys would be irreversibly damaged. And though he had developed serious symptoms related to his dehydration fever, Ninoy had refused to accept intravenous fluid feedings. Once again Cory explained that her husband was risking his life to protest the Marcos regime and its illegal acts against him and against all the people of the Philippines. Once again, Cory asked for the prayers of the people on her husband's behalf.

During his fast, Ninoy's weight dropped to 127 pounds. He was on the verge of death. For the past weeks, Cory and Ninoy's mother, Doña Aurora Aquino, had begged Ninoy to end the fast. Finally, Ninoy consented. He took his first bite of food after fasting for 40 days as he had promised.

As Senator Aquino's strength returned, he was called before the Military Commission once again. And once again he refused to participate in a proceeding which he considered ". . . a conscienceless mockery of justice."[8]

On 25 November 1977, after five years and two months of imprisonment, the Military Commission sentenced Senator Ninoy Aquino to death before a firing squad. Ninoy and Cory both remember the horrible loneliness of that moment. For more than five years they had fought the battle almost alone. The Filipino press, controlled by the Marcos military regime, had been silent. No ranking American officials, either from the American Embassy in Manila or from the

Cory and her grandsons

Cory
and her
grandsons

Cory and Cardinal Sin

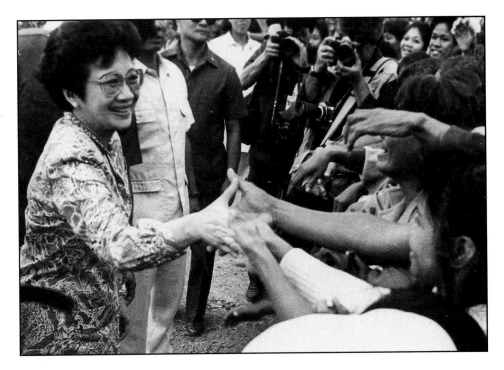

(above)
Cory and well wishers

(left)
Cory plants a seedling

President Aquino and Director Frankie Batacan of the Bureau of Broadcast Services

Cory confers the Phillippine Legion of Honor, Degree of Chief Commander upon Don Joaquin Roces

The president with the Roces family at the funeral of Don Joaquin "Chino" Roces

Cory kisses her grandson goodbye before boarding a flight to attend the funeral of Emperor Hirohito of Japan

The president delivers her second State of the Nation address

The president and her family

Cory reviews her troops

Mel White, the author, and Doña Aurora Aquino, Ninoy's mother and Cory's mother-in-law

A TIME COMES IN A MAN'S LIFE WHEN HE MUST PREFER A MEANINGFUL DEATH TO A MEANINGLESS LIFE.

BENIGNO S AQUINO, JR

Mel White stands in front of a wall mural honoring Ninoy Aquino

State Department in Washington, D.C. had even bothered to visit Senator Aquino or to inquire of his well-being. Everyone seemed to believe Marcos's allegation that Aquino was a subversive who needed to be imprisoned. There were faithful friends in the Philippines who struggled alongside Cory on Ninoy's behalf, and there had been occasional articles in the world's press discussing the Aquino case, but generally Ninoy and Cory had struggled alone.

The same year that Senator Aquino was sentenced to death, Jimmy Carter began his term as America's thirty-ninth President. He appointed Patricia Murphey Derian to head his Human Rights Bureau. Under previous administrations, that particular desk in the State Department had served primarily to gather information on human-rights abuses. Mrs. Derian's nomination was approved without reservation; after all, she was a woman in a male-dominated branch of government and totally inexperienced in foreign policy. What harm could she do?

Shortly after Ninoy Aquino was sentenced to death, Mrs. Derian made an official visit to the Philippines. She confronted President Marcos about his human rights abuses and in the heated argument that followed she warned him that President Carter might use his power with the world banking system to keep Marcos from getting further loans if he didn't stop those same abuses. Next, she confronted Marcos's defense minister, Juan Ponce Enrile. When Enrile, who was trained in the United States, began an elaborate public relations presentation complete "with slides, charts, pointers, and officers in crisp uniforms to deliver the performance," Derian interrupted with the questions she had come to ask.

What about the people Marcos was holding in jail without a trial? What about the rumors of torture and murder carried out by the military? Why was the press censored, and television and radio stations closed down? Why had Senator Benigno Aquino, Jr., the leading member of the Marcos's opposition, been sentenced to death?

Later that night at an American Embassy dinner for Derian, the CIA Chief in Manila asked her if she would like to visit Ninoy Aquino in prison. The visit had been mysteriously arranged for that same night. Whoever arranged it assumed that Under-Secretary Derian would refuse the invitation at such an inopportune moment. Mrs. Derian fooled them once again. Though she was wearing a strapless, formal gown to an embassy party in her honor, Mrs. Derian accepted the challenge, borrowed a wrap from another guest and was driven to Fort Bonifacio in the middle of the night.

Apparently, the American CIA chief spent the ride trying to convince Under-Secretary Derian that Ninoy Aquino was just another subversive, "a rich playboy, an adventurer, a seamy character."[9]

But in Fort Bonifacio, Derian sat with Ninoy for ninety minutes, listening to his side of that story. She was impressed by the man who emerged from their conversation. She called Ninoy "a small d democrat, with an honest-to-God full understanding of the history of the idea of democracy, of the necessity of it, the mechanism, the games of it. It was simply a breathtaking exposition," she said later, " . . . and we came away with the sense that we had met somebody of monumental stature, intellectually and in terms of democracy. Like Churchill. A giant."[10]

Researchers aren't sure exactly what happened next. They don't know how the head of President Carter's Human Rights Bureau affected her hosts in Manila, but after Ninoy made his appeal to the Supreme Court in the Philippines, no other hearings were held. And even as Ninoy sat on death row waiting for the firing squad, Marcos offered him the chance to run as a candidate in the "transition elections" scheduled for 7 April 1978.

To allow a prisoner on death row, condemned for murder, to run for public office was just one of the many ways President Marcos demonstrated his love-hate relationship with Senator Aquino. Both Ferdinand and Imelda seemed to have a grudging respect for the senator. To silence him (and to take advantage of his skills), they offered him official positions in their government. And though Ninoy's constant and insightful criticism was the greatest single threat to the Marcos regime, the president and the first lady continued to vacillate in their response to the fiery Aquino. They hated Ninoy but they had to admire him at the same time.

Marcos allowed Ninoy to run for office but refused to let the former Senator out of prison to mount his campaign for a seat in the interim Batasang Pambansa (National Assembly). Defense Secretary Juan Ponce Enrile went on network television to defend the president's ruling. Enrile claimed that Ninoy had connections with the New People's Army and that he worked for America's Central Intelligence Agency.

Ninoy demanded equal television time to respond to both lies and Marcos was so overconfident of his hold on the nation that he granted Senator Aquino his request. On March 10, Ninoy answered the charges against him on a network television broadcast. For ninety minutes he held the nation spellbound. The streets of Manila emptied of traffic as Ninoy made his case known to the people.

Ninoy asked that the people register their protest against Marcos's military regime with a noise barrage on April 6, election eve. At exactly 7:00 that night, women picked up cooking pans and began to bang them together. At the same time, the drivers of cars, trucks and jeepneys began to blow their horns. Church bells rang. Sirens sounded. The streets were filled with young and old alike banging pieces of steel together, shouting their protests against Marcos and martial law, and making the "L" sign of Ninoy's Laban party to the lines of police and soldiers Marcos had called up to keep order. The noise barrage that Ninoy had requested echoed across Metro Manila through the open windows of the presidential palace and among the islands of the Philippines.

With the incredible show of public support, everyone felt confident that Ninoy and his slate of candidates would defeat the Marcos cronies, including Imelda, who stood against them. But once again, Marcos won the election through massive fraud.

In a statement issued from his cell, Ninoy condemned "yesterday's brazen and massive cheatings, the use of naked terrorism, the ballot stuffings and the changing of actual tallies—and the sabotage." He called the noise barrage on election eve, "an unprecedented outpouring of unity . . . ." and he said it was "proof of a great moral victory that crowned a mission set out to reactivate the consciousness and rekindle the awareness of our people . . . . The real victors are the Filipino people," Ninoy concluded. "They have finally succeeded in overcoming their collective fear that has stood guard over the locked doors of their freedom."[11]

President Marcos kept Senator Aquino in prison for another twenty-one months. But the president was being criticized for holding Ninoy. He couldn't kill the senator. That would be bad for Marcos's "image." But he couldn't release Ninoy, either. Aquino was just too great a political threat. Finally, in December, 1979, Marcos offered to free Ninoy if he would leave the country. Ninoy talked at length to Cory and to his political allies and advisors. Everyone agreed that Ninoy and his family should seek asylum in America.

Then one spring afternoon in 1980, while the senator exercised in the Fort Bonifacio prison courtyard, he felt pains in his chest and numbness in his left side and arm. Arteries were clogged. Ninoy needed triple bypass surgery. Even President Marcos must have laughed in disbelief when his wife, Imelda, offered Ninoy the services of her brand new heart center in Quezon City. The Senator chose instead a famous Filipino doctor in Dallas. In May, 1980, Ninoy, Cory and their children left the Philippines for Texas. Ninoy had been in prison for seven years and seven months.

Cory had devoted those endless prison years to Ninoy and their children. Every day she lived with the fear that she might not see her husband again. She was abandoned by many old friends and even members of her wider family who believed the president's lie that Ninoy was a subversive intent on undermining the government.

There were long periods of time when Cory stood almost alone in his defense.

In a speech in 1986 to her old classmates at Saint Vincent College, Cory described those years of Ninoy's imprisonment as her "first great suffering." And in a question-and-answer session that followed, Cory claimed that only God could have supplied the strength, hope and comfort she needed for those trying times.

Even with her husband in prison, Cory took time to begin and to end each day with a time of meditation on the life of Jesus. Every Sunday she and her family went to church. She read gospel stories to her children and studied the Gospels to gain insights and comfort for her own life. And she prayed "without ceasing" for God's guidance and presence in her life.

No one even guessed it then, but those seven years that Ninoy spent in prison were Cory's graduate school preparing her for the political and spiritual tasks of the presidency. She was trained in political science by her husband, who used his weekend sessions to pass on to her his own political skills and commitment. At the same time, God was teaching Cory about the spiritual disciplines that would sustain her in the days ahead.

Above all else, Cory learned about the price of Christian leadership. "If we are to be real Christians," she said in a speech in 1986, "we have to accept suffering as a part of our life."[12]

7

Ninoy and Cory:
In Exile
(May, 1980–21 August 1983)

The consolation of slavery is that one is spared the anxiety of being responsible for yourself and your country . . . . Freedom is different. The shackles are struck from your wrist and your hands are full of responsibilities . . . .

President Corazon C. Aquino

I believe the cause delaying our liberation may be found in ourselves, in our reluctance to assert our rights and frontally confront the forces of evil. We are afraid to die and our fear has immobilized us. We have forged our own chains with our cowardice.

Senator Benigno Aquino, Jr.

Cory Aquino and her children hurried after Ninoy as he walked with a small crowd of friends and reporters toward gate 21 at the Manila International Airport. After almost eight years in prison, Ninoy was just a few steps away from freedom. Cory still remembers that moment of their release from Marcos's captivity. "We always believed that God works in wondrous ways," she said. "Who would have thought that a frightening thing like his heart attack on March 19, 1980, would be the instrument of his release?"[1]

Ninoy Aquino's popularity with the people was a terrible threat to Ferdinand and Imelda Marcos. They wanted to rule the Philippines forever. As Imelda had been prepared to succeed her husband, so their son, Ferdinand, Jr., had been prepared as Imelda's political heir. Ninoy Aquino was perhaps the only man in the Philippines with the political clout to end the Marcos family dynasty.

It isn't difficult to imagine why President Marcos released Ninoy Aquino from his prison cell that day. Ninoy's death sentence was still pending, but the president knew that the public's reaction to the popular young senator's execution might bring down the Marcos regime. (Later events would justify his fear.) For awhile, the president thought that keeping Ninoy in jail would silence his powerful voice. But even locked away in his cell at Fort Bonifacio, Ninoy's cry for the end of martial law was echoing louder and louder across the land. Ninoy's need for heart surgery gave Marcos his only acceptable option: send Aquino into exile.

But Ninoy's freedom came with strings attached. Imelda Marcos visited Ninoy and offered him the opportunity to travel to America on two conditions. First, he would return to his cell in Fort Bonifacio after his surgery and after an appropriate time of recuperation. Second, he would not comment on partisan Philippine politics while he was abroad.

Ninoy agreed. But 87 days after his release, Ninoy broke his promise. "A pact with the devil," he announced, "is no pact at all. My goal is to restore freedom to my people."[2] After his successful triple bypass surgery in Dallas, Ninoy launched his three-year American exile with a rousing speech to the Asia Society in New York City. In his first few months in America, he had conferred with most of the Filipino leaders in exile.

"All . . . have one demand," Ninoy exclaimed. "That Mr. Marcos step down and dismantle his martial law regime as a basis for national unity."

Next, Ninoy sounded the warning of "A massive urban guerrilla warfare being built up by young patriots to bring the Marcos regime to its knees." Across the Philippines and in various exile centers in Asia, Europe, North and South America young Filipinos were plotting the end of Ferdinand and Imelda's fifteen-year rule. And though the hard-core NPA leadership may have been devoted to communist ideology, the New People's Army was swelling with volunteers who had no interest in or direct connections to the international communist movement. The young farmers, blue collar workers and students who were taking up arms against President Marcos were signing up with the NPA because they could see no other option to the corruption, the deceit and the terror of the Marcos regime.

During his exile in America, even Ninoy was having trouble deciding between the violent and nonviolent options.

"I have," Ninoy explained to the Asia Society, "chosen to suffer long years of solitary confinement rather than urge my followers to put our country to the torch because, like the average Filipino, I put the highest value on human life. And I dread the weeping of mothers whose sons will surely be sacrificed at the altar of revolution."[3]

In those first months after his release, Ninoy traveled to Saudi Arabia to talk with Nur Misuari, the leader of the Muslim National Liberation Front in the Philippines. The Muslim insurgency in the southern Philippines had already cost the lives of 100,000 Filipinos, Muslims and Christians. At least one million more had suffered homelessness during those years of endless terror in the war of secession of the Philippines' Muslim south.

Ninoy also traveled to Managua, Nicaragua, to study the Sandinista revolution there. President Ortega welcomed Ninoy as "a head of state" and Ninoy was greeted in Nicaragua by the Cuban ambassador who offered him military support for a revolution in the Philippines.

"Should Marcos remain obstinate," Ninoy told the Asia Society in his first major speech in America, "the only alternative will be to remove him by force along the Iranian or Nicaraguan model. It could be done," he affirmed. "The most entrenched dictator can be toppled."

Ninoy was angry that the United States government continued to prop up dictators in Central and South America and in Asia through direct financial aid and clandestine CIA support. He was surprised and disappointed that President Reagan could label Ferdinand Marcos as America's "best friend in Asia" or that after the sham elections in 1981, Vice President George Bush could announce at Marcos's inauguration that "We love your adherence to democratic principles and the democratic process." Still, the young senator found it increasingly difficult to believe that violent communist revolution was a viable option.

"If Marxism is so good," Ninoy would ask a reporter in 1983, "how come the traffic has been from East to West?" After his visit to Nicaragua, Ninoy said, "[It's] very sad. After the revolution, the Russians are now the new lords of these people. We can't accept the offer of the Cuban ambassador. We'll be tied up by the necks. If we'll be asked to choose between the Americans or the Russians, we'll go for the Americans."[4]

Ninoy knew that democracy could not come to the Philippines until Marcos had been deposed. Nonviolence was a preferable option, but the Marcos regime had proved itself ruthless in its successful efforts to get and to keep power over the people. There were times it seemed that the only way to rid the Philippines of Marcos's rule was to use violence against violence.

As Ninoy puzzled over the options, one thing became perfectly clear: he might be called upon to sacrifice himself to help free the Filipino people.

"I have asked myself many times," he said, "Is the Filipino worth dying for? Is he not a coward who will readily yield to any colonizer, be he foreign or homegrown? Is a Filipino more comfortable under an authoritarian leader because he does not want to be burdened by the freedom of choice?

"I have carefully weighed the virtues and the faults of the Filipino," Ninoy went on. "I have come to the conclusion: He is worth dying for . . . ."[5]

Ninoy Aquino had been offered fellowships to teach and to research and write at several great universities in Australia, Japan, Europe and the United States. In 1980, after his successful heart surgery and several quick trips abroad, Ninoy began a one-year fellowship to teach at Harvard University. His fellowship was renewed in 1981 for a second year and Senator Aquino spent his third year in America, 1982–1983, teaching and researching for his own book at the prestigious Massachusetts Institute of Technology.

Cory Aquino still looks back on those three years in Boston with grateful memories. Even before Ninoy's imprisonment, their life together as a family had been chaotic and stressful. Cory had given those first years of her married life to bring stability and calm to their busy household. The demands on Ninoy as a public servant had left almost no time for just being together as a couple or a family.

In Boston there would be time for the entire Aquino family to sit around a fireplace or make a snowman or watch the trees change colors along the banks of the Charles River. Ninoy and Cory purchased a beautiful old red-brick home on Commonwealth Avenue in Chestnut Hill, a quiet, distinguished suburb of Boston, just south of Cambridge and the Harvard Campus. The senator would have an office in his home. The libraries and classrooms of Harvard where he would write and teach were only a few minutes away. Boston College was just across the street. During the humid eastern summers, the Aquino family could walk together in the shade of the chestnut trees that shelter that beautiful campus and in the winter they would join the students bundled up in winter coats and gloves to frolic in the freshly fallen snow.

From the beginning, in summer and in winter, there was a steady line of old friends, co-workers, reporters, cameramen and favor seekers making their way up Commonwealth Avenue to the home of Ninoy and Cory Aquino. There must have been many times that Cory resented that house full of visitors who wanted to talk to her famous husband. Once again, she found herself hurrying in and out of the kitchen and guest room preparing food and making up the beds for Ninoy's guests.

People who visited Ninoy during his Boston exile remember that Cory seldom had time to enter into their discussions about current events in the Philippines. She insisted on maintaining her own personal privacy and there was still a large family to care for. The two oldest Aquino daughters were in their twenties. In 1976, Ballsy had graduated from Manila's Assumption College with a degree in accounting. Pinky graduated from the University of the Philippines in 1979 with a degree in Business Economics. Ballsy and Pinky had accompanied their father into exile. Only the Aquino son, Noynoy, had stayed in Manila to finish his Economics degree at the Ateneo University. Viel (19) was a college sophomore living at home and attending classes at Boston College just across the street from their home in Chestnut Hill. The youngest daughter, Kris, was just nine years old.

In spite of the demands placed upon their family by Ninoy's celebrity status, Cory guarded the family's privacy and maintained the family's traditions. Every Aquino birthday required a celebration. From October to February there was at least one birthday party every month. In February there were two. In an interview, Ballsy Aquino remembered that Ninoy's first birthday celebration in America fell on Thanksgiving day, 27 November 1980.

The day began with a birthday breakfast with at least fifteen relatives dropping by for the occasion. The whole family attended Mass at a chapel on the nearby campus. Then, while Ninoy and his cousin (Midjie Aquino) installed a stereo in Pinky's car, Cory stayed in the kitchen preparing chicken with walnuts, the Filipino adobo and kare-kare and Ninoy's favorite dish, Peking Duck. A huge table was spread. Before the day had ended more than 40 friends and family had joined the celebration. After dinner, Ninoy unwrapped his gifts: neckties, cakes, "another attache case," and a portable snow shovel for his car.

"We had a lot of fun," Ballsy recalls, "as Dad loved to joke." Someone brought out a guitar and as Ballsy remembers it, ". . . there was a lot of singing."[6] The party lasted until 3 A.M. The Aquino family took advantage of every moment like this that they had together. They knew that one day this peaceful, happy time might end.

"Throughout our three years in the United States," Cory wrote, "we were always aware that our life there was temporary. Ninoy never ceased talking about returning to the Philippines."[7]

And though Cory missed her homeland, it wasn't easy to think about returning to Manila. She knew that Ninoy might be imprisoned again or even killed. While that stream of visitors talked to her husband about the future of the Philippines, Cory continued to pray that God would guide Ninoy in his search and give them both strength for those troubled days ahead. Cory spent time every day in prayer. She studied the Scriptures and other devotional literature and continued to meditate daily on the mysteries of the life of Jesus. And she attended church and went to confession regularly.

Cory and her husband had spent long, uninterrupted hours together on their weekend visits in his cell at Fort Bonifacio. During those visits they had talked of everything. In Boston, it was a battle to maintain their regular times together.

After all, Ninoy was seen as the leader of the expatriate Filipino community. He was the one person who might rescue their nation from tyranny. Their business with him was urgent, even historic. Once again the needs of Ninoy's wife and his family took a back seat to the needs of his nation. Besides, this was a male-dominated culture. Even Cory has admitted that from time to time she was frustrated by her husband's "chauvinism." Everyone, including Ninoy, expected Cory to care for her man and his guests—and Cory obliged.

Yet Cory must have had her own strong feelings about martial law and how it might be ended. After all, she, too, had been a victim of the conjugal dictatorship of Ferdinand and Imelda. While Ninoy was in jail, Cory had to fight her husband's battles. She carried his messages and spoke his words before the microphones and bright lights of the media. To his political allies and even to his foes she stated and explained his positions. And through it all she struggled selflessly to parent his family and to gain his freedom. And yet almost immediately upon their arrival in America, Cory found herself assigned the back row once again. Ninoy took center stage while Cory played the traditional supporting role as wife and mother.

Cory did have her limits. When one of Ninoy's visitors presented her a pile of his dirty underwear to wash and fold, Cory was heard to threaten, "Either he goes, or I go!"[8] But that steady stream of Filipino visitors was also a blessing, even to Cory.

"We adjusted," she recalls of those three years together in America, "and what made life so much easier, although we were far from the home we loved, were the many friends we made in the Filipino community in Boston."[9]

One of their visitors was a real surprise. In December, 1980, Imelda Marcos called, inviting Ninoy to meet with her in Imelda's ($1,700 a day) Waldorf-Astoria Suite in New York City. It was an unpleasant encounter to say the least. Imelda accused Ninoy of sending assassination teams to Manila to "knock off her people." She warned Ninoy to stop his death squads and threatened that the Reagan administration would go after Ninoy in America if he didn't obey.[10]

Ninoy denied the charges. He had thought seriously about using force to depose Marcos, but Ninoy's spiritual conversion in prison, his visit to Nicaragua and his study and discussions in America were all leading Ninoy toward the position of Christian nonviolence.

"Shortly after I arrived in Boston," Ninoy told a congressional committee, "I was visited by some of my countrymen and asked to join the ranks of the freedom fighters who have chosen the path of revolution to liberate our people. I considered their appeal very seriously and I re-directed my academic research to a close scrutiny of the advantages and disadvantages of the use of force and violence to attain national liberation."

After detailing the history of his travels to the Middle East, to Southeast Asia and to Central America where he interviewed "the victors and the vanquished of the most recent successful revolutions," Ninoy concluded "that revolution and violence exact the highest price in terms of human values and human lives in the struggle for freedom. In the end there are really no victors, only victims."[11]

Ninoy Aquino could look Imelda Marcos straight in the eye and deny without equivocation that he was behind the urban terrorists who threatened her. There were Filipinos at home and abroad who were plotting Imelda's assassination. But it wasn't Ninoy's lectures against martial law or his call for the restoration of democracy in the Philippines that motivated Imelda's enemies. Her own arrogant and insensitive actions inspired the plottings against her. Imelda's shopping sprees on those New York visits are a case in point.

While millions of Filipinos were starving Imelda Marcos was dazzling New Yorkers with her extravagant spending. It didn't matter that the national treasury of the Philippines was practically bankrupt. Imelda still tipped bellmen with hundred-dollar bills and ordered thousand-dollar floral displays created for her hotel bedrooms and parlors. Billions of dollars in foreign loans were propping up the economy of the Philippines (and saddling the nation with interest payments that could destroy it), while Imelda used much of those same monies to purchase diamonds, stocks, bonds and an impressive hunk of the New York City skyline.

According to author and historian Raymond Bonner, during Imelda's 1981 visit to the U.S., she spent $1.1 million for a heart-shaped necklace with pearls and matching earrings, $130,000 for another ruby and diamond necklace, $225,000 for a necklace of Egyptian coral and onyx. Two days later she spent more than $610,640 on antiques, including a rare mahogany China cabinet for $100,000 and two eighteenth-century carved and gilt wooden Georgian armchairs, for $41,600. Three weeks later she bought an entire New York estate for $5.95 million that included paintings by the masters, rare books and antique furniture.[12]

Ninoy knew that Imelda and her husband were destroying the nation's economy with their extravagance. He knew, too, that the opposition to Marcos's regime was growing and that the Communist Party of the Philippines and their New People's Army was taking advantage of the people's growing discontent.

In a letter to a friend, Senator Eva Kalaw, marked "personal and confidential," Ninoy wrote: "I sincerely believe that if current trends are not reversed, by 1985 the CPP/NPA will be a real threat to our Republic and way of life."[13]

After sharing his fears about the growth of communism in the Philippines, Ninoy stated his belief that "Only a hopeless people will turn to communism. We must therefore exert every effort to convince Marcos that a genuine return to democracy is the only sure path out of the enveloping red tide. Only more democracy can defeat communism," Ninoy concluded. "Increased repression will only hasten the communist victory."

Ninoy and Doy Laurel had agreed to try to begin a dialogue with Marcos. "Should Marcos die tomorrow," Ninoy warned, "there won't be anyone in our country with enough power and/or legitimacy to restructure our democratic form of government and/or re-establish the necessary institutions to restore democracy."

One last time, Ninoy warned against the ultimate cost of violence: "Every bloody revolution has inevitably consumed its own children. What will be our future if the killers of today will become our leaders tomorrow? The lessons of Iran and Nicaragua are too fresh to be forgotten."

Ninoy Aquino was a realist. Violent revolution was a costly business. Too many innocent people would be killed and wounded. Too many homes, schools, churches, farms and factories would be damaged or destroyed. And the waste in money and natural resources would be incalculable.

During his years as a war correspondent in various Asian nations, including his own, Ninoy had seen the corpses of the children and of old men and women lined up along the roadway. He had heard too many screams of pain and looked into too many eyes clouded with terror and despair. He had walked through too many ruined cities, towns and villages. Firsthand he knew why violent revolution was not the best way to overcome tyranny. But he still wasn't sure that nonviolence could be effective against a tyrant like Marcos—or why it was the only real option to consider.

Ninoy seemed destined to lead a revolution that would end the Marcos era and bring democracy to the Philippines. But what kind of revolution would it be? Both Cory and Ninoy had been praying for God's answer to this important question. God heard their prayers and answered them.

At Harvard, Ninoy spent time reading the biographies of the great pacifists. He was fond of quoting Gandhi and telling stories in his speeches or class lectures about Martin Luther King, Jr. Ninoy was beginning to feel a growing commitment to the ways of Christian pacifism, but nonviolence required incredible patience, and violence was already taking hold in the Philippines.

"If we wait too long," Ninoy wrote, "events might overtake us. I am afraid when the present trickle of bloodshed becomes a flood, violence would develop a momentum of its own and we will all be sucked into the vortex. I pray to God this won't happen."[14]

Ninoy had to decide. Would he go back secretly to the Philippines and join the freedom fighters training in the mountains above Manila? Or would he go back in peace? Would he carry a machine gun on his return journey or would he arrive in Manila empty-handed? Either way he was risking his life.

During Ninoy's three years in exile, there were at least two brief encounters with evangelical Christian leaders who helped Ninoy make his ultimate choice. One Sunday morning, shortly after his arrival in the United States, Ninoy Aquino was invited to attend the North Shore Baptist Church in Chicago. Many of the church's members were Filipino expatriates who had to flee the Marcos regime.

The Old Testament reading that Sunday morning was from the Prophet Zechariah. "Not by might, not by power, but by my spirit, says the Lord of Hosts" (Zechariah 4:8). The pastor picked up on the words of that ancient text and spoke directly to Ninoy's heart.

Months later he wrote his host in Chicago, Eddie Monteclaro, a former president of the Philippines Press Corps, admitting that he had been struggling to know exactly how he should proceed in his efforts to oust Marcos. "The message of Zechariah 4:8 in that morning worship experience had crystallized his thinking: he would return in peace."[15]

In 1982, when Ninoy was doubting his decision, he heard a lecture by Anthony Campolo, a Protestant Christian author and public speaker. Campolo remembers lecturing that day about Jesus' teachings concerning the difference between power (that comes from military might) and authority (which comes from right and truth). After the lecture, Ninoy thanked Campolo with these words:

"You have given me hope," he said. "I know that when I return to my homeland I will be powerless; but you have helped me to see that I will have authority. What I say is right, and people know it. What I believe to be true, I am willing to die for. I now believe I will have a great influence in the Philippines, even though I hold no power at all."[16]

Often during their exile in America Ninoy and Cory Aquino talked about going home. During his second meeting with Imelda Marcos in 1982, Ninoy shared his growing conviction that it was time to return to Manila. When he showed Imelda his expired passport, she took it from him, promising to have it renewed. Ninoy never saw his own passport again.

When Ninoy did board the airplane for his final journey home, he was carrying two false passports. On one his real name was written, Benigno S. Aquino, Jr. The other bore the name Marcial (for martial law) Bonifacio (for the military prison where he had spent almost eight years in solitary confinement and where he thought the soldiers might take him after his return).

On 21 May 1983, Imelda and Ninoy met for the third time in New York City. No one knows for sure exactly what Imelda said that day. Apparently, she and her husband were willing to make some kind of compromise to get Ninoy on their side. It is alleged that Imelda even offered Ninoy the position of prime minister if he returned—or a large financial stake if he would stay and go into business in America.

Ninoy refused. He knew that Marcos was the key to peaceful change in the Philippines, but there was no way that Imelda could bribe Ninoy to become a member of her corrupt regime.

"Ninoy believed that it was imperative for him to speak to Marcos," Cory said later, "and appeal to him to return our country to democracy before extreme forces were released that would make such a return impossible."

Cory tried to persuade her husband that Marcos would not listen. "That man is completely calloused," Ninoy replied, "[but] I will never forgive myself if I do not at least try."

"When I heard this," Cory remembered, "I knew there was nothing I could do to stop him from returning, not even after we were warned about the threats on his life. The smallest hope that there could be a peaceful, painless and graceful restoration of democracy was enough to convince Ninoy he had to try it."[17]

On their last Christmas in Boston, the family attended Midnight Mass together and then returned to their home on Commonwealth Avenue for their traditional Christmas eve sharing of gifts.

"Being a Christian," Cory recalled, "Christmas is Christ." Every year Cory sent out the family Christmas card with a Bible verse announcing the birth of the Savior. On their Boston mantle she placed a Christmas creche made of Filipino *narra* wood with the familiar figures of the wise men, shepherds, angels, Joseph, Mary and the baby

Jesus. And on Christmas Eve the family prayed and sang carols together at the nearby church of St. Ignatius.

"Christmas means being together for the entire family," Cory added. "Ever since we were married, Ninoy and I were never apart for Christmas."

On that last Christmas Eve together in Boston the family returned from church to a blazing fire on the hearth and a pile of colorful packages beneath a pine tree decorated with lights. After midnight Ninoy telephoned friends and family in Manila where it was 12 noon on Christmas Day. It was late when the last gift had been unwrapped and the final snapshot taken of the Aquino family grouped around the Christmas tree.

In June, 1983, Ninoy's teaching fellowship at M.I.T. was due to expire. During those last six months in America, Ninoy became more and more certain that the only way to save the Philippines was to convince President Marcos to hold a genuinely free election. Ninoy knew that more, not less, democracy would weaken the communist insurgency and set the nation on the path to moral and economic renewal.

"I am sure," Ninoy wrote Senator Eva Kalaw, "the CPP/NPAs [New People's Army of the Communist Party of the Philippines] will be most unhappy by the holding of a clean and honest election because this will delay their timetable."[18]

Again, Cory tried to convince her husband that President Marcos would not listen. But Ninoy Aquino was already making plans for his journey home.

"The smallest hope that there could be a peaceful, painless and graceful restoration of democracy was enough to convince Ninoy he had to try it."[19]

He was willing to risk his own life in the hope that a bloody revolution could be avoided.

"The funny thing about Ninoy," Cory wrote, "was that, while his own suffering had convinced him of the inexhaustible capacity of man to endure pain, he never wanted anyone else to go through the same experience. He was half convinced that suffering ennobles, but he was not prepared to experiment with other people's lives. Only with his own."[20]

"Ninoy is coming home!"

The rumors spread quickly from Boston to Manila and up and down the islands of the Philippine archipelago. In May, 1983, during Aquino's last visit with Imelda Marcos in New York City, she pleaded with him to cancel or delay his plans to return. "It's not advisable, Ninoy," she warned him. "Believe me: there are people who would like to kill you. The intelligence community tells us this." In an interview with *Time* magazine, Senator Aquino quoted Imelda as saying, "Ninoy, there are people loyal to us who cannot be controlled." Imelda herself told a *Newsweek* magazine reporter, "If he [Ninoy] comes home, he's dead."[21]

When Ninoy finally made it official that he would soon return to Manila, Marcos wired Ninoy a summary of intelligence reports in the Philippines that "confirm certain groups plan to assassinate you when you come to the Philippines. Since the government will be blamed for anything that happens to you, it prefers to assume a prudent approach." Marcos urged Ninoy "to stay in the United States until such time that we can identify and neutralize these groups."[22]

Two weeks later, on 31 July 1983, Defense Minister Juan Ponce Enrile warned Ninoy in another telegram that government agents were "convinced beyond reasonable doubt there are plots against your life upon your arrival in the Philippines." He, too, urged Ninoy to delay his travel plans for at least a month while the government neutralized the plots against him. Enrile appealed in the name of "national unity and reconciliation."

Ninoy consented. He promised to delay his return for another thirty days. Then, on 13 August 1983, in spite of the rash of warnings, Ninoy, Cory and the family left their home on Commonwealth Avenue and drove to the Boston International Airport where Ninoy would begin his final journey home.

"The last time I saw Ninoy alive," Cory remembers, "was on August 13, 1983. We had all gone to Mass that morning and, although we tried to hide our apprehension, Ninoy and I could feel each other's sadness. When we said good-bye to him at the airport, the children and I said: 'See you in two weeks' time.' We saw him even earlier."[23]

Ninoy flew directly to Los Angeles where he spent two days in conferences with Filipino friends and supporters. He explained that he was going back to Manila as a man of peace. He was willing to exchange another jail sentence for a chance to speak to President Marcos for even ten or fifteen minutes.

Ninoy knew the risk. During Ninoy's three years in Boston, General Fabian Ver, Marcos's Chief of the armed forces, had conducted an extensive intelligence campaign against him. Philippine embassy and consular officials were monitoring Ninoy's movements. In an attempt to throw off any agents of the Marcos government who might be pursuing him, Ninoy flew from Los Angeles by way of Tokyo, Hong Kong and Singapore to Kuala Lumpur. The senator suspected that General Ver and his agents might try to stop him from traveling to Manila. To guarantee his own safety and the safety of his fellow passengers, Ninoy tried to keep his travel plans secret.

But Ninoy wanted to explain to leaders of the Philippines' neighboring Asian nations and to the people of the Philippines that he was coming home in peace. In Kuala Lumpur, Ninoy held meetings with the prime minister of Malaysia and key officials from Indonesia and Thailand. Then, still anxious to elude pursuit, Ninoy flew back to Singapore and north through Hong Kong to Taipei, Taiwan.

On August 19, one day before the final leg of Ninoy's journey, General Fabian C. Ver, the Chief of Staff of Marcos's Armed Forces, announced to the press that Aquino would not be allowed to land on Philippine soil. And if he landed, he could not disembark but "would be flown out on the same aircraft."[24]

That next day, Ninoy, his brother-in-law, ABC newsman Ken Kashiwahara, and a rather large party of newspaper, newsmagazine, radio and television reporters boarded CAL (China Airlines) Flight 811 to Manila. In Boston, Cory and her family waited nervously for news of Ninoy's safe arrival. In Manila, thousands of Ninoy's supporters were converging on the Manila International Airport carrying posters and waving banners of welcome. In the airport's VIP waiting room, Ninoy's youngest sister, Lupita Aquino-Kashiwahara, opened a large envelope that Ninoy had sent her and began to distribute copies of the arrival address that Ninoy had written but would not live to deliver.

"I have returned of my own free will to join the ranks of those struggling to restore our rights and freedoms through nonviolence. I seek no confrontation. I only pray and will strive for a genuine national reconciliation founded on justice. I am prepared for the worst, and have decided against the advice of my mother, my spiritual adviser, many of my tested friends and a few of my most valued political mentors. A death sentence awaits me . . . ."

Ninoy's mother, Doña Aurora Aquino, waited in the airport's VIP Lounge to be the first to greet her son. Doña Aquino was surrounded by her family and by a distinguished group of Filipino leaders who had come to support Ninoy and to guarantee his safety by their presence.

"I could have opted to seek political asylum in America, but I feel it is my duty, as it is the duty of every Filipino, to suffer with his people especially in time of crisis. I never sought nor have I been given any assurances or promises of leniency by the regime. I return voluntarily

armed only with a clear conscience and fortified in the faith that in the end justice will emerge triumphant . . . ."

At 1:04 P.M. CAL Flight 811 landed at the Manila International Airport and taxied to Gate 8. More than 2,000 officers and troops had been mobilized supposedly "to guarantee Senator Aquino's safe return." In fact, Operation Homecoming (Oplan Balikbayan) had been conceived by General Fabian Ver and by Major General Prospero A. Olivas to guarantee that Ninoy Aquino would not leave the airport alive.

"According to Gandhi, the willing sacrifice of the innocent is the most powerful answer to insolent tyranny that has yet been conceived by God and man. Three years ago when I left for an emergency heart bypass operation, I hoped and prayed that the rights and freedoms of our people would soon be restored, that living conditions would improve and that bloodletting would stop. Rather than move forward, we have moved backward. The killings have increased, the economy has taken a turn for the worse and the human rights situation has deteriorated."

As Flight 811 rolled to a stop at Gate 8, military vans raced into position around the plane. Team Delta (six SWAT soldiers in full battle gear led by Capt. Llewelyn Kavinta) positioned themselves under the airplane's nose. The seven SWAT soldiers in Team Charlie lined up to guard the right side of the airplane; while Team Bravo's seven soldiers fanned out between the left wing tip and the tail. There were no fewer than forty persons, most of them military, waiting at the jetway. Ten soldiers accompanied the official six-man boarding party as they rode the movable tube toward Flight 811. These men would claim to President Marcos's Fact Finding Board that they had been assigned the task of protecting Senator Aquino. In fact, they were there to murder him.

"The country is far advanced in her times of trouble. Economic, social and political problems bedevil the Filipino. These problems may be surmounted if we are united. But we can be united only if all the rights and freedoms enjoyed before September 21, 1972 are fully restored . . . . Yes, the Filipino is patient, but there is a limit to his patience. Must we wait until that patience snaps?"

Constable Mario Lazago was the first soldier onto the plane. He didn't recognize Senator Aquino and walked past him. Air Force Sergeant Arnulfo de Mesa spotted Ninoy and paused. A second Air

Force sergeant, Claro Lat, reached out to shake Ninoy's extended hand and then lift Ninoy gently by the elbow.

"Boss, the armed forces is inviting you," Lat said in Tagalog.

"Where are we going?" Ninoy asked, responding in Tagalog, his native Filipino dialect.

"Just here," Lat replied. "Please come with me."

Ninoy stood up and then reached down under his seat.

"I'll just bring this, Brod," he said kindly, picking up his rosary.

Eyewitnesses report that as Ninoy took his first step toward Philippine soil, his smile disappeared. "Sadness appeared across his face. He bit his lips. The most dreaded of fears must have crossed his mind."[25]

"The nationwide rebellion is escalating and threatens to explode into a bloody revolution. There is a growing cadre of young Filipinos who have finally come to realize that freedom is never granted, it is taken. Must we relive the agonies and the bloodletting of the past that brought forth our Republic or can we sit down as brothers and sisters and discuss our differences with reason and goodwill?"

As the three members of General Ver's boarding party led Ninoy from Flight 811, cameras and tape recorders whirred to life. Reporters from *Time, Newsweek, Asiaweek* and television crews from ABC, NBC, Japanese JNN and TBS struggled to follow Ninoy and his escorts through that airplane door.

Suddenly, "a whiteclad arm, brawny and dark" pushed against the crowd of reporters, causing several to fall. That same arm tried to slam the door closed, but it swung back and forth as the reporter's cameras continued to record the scene. Finally, the door slammed shut.

The soldiers assigned as Senator Aquino's "official escort" had managed to separate Ninoy from the protection of his friends and representatives of the world's press. Instead of taking him up the loading tube and into the airport, the soldiers guided Ninoy through an emergency door and across a small platform connected to the tarmac by seventeen narrow metal steps.

"I have often wondered how many disputes could have been settled easily had the disputants only dared to define their terms. So as to leave no room for misunderstanding, I shall define my terms:

1. Six years ago, I was sentenced to die before a firing squad by a military tribunal whose jurisdiction I steadfastly refused to recognize. It is now time for the regime to decide. Order my IMMEDIATE EXECUTION OR SET ME FREE.

"I was sentenced to die for allegedly being the leading communist leader. I am not a communist, never was and never will be.

"2. National reconciliation and unity can be achieved but only with justice, including justice for our Muslim and Ifugao brothers. There can be no deal with a Dictator. No compromise with dictatorship.

"3. In a revolution there can really be no victors, only victims. We do not have to destroy in order to build.

"4. Subversion stems from economic, social and political causes and will not be solved by purely military solutions; it can be curbed not with every increasing repression but with a more equitable distribution of wealth, more democracy and more freedom, and

"5. For the economy to get going once again, the workingman must be given his just and rightful share of his labor, and to the owners and managers must be restored the hope where there is so much uncertainty if not despair."

Videotapes trapped behind the airplane door continued to record the sounds of that tragic scene.

"Ako na, ako." (I'll be the one, I.)

"Pusila! Pusila!" (Shoot him! Shoot him!)[26]

The television sound track captured that brief exchange between Ninoy's guards. Exactly 8.5 seconds passed before the first shot was fired from behind Ninoy (apparently by one of his "guards") directly into his brain.

"On one of the long corridors of Harvard University are carved in granite the words of Archibald Macleish:

'How shall freedom be defended By arms
when it is attacked by arms; by truth
when it is attacked by lies; by democratic faith when it is attacked by
authoritarian dogma. Always, and in the
final act, by determination and faith.'

I return from exile and to an uncertain future with only determination and faith to offer —faith in our people and faith in God."

Benigno S. Aquino, Jr.

8

Ninoy, the Martyr;
Cory, the Widow and Mother
(21 August 1983–21 November 1985)

"I have decided to challenge death. I do not believe I'm sinning against my Creator because in the end, I am not really my own executioner. By my example, I hope I can inspire others. Like the dominoes, one has to fall to create the chain reaction."
Senator Benigno Aquino, Jr.

"We know by faith that nothing happens by accident. Christ knows full well what He put into us and what He must put us through to make us what we must be."
President Corazon C. Aquino

Cory and her children learned about Ninoy's death on Sunday morning, 21 August 1983. The family had spent that long, restless night together in their home near Boston on Commonwealth Avenue. Neither Ballsy Aquino nor her mother had slept that night. Ninoy had promised to call them when he landed safely in Manila. They were waiting for his call. About 1:30 A.M., after a long mother-daughter conversation, Cory had closed the door to the master bedroom so that she could be alone to pray. Noynoy was in the den watching the Cable News Network, also hoping for some word about his father's safe return to the Philippines.

At 2:30 A.M. the telephone finally rang. Ballsy rushed to answer it. She hoped it was her father. "We are calling," the stranger's voice began, "to confirm reports of the assassination of Benigno S. Aquino, Jr." Ninoy's oldest daughter was stunned and confused. Cory took the telephone from Ballsy's trembling hand.

"What's this?" she asked.

"We've heard from Tokyo that your husband has been shot."

"Are you sure?" Cory questioned.

The reporter from the Kyodo News Agency in New York City seemed quite certain.

"Yes," he answered. "Have you heard anything?"

"No," Cory replied.

In the next thirty frantic minutes, Cory called contacts around the world hoping against hope that Ninoy was alive. Then the telephone rang again.

"Cory," began the familiar voice of Congressman Shintaro Ishihara, a friend of the Aquino family calling from Tokyo, "I'm very sorry but I think that Ninoy is dead."

A Japanese journalist who had seen Ninoy lying on the tarmac bleeding from his fatal head wound had called the congressman with his eyewitness report.

Slowly, Cory put the telephone receiver back in its cradle. Her children were weeping. For a moment she wrapped her arms about them joining her tears with theirs. Then she asked them to join her in prayer. "There's nothing else for us to do," she said to her devastated family. By 3:30 A.M. friends began to arrive at the Aquino house on Commonwealth Avenue to comfort Cory and the children and to share their grief.

At 6 A.M., Cory took the children to Mass. In spite of Ninoy's assassination, Cory's faith in a loving, caring God was unshaken. Reporters and television crews were gathered outside waiting for an interview. They still remember Cory's sad smile as she led her family past their waiting microphones to the campus church where they knelt and prayed together. Cory knew how much she needed strength to face the days ahead and she refused to let anyone keep her from the source of that strength.

On leaving for church that morning, Cory remembers how awful it felt to leave the telephone knowing that her family would be calling from the Philippines. That call didn't come until later.

"They didn't know how to tell me," Cory explained later. "They didn't know how to break it to me, and anyway they weren't sure themselves until my mother-in-law had seen Ninoy's body. They were still hoping it was a false rumor and that Ninoy was still alive."[1]

After a cruel and frantic search, Doña Aurora Aquino found her son's body in a military hospital. She refused to allow the attendants to cover the ugly facial wounds that Ninoy had suffered or to change his torn and bloody clothing. The Filipino people must see what Ninoy's assassins had done to him. She wanted his countrymen to know exactly how he had suffered on their behalf. Doña Aurora accompanied Ninoy's body to the Aquino home on Times Street in

Quezon City. Early on that Monday afternoon, 22 August 1983, crowds of mourners began to line up to honor their martyred hero.

Doña Aurora Aquino stood watch over her son's wake.

"I think it was faith which kept me strong," she says. "I am convinced that nothing happens without the permission of God. The whole time, I was repeating to myself: 'Lord, You know best. You know best . . . .' I was numb that first day," she added. "I could not cry. It was only the next day when I really gave way. I was alone in the room and I cried and cried. I said: 'Lord, I know that something good will come out of even this.'"

Doña Aurora also remembers being comforted by the New Testament story of the widow of Nain in the Gospel. Jesus touched her dead son and brought him back to life again.

"I told our Lord," Doña Aurora said, "'I don't expect You to give my son back to me right now, in flesh and blood. But I know that he will rise again in the next life with You.' And I told Him again: 'Lord, You know best and someday, I will probably see the light.'"[2]

Ninoy's old friends and co-workers clustered about the casket in shock and bewilderment. After praying for Ninoy and his family, Jaime Cardinal Sin stood staring down at Ninoy's battered body. The Cardinal's hands, clasped in prayer, were pressed to his lips. Still cameras flashed. Television cameras whirred. And though he knew the world was watching to see how the most powerful cleric in the Philippines would react to Ninoy's death, even Cardinal Sin could not hide his disbelief and growing anger at this arrogant, brutal murder. His eyes reflected the nation's growing horror. This time the enemy had gone too far. In Ninoy's death, something was coming to life in the Philippines that could change that nation forever.

Outside the Aquinos' sprawling bungalow, journalists from the world's press were beginning to gather. Television and radio cables were spread. Lights burned brightly. Through communication satellites passing far overhead, the scene was being broadcast to the islands of the Philippines and to every nation of the world.

Later that day, in Boston, Cory heard from her sisters that huge crowds were besieging her house on Times Street. Cory could hardly believe it. She thought the people had forgotten Ninoy. After almost seven years in prison and another three years in exile, she was afraid that Ninoy had "very few friends," but Cory could see on the evening news that her sisters had not exaggerated their report. Mourners were passing by Ninoy's body at a rate of forty or fifty people per minute and the streets were jammed with people waiting quietly, tearfully to see him. Someone in the crowd held up a T-shirt printed with these words: "Who killed our hero?"

On that same Monday afternoon, President Marcos sat in his high back, golden chair to answer that same question before the world's press. As usual, he blamed the communists. But on the day of Ninoy's assassination, when Imelda Marcos, General Ver and their entourage reported the news of Aquino's death to President Marcos, one eyewitness said that the ailing president "seized a small dish from his bedside table, and threw it at Ver, saying: 'You fools, they will all blame me.'"[3]

In his news conference, President Marcos added, ". . . no matter what explanation we make now, there will be some kind of shadow over the government, and this was never, never our purpose. We had hoped the matter could be handled with a little more finesse."[4]

Most Filipinos blamed the Marcos regime. Many thought Imelda and General Ver had conspired against Ninoy without the president's knowledge. Almost no one was convinced by General Ver's explanation that the assassination had been planned by the Communist Party of the Philippines/New People's Army or executed by Rolando D. Galman, a hired hitman who seconds later killed himself.

At first, the news of Ninoy's death led to a kind of panic in the Philippines. Wealthy Filipinos rushed to draw their money out of banks. They emptied grocery stores and gasoline stations. Businesses were closed. Fearing an economic collapse, businessmen smuggled millions of dollars out of the country. As the days passed, the value of the Filipino peso dropped on world money markets. Prices soared. Everyone knew that the Philippines stood on the edge of chaos.

And rich or poor, the Filipino people were angry and discontented. Troops were drawn up around the Malacañang Palace to protect President Marcos and his family. No one knew exactly what would happen next. And every eye seemed focused on Times Street where the nation's grief was being shaped into a mighty force.

During the first twenty-four hours after the assassination, at least 100,000 mourners had passed by Ninoy's body at a rate of one person every two seconds. A member of Parliament, standing next to an old woman in the crowd, remembers hearing her say, "They are so cruel. He was returning to his country; they didn't even let him step on the soil of his native land."[5]

Tuesday, August 24, Cory and her children arrived in Manila. She was stunned by the crowd of reporters waiting at the airport to greet her—and by the tens of thousands of people waiting to pass by her husband's bier. When he was alive, Ninoy had been pleased when a crowd of 500 people gathered to hear him speak. *I have to tell this to Ninoy,* Cory remembers thinking as she passed through the crowd.

Throughout their married life, Cory had especially enjoyed those times when she could bring good news to Ninoy. She loved to see his eyes light up and hear him laugh. Although he was fifty years old, when something happened that gave him hope, that excited him, that made him feel their dreams were coming true, he would jump up and walk about the room talking and gesturing like a little boy. When Cory saw thousands of people wearing his name and carrying his banners, her first response was to rush to Ninoy and tell him all about it. "Then," she said, "I realized that that was no longer possible."[6]

When Cory finally looked down on her husband's bloody face, she wept. There are still times that Cory cries when she thinks about Ninoy's death, but from the moment she heard about his assassination she showed amazing strength.

"Mom has always been cool under pressure," her son recalled. "When my dad was arrested in 1972, she was upset, yes, but she was in perfect control. We could always look up to her as a source of strength."[7]

Prayer is at the heart of Cory's strength. Her worst critics do not doubt for a moment Cory's genuine faith in God. Friends and foes alike know that when the pressure rises, Cory turns first to prayer. When she first heard the news of Ninoy's death, she asked the children to pray with her. At 6:00 that next morning, after a sleepless, tearful night, they prayed together again in a nearby church. On the long flight from Boston to Manila, Cory spent much of her time in prayer, meditating once again on the mysteries in the life of Jesus.

At her home on Times Street, as hundreds of thousands walked past her husband's body, Cory searched for a quiet space in the bedroom she had shared with Ninoy to pray and meditate. And when she bent down to kiss him one last time, she prayed again for her beloved Ninoy, and for their family now entirely in her care. Again, in the middle of the week, when they took her husband's body to his home town in Tarlac, Cory led her family in prayer.

She had thought that Ninoy's last visit home would be a rather private affair. The townspeople wanted to honor their favorite son in their own, quiet way. But thousands of mourners joined the family on their route. The mourners were carrying yellow banners and wearing yellow armbands printed with the single word: "Ninoy." Because of the huge and enthusiastic crowds, that march to Concepcion took twelve long, terrifying hours. Masses of people anxious to express their outpouring of love for Ninoy, for Cory and their family pressed against the car with such force that bumpers were torn away and lives were endangered. "Dear Lord," Cory prayed, "please make sure that nothing happens."

The people's grief was mixed with anger and frustration. For fifteen years they had felt helpless in the face of Ferdinand and Imelda's ruthless power. Ninoy's death seemed to be releasing the people from their helplessness. A Filipino television documentary on Ninoy's life begins with these words:

> "With his murder, a cowering, silent Filipino spirit
> broke free in a flood of tears demanding justice
> and freedom for all."

From Tarlac, Ninoy's body was transferred to the St. Domingo Church in Metro Manila. Jaime Cardinal Sin presided at Ninoy's Funeral Mass at 8:00 on Sunday morning, 31 August 1983. Cory's small voice echoed across the packed church and out through huge speakers mounted for the mass of mourners who could not get inside.

"Ninoy who loved you, the Filipino people," she said, "is now loved in return."

At 10:00 A.M. the funeral procession began its journey across Manila to the Manila Memorial Park in Paranaque where Ninoy would be buried. It was the largest funeral cortege in the history of the Filipino people. One journalist who viewed the scene from a helicopter said it was the largest funeral cortege in history. Millions of people began that march at 10:00 A.M., walking for hours in the sweltering noonday sun. The march ended eleven hours later at 8:00 P.M. in a thunder and lightning storm that left the huge crowd cold and soaking wet.

One reporter claims that if Cory Aquino had asked the crowd of mourners to march on Malacañang Palace that night, 2,000,000 would have obeyed without a question. And though Imelda Marcos ignored Ninoy's funeral by throwing a lavish party at the palace for a visiting American senator, Ferdinand Marcos had helicopters on ready alert to whisk his family and their guests to safety, just in case.

But the nation's first family had little reason to suspect that Cory might ever lead a revolution against them. In spite of her husband's prominence, Mrs. Aquino was entirely unknown. She had consciously avoided the public spotlight. During Ninoy's political campaigns, she had knocked on doors and passed out handbills with the rest of her husband's volunteers. And during his years as governor and senator she had her fair share of influence on his decisions, but she was not a public person. She had no ambition to compete with her husband for the people's acclaim. Cory and Ninoy agreed. He would be the politician. She would be his wife.

But the moment Ninoy died, a new Cory emerged. The first step in that direction came during the week of Ninoy's death and burial. Thanks to the world's press, unknown and unrecognized Cory suddenly became a symbol of the nation's grief and anger. The whole world was amazed at her quiet strength. Television cameras recorded her praying beside her husband's body. She was interviewed and profiled on the evening news. The cameras followed her everywhere, even into church where she knelt and prayed without apology or explanation. In the press conferences she answered reporters' questions directly, without fear or equivocation. Already, members of the press were beginning to doubt Cory's oft repeated claim that she was a "mere housewife." This "mere housewife" was bright, articulate, cool and courageous.

On the front pages of the world's newspapers and newsmagazines, Cory was pictured in quiet, intimate conversations with political and religious leaders who had come to offer their respect. She was filmed and taped from mobile units on the ground and in the air as she walked or rode behind Ninoy's body in those incredible masses of mourners. This non-stop, close-up media coverage elevated the unknown Cory from obscurity into instant celebrity. Still, it was too early to tell what Cory might do with the power that accompanies such world acclaim.

There were clues. Ninoy's sister, Lupita Aquino-Kashiwahara, shared one of those intimate looks into the metamorphosis of Cory from housewife to world leader. As she walked behind her husband's casket on the way from their home on Times Street to the St. Domingo Church, Cory told Ken Kashiwahara that President Marcos was reaching out to make peace with her through the press. But Cory had decided to refuse the president's offer "unless he released all political prisoners as a proof of his sincerity."[8]

As Cory began to flex her new political muscles, President Marcos's physical and political strength continued to decline. At the same time, the nation's economy grew weaker by the day. The peso was devalued by almost 40 percent. Even food staples like rice and fish were not affordable to 70 percent of the Filipino people who were living below the poverty level. Millions of squatters were struggling to survive in cardboard shacks on the empty lots and crowded streets of Manila. The city reeked of garbage and human excrement. Brutal, bloody crimes were perpetrated on rich and poor alike. Child prostitution had reached epidemic proportions. And all the while, the nation's incredible natural resources were being pillaged by a handful of rich Filipino families and corporations and operated in Ferdinand and Imelda's favor.

During the months following Ninoy's burial, the nation, with Cory's example, turned to prayer. Up against the Marcos tyranny, prayer seemed at first to be the only alternative. Not even the Marcos regime could legislate against prayer meetings and get away with it. Almost every day prayer rallies were held in churches and cathedrals, in public parks and squares, in homes, in business lobbies, even in government buildings, to protest Senator Aquino's assassination and to beg God to intervene on behalf of the Philippines' uncertain future.

If Imelda and General Ver thought that the people would forget Ninoy's murder, they were wrong. Those public prayer meetings kept Ninoy's memory very much alive. But there were secret, private meetings being held in homes and hotel suites, in private offices and conference rooms, in university dorms and gymnasiums around Manila and across the Philippines. It was not enough to pray. The time was growing closer when brave Filipinos would also finally act on the nation's behalf.

Soon after Ninoy was buried, a small group of business leaders and politicians dared to propose a public rally to be held in Makati, Manila's business center, to protest the senator's assassination and to help bring an end to the eighteen-year rule of Ferdinand and Imelda Marcos. The organizing committee signed up 500 volunteers from outside Manila to guarantee at least some kind of crowd at this first anti-Marcos rally.

The leaders had worried needlessly. On that day in mid-September, 1983, at least 100,000 Filipinos gathered at Ugarte Field near the Stock Exchange. Wearing yellow, the color of protest, students and workers, businessmen, nuns and priests chanted in unison, "Ninoy! . . . Ninoy! . . . Ninoy! . . ." Workers looking down from the modern, high rise office buildings nearby shredded every piece of yellow paper they could find and rained yellow confetti down from their windows to the streets below in support of the marchers. Their voices, too, echoed the cry, "Ninoy! . . . Ninoy! . . . Ninoy! . . ."

The weekly Makati protest rallies grew in size and enthusiasm. On 22 September 1983, the eleventh anniversary of the declaration of martial law, Cory made her first political address at one of those Makati rallies. Her voice was quiet and uncertain but her presence mobilized the mass of protesters who had assembled to hear her speak.

After the rally, a group of angry students marched on Malacañang. The forces of President Marcos overreacted. Eleven young people were killed and several hundred more were burned and bloodied when police and soldiers opened fire on the demonstrators.

Once again President Marcos blamed the communists and communist sympathizers like Cory and her friends for the students' deaths. In fact, Cory, like Ninoy, had never been a communist or a communist sympathizer. And like her husband, Cory was totally committed to nonviolence. But all Filipinos who opposed the Marcos regime did not agree.

The anti-Marcos protest rallies were supported by Filipinos from two very different positions. "The Yellows" were primarily members of the rising middle class: businessmen, politicians, priests, nuns, university students, workers, teachers, mothers and housewives who represented a more moderate, centrist position. Their one goal was to replace Marcos and to reinstate democracy in the Philippines. "The Reds" were avid nationalists, politicians, trade unionists and more radical students who wanted to end the Marcos regime, but they also wanted to end eighty-three years of U.S. domination of the Philippines and to remove the U.S. military bases from Filipino soil.

Cory was caught in the middle of these two political movements. Both sides revered her husband. The memory of his life and death inspired the "Yellows" and the "Reds" alike. But from the beginning it was plain that it would be difficult for Cory to speak or act on any issue besides the end of the Marcos regime without displeasing one side or the other.

On Ninoy's fifty-first birthday, 27 November 1983, just three months after his death, a huge memorial rally was held at Rizal Park, that spacious, grassy, tree-lined strip of land nicknamed "Luneta," stretching north from the Quirino Grandstand on Manila Bay to Taft Boulevard in the heart of the city of Manila. This time several hundred thousand Filipinos wearing yellow Ninoy sun visors, T-shirts and armbands gathered to sing the new songs of protest and to hear speakers demand the resignation of Ferdinand and Imelda Marcos.

In her short speech that day, Cory's voice seemed stronger, her political intent more clear. "Thank you," she said to that endless sea of faces smiling up at her. "Your presence is the most extraordinary birthday gift in the world . . . . You cannot tell how much loneliness has been relieved by this outpouring of love by so many people."

Then she added, almost as an afterthought, "I hope Marcos listens to us and resigns!" In the midst of their thunderous applause, someone began to shout again, "Ninoy! . . . Ninoy! . . . Ninoy! . . ." Cory's eyes were damp as she stood before them acknowledging their tribute to her husband. Then, slowly, the chant began to change. Suddenly she noticed. With their arms extended overhead and their thumbs and forefinger shaping the "L" sign of her husband's Laban Party, they were shouting her name, not his. "Cory! . . . Cory! . . . Cory! . . ." was echoing across the Luneta. For a moment the Senator's wife stood before them still smiling and waving. But when she heard her own name being chanted by the people, Cory turned and walked quickly to her seat.

Cory was not guilty of ambition. She had enjoyed being a wife and mother. In the fall of 1983, she returned to Boston to help pack their household belongings and return them to Manila. And though she made occasional public appearances and continued to speak on those rare occasions she thought appropriate, Cory Aquino continued her fight to be a private person.

At Christmas she took time to prepare chicken-liver pâté to send to family and friends. She took painting lessons from Raul Isidro, a Filipino artist she admired. She even served on the board of the Parent-Teacher Association of the Poveda Learning Center where her daughter, Kris, had enrolled for her first year in high school. A family friend, Betty Go Belmonte, notes "that Cory attended the meetings faithfully and was always very punctual."[9]

Cory sincerely wanted to stay in the background, but the invitations for her to speak increased almost daily. And as the political and economic conditions of the people of the Philippines continued to decline under the excesses of the Marcos regime, Cory began to accept more and more of the invitations. Along with the political rallies and the mass meetings commemorating Ninoy's life and death, Cory began to speak at the many Rotary Clubs across Manila, to schools, to churches and to civic organizations.

In February, 1984, when Cory decided to campaign for candidates opposing loyal Marcos supporters for seats on the national assembly, she was criticized by friends and even by her family who had decided to boycott Marcos's elections. Prayer and her long meditative discussions with Ninoy led her to that controversial decision.

To those who insisted on a boycott, Cory quoted Ninoy who believed that the democratic election process "was the only system available whereby we could have a peaceful change of government." And though Marcos was famous for using "gold, guns and goons" to control the final outcome of an election, Cory determined to give the democratic process one last chance.[10]

The quiet, cautious widow threw herself into the campaign of 1984. She traveled up and down the Philippines encouraging people to vote for the opposition candidates of every party. And though Marcos and his henchmen invested millions of pesos to interfere with the fair election process, 59 opposition members were elected. Many more Marcos candidates would have been defeated if voters' lists hadn't been destroyed, polling places vandalized, workers threatened, beaten and murdered, ballots ruined or replaced and the counting process corrupted. Still, in spite of Marcos's massive election fraud, 30 percent of the 183 delegates to the National Assembly (the Batasang Pambansa) were elected on platforms opposing the Marcos regime. Their victories were due in large part to the courageous support and tireless campaigning of Cory Aquino.

And though Cory's popularity was surging, she still refused even to think about running for any political office herself. She continued to speak at public meetings, now called the "Parliament of the Streets." Wherever Cory spoke, crowds of hopeful Filipinos mobbed her enthusiastically. On 21 August 1984, the first anniversary of her husband's death, two bronze statues of Ninoy were unveiled. At one dedication in the Santo Domingo Church, Cory heard Cardinal Sin's call for national unity. "Where do we go from here?" he asked.

Cory's speech to the more than 5,000 people who had crammed into the sanctuary held a hopeful if still veiled response to the Cardinal's question. "It has been a year of justice delayed," she admitted, "but it has also been a year of courage and sacrifice by the Filipino people. It was a year of the people's victory over themselves, over their timidity before their rulers, over their fear before their oppressor's might."[11] Following that Mass, Cory led two million Filipinos on a four-hour march to the Luneta for a massive memorial to Ninoy's sacrifice.

In September, 1984, on the thirteenth anniversary of martial law, students and workers walked hand in hand toward the palace singing songs of protest and chanting "Down with the Marcos regime." Once again, the president used force against the peaceful marchers. Soldiers and police beat demonstrators with clubs and turned tear gas and water cannons against them. Two young people were killed. Dozens were seriously injured.

In 1971, when martial law had been declared, the Armed Forces of the Philippines had 50,000 men whose primary task was to defend the nation from outside invasion. With American military aid and advisors, Marcos had united local police forces, the nation's constabulary and the armed forces under his own command. In 1984, after thirteen years of martial law, there were more than 200,000 heavily armed soldiers used by the president to enforce his one-man rule over the people of the Philippines.

Using "the communist threat" as his excuse, Marcos managed to crush democracy in the Philippines, end free elections, abolish the Congress, make laws by presidential decree, neutralize the power of the courts, abolish all political opposition and end the traditional checks and balances of a democratic society. He used police and military forces to terrorize the nation and to torture and murder his opposition. And his American supporters in the White House, the State Department and the Congress continued to support Marcos's totalitarian regime with billions of dollars in "aid" because he was

strongly anti-communist and because he allowed the American naval
and air bases to remain on Filipino soil. Now we are discovering that
hundreds of millions of those same dollars were squandered and
stolen by Ferdinand and Imelda and their cronies.

When those brave young Filipinos marched on Malacañang in
1984, Marcos had been the dictator of the Philippines for more than
thirteen years. Throughout those years the president's agents had
beaten, kidnapped, tortured, imprisoned and murdered the president's opposition. There was even a torture cell in the basement of
the palace just below the formal banquet halls and guest salons
where Ferdinand and Imelda entertained their grateful guests.

On 24 October 1984, the "fact-finding board" appointed by
President Marcos to conduct a thorough investigation of Ninoy
Aquino's assassination reported to the president. The Board had
examined 1,294 documents, 1,472 photographs, 14 videotapes and
91 pieces of physical evidence. Between 3 November 1983, when
Marcos appointed the Commission and 20 August 1984, when the
five-member blue-ribbon commission formally ended its investigation, they had conducted 125 public hearings involving 193 witnesses with 20,377 pages of recorded transcripts.[12]

Joker Arroyo, Cory's executive secretary, a human rights attorney
and long-time Aquino family friend, announced that the hearings did
more than investigate Ninoy's assassination. "They put Marcos and
his government on trial," he said. In fact, board members indicted
three of the president's generals (including Fabian Ver, Marcos's
Chief of Staff), two colonels, two captains, one lieutenant, twelve
sergeants and four enlisted men "for the premeditated killing of Senator Benigno S. Aquino, Jr., and Rolando Galman [the supposed hit-
man] at the Manila International Airport on August 21, 1983."

Exactly who issued the order for Ninoy's assassination is still
unclear. Ferdinand Marcos was "gravely ill" during the crisis, or so
he claimed in his defense. In fact, Marcos was too smart to order the
senator's death in such a public fashion. Imelda and/or General Ver
are still the primary suspects.

Justice Corazon Agrava, the Board's Chairperson, turned in her
own minority report claiming against all the evidence that Senator
Aquino was shot and killed by Galman in an assassination "planned
and executed by the Communist Party." President Marcos accepted
the minority report. And though he granted General Ver "a leave of
absence" until Ver's reputation "could be totally cleared," President
Marcos attacked the majority report and with 68 other high-ranking
military officers declared his "unfailing loyalty and support" to the
indicted general. Days later, Cory Aquino repeated what she had been
saying since 1983: "Justice is not possible while Marcos is in power."

Public protests against Marcos continued to grow in numbers and in enthusiasm across the Philippines. The New People's Army struck military bases, town halls, police and constabulary stations. There were as many as ten to eleven insurgency-related incidents of violence daily. And general strikes involving tens of thousands of workers threatened to paralyze the nation.[13]

Once again Ferdinand and Imelda had strained the limits of credulity. Even their American allies were beginning to wonder about the arrogance and cruelty of the Marcos regime. And though his "term" in office was not scheduled to end until June, 1987, there was a growing hope that Marcos might call an election even before that time to prove to his critics, Filipino and American alike, that he was still "the people's choice." With that hope came a growing conviction among the people that Cory Aquino was the only person who might defeat him.

On 27 November 1984, when Cory accepted the invitation to speak briefly at the massive celebration of Ninoy's fifty-second birthday in downtown Manila, the crowd was chanting her name even louder than his. "Cory! . . . Cory! . . . Cory! . . ." echoed out from the streets of Manila to every village, town and city throughout the islands of the Philippines.

Still, Cory refused to consider running for public office. She claimed no political experience. "I was wife and mother," she argued. "Ninoy took care of all the rest." She did accept an appointment in 1984 to serve on a Convenor Group to help select a candidate who could defeat Marcos, but when the other members suggested that Cory should be that candidate, she refused again. In December, 1984, Cory read an interview with the dean of the Law School at the Far Eastern University suggesting that she was the only candidate who could defeat Marcos. She called the dean to correct him. "Please," she urged him, "stop your crazy ideas."[14]

Marcos would be difficult to defeat. Too many times he had demonstrated his power to control the election process. It would take a kind of miracle to end his totalitarian regime and give democracy its first real chance in the Philippines. The growing opposition groups could not begin to defeat the tyrant without coming together under one strong candidate.

In March, 1985, a National Unification Conference was held. Former Supreme Court Justice, Cecilia Palma, a woman of great integrity and commitment, suggested that Cory was the only candidate who could mobilize the people enough to bring down the Marcos regime. Still Cory refused.

In May, 1985, the leading opposition candidate, Doy Laurel, offered Cory the vice-presidential spot on his Unido Party ticket. She declined his invitation. That summer, the San Jose *Mercury*, a California newspaper that served a large Filipino expatriate community, began a Pulitzer Prize-winning investigation on "The Hidden Wealth" of the Marcos regime. At last, the truth was being told in America about the pillage and the destruction of the Filipino economy by Ferdinand and Imelda and their cronies. The possibilities of a real "Cory-for-President" movement were growing in the Philippines and in America.

On 21 August 1985, the second anniversary of Ninoy's death, banners begging Cory to run against Marcos were unfurled at the memorial Mass at the Santo Domingo Church and carried through the streets of Manila to another huge protest rally in Makati. Once again, the people cried "Cory! . . . Cory! . . . Cory . . ." This time they wouldn't take "no" for an answer.

Joaquin "Chino" Roces, former publisher of the Manila *Times* and the man who gave Ninoy his first job as a reporter, organized a "Draft Cory" movement and opened a "Cory Aquino for President" headquarters in downtown Manila. In the face of this genuine people's movement, Cory agreed to run against Marcos on two conditions: First, her backers had to get the signatures of a million Filipinos who would support her candidacy and second, Marcos had to call a "snap election."

And though Senator Paul Laxalt, President Reagan's personal envoy to Manila, suggested in a visit in October, 1985, that a "snap election" might prove that Marcos still had the support of the Filipino people, there was no real reason for Marcos to take the risk. Elections weren't scheduled until 1987. Marcos was ill. His administration was under fire from critics at home and abroad. Marcos was a wily politician. No one really expected that he would call the "snap election," but he did.

On 3 November 1985, Ferdinand Marcos was the featured guest on a live television satellite interview news program, "This Week with David Brinkley." The conservative columnist, George Will, popped the question.

"I am ready to call a snap election," Marcos fired back, "perhaps earlier than eight months, perhaps in three months or less than that . . . ."

The ABC White House correspondent, Sam Donaldson, pushed Marcos for details.

"Mr. President," he said, "are there any catches? Can anyone run in this election? If Corazon Aquino wants to run? If Senator Laurel wants to run? Everyone can run?"

"Oh yes," Marcos replied without hesitation. "Anyone."

After a commercial, Donaldson asked, "Since the allegation

against you is that you have conducted massive voting fraud in the past, if you hold elections in sixty days or so, will you allow outside observers into the Philippines to oversee the elections to make certain they're fair?"

"You are all invited to come," Marcos shot back, "and we will invite members of the American Congress to please come and just see what is happening here."[15]

That same day, Cory Aquino left her home and family to go on a spiritual retreat. As the pressure had increased on Cory to run for the presidency, she had prayed and fasted on a regular basis, seeking God's will. She had spent many long weekends in a tiny cell in a Christian retreat center reading the Bible, meditating on the life of Jesus, seeking counsel from Christian writers, ancient and modern, talking to religious leaders whom she admired, and praying without ceasing that God's will would be done in her life and that of her nation.

Her need for God's direction was urgent and heartfelt. Marcos's call for a "snap election" had eliminated one of the two obstacles to her candidacy. But her husband's long-time friend, Doy Laurel, had already mounted his own national campaign. Within days "Laurel for President" posters would be seen across the nation. She had turned down his offer to run as vice-president. And until those last few weeks, she had told everyone that she would not be a candidate herself. It was an awkward and painful moment.

Then on November 25, Chino Roces presented Cory with petitions signed by more than one million Filipinos, begging her to run. Again Cory went on retreat. Again she prayed and fasted about her decision. The last two obstacles had been swept away. Still Cory hesitated.

Then, on November 31 the Supreme Court announced their verdict on the charges against General Ver and his fellow officers who had been indicted by the fact-finding board in the assassination of Senator Ninoy Aquino. They exonerated Ver and the twenty-six military men accused with him. The Supreme Court, in its final, unappealable verdict, declared that Ninoy had been shot and killed "by a lone communist-hired gun."[16]

"My number one suspect is Mr. Marcos," Cory answered when she heard the Supreme Court's verdict. "Since he was not even mentioned among those accused, it's really not of much concern to me whether one or all would be acquitted."[17]

The same day, Cory Aquino agreed to run against Ferdinand Marcos for the presidency of the Philippines. In Chino Roces's words, Cory was "the first Filipino presidential candidate nominated and drafted by the people."[18]

9

Cory:
The Presidential Candidate
(22 November 1985–20 February 1986)

> Ours is to keep lighting the beacon light of freedom for those
> who have lost their way . . . . Ours is to articulate the fervent
> hopes of a people who have suddenly lost their voices . . . .
> Ours is to adopt the solid stance of courage in the face of
> seemingly hopeless odds so that hope, no matter how dim or
> distant, will never banish from sight.
>
> *Senator Benigno Aquino, Jr.*

> The time for talk and hesitation and criticism is over. The time
> for action is now.
>
> *President Corazon C. Aquino*

On 11 December 1985, Cory Aquino drove through the darkened streets of Manila to the private residence of Jaime Cardinal Sin.
He welcomed her at his front door and led her into a quiet study
where they could talk. Cory got right down to the business at hand.

"I am going to run," Cory said quietly. "I am inspired by my
husband."

For more than a year Cardinal Sin had been waiting to hear those
words. After more peaceful protestors had been bludgeoned and
killed by Marcos's men in 1984, the cardinal had called on President
Marcos to end "the saturnalia of sadism and violence." When Marcos
did not respond, Sin knew that it was time to end his own years of
"critical collaboration" with the Marcos regime. "The whole nation
wanted Marcos out of Malacañang," the cardinal said, "but at that
time the only weapon we had against him was prayer."

Cardinal Sin was determined to use what power he had to help
restore freedom to his people. He dedicated 1985 as a year for prayer

and fasting and he mobilized millions of Filipino Christians around a simple Old Testament prophecy.

"Have you read 2 Chronicles 7:14?" Cardinal Sin asked me during our interview. "If my people," the cardinal quoted enthusiastically, "who are called by my name, will humble themselves, and pray and seek my face, and turn from their wicked ways, then will I hear from heaven and will forgive their sin and will heal their land."

"We were a land in need of healing," the cardinal continued. "So we began to make plans for 1985 that would unite the people in prayer. We needed a theme. So we chose COR, in Spanish the root of the word corazon, in English, heart. But it is also an acronym," the cardinal explained. "C for conversion; O for offering our lives to God; and R for reparation."

"You see?" he explained. "In those three letters is God's plan for the healing of a nation. First, you must ask for God's forgiveness. Second, you must offer God your life. Third, you must do penance for your sin. Then, God will restore your freedom and renew your nation's life."

During that entire year, 1985, the cardinal traveled up and down the Philippine island chain by car and jeep, by bus and airplane. "I went all over the country," he told me, "preaching God's Word and calling the people to repent. Our pastors and lay leaders were overwhelmed by the people's response. The churches were filled. Young and old alike rushed to seek forgiveness. They offered God their lives to be used in whatever way God saw fit. And they brought forth gifts worthy of their repentance."

On 8 September 1985, three million Filipinos gathered to pray and fast for their nation's renewal. Cardinal Sin remembers looking out over that massive sea of faces and thinking to himself, "We have obeyed God's living Word. Now, we can trust that something will happen to save our nation."

Just a few months after that huge prayer rally, President Marcos called for the snap election. And just a few days after that, Cory Aquino stood before Cardinal Sin with news that made him tremble.

Cory's announcement, "I'm going to run," was an answer to the cardinal's prayers and to the prayers of millions of Filipino Christians. But the cardinal knew that Cory must find a way to reconcile with opposition leader Doy Laurel or they would divide the vote and both lose to Marcos.

"If you are united," the cardinal said, "you will win. But if you are not, you are crazy to run."

Cory nodded slowly. Months before, Doy Laurel had offered her the vice-presidential spot on his Unido Party ticket, and she had refused. Laurel, Ninoy's boyhood friend, had spent his political lifetime seeking the presidency. Long before Cory decided to run, he had announced his candidacy. The opposition was divided between Cory and Doy. The cardinal knew how difficult it would be to bring those two candidates together. He also knew that if some kind of reconciliation didn't take place in the next few hours, it would be too late. The deadline for candidates to file was at twelve midnight that same night and the clock was ticking.

"I think you are going to win," the cardinal added in his advice to Cory that day. "You are a woman. It is humiliating for Marcos to lose. But that is the way God works to confound the strong."

Cory knelt to receive the cardinal's blessing.

"You will be our Joan of Arc," the Cardinal said just before he prayed. "Cory, you are going to win, in the name of the Father, Son and Holy Spirit. Amen."

"I didn't know by what providence of God Doy Laurel also came to my house that day," the cardinal added. "But it was a kind of miracle. Doy's political machinery was in place. He had a campaign committee organized in every city in the Philippines. They had banners printed and posters hung. 'Laurel for President' T-shirts, buttons, and badges were already printed and in place."

"Let us be practical," the cardinal advised. "Between you and Cory, she is the most powerful. She is more attractive to the voters because of the popularity of Ninoy. If you run against her, you both will lose. It is simple arithmetic."

Doy Laurel was saddened by the cardinal's words. He sat listening in silence, his head bent, his eyes focused on the floor.

"If you really love your country," the cardinal continued, "then you will run as Cory's vice-presidential candidate. I am sorry," he added, "but this is my assessment."

"Why don't we put numbers in a box?" Laurel suggested. "If she gets number one, then she runs as president. If I get number one . . . ."

"This is a serious matter," the cardinal interrupted. "We can't settle it with lucky numbers."

Laurel paused. "All right, Cardinal," he replied, "if that is what you say, I will follow you."

The Cardinal blessed Laurel and thanked him for his sacrifice.

"Now, you must find Cory quickly," the cardinal added, "and go to the Commissioner of elections before midnight."

The representatives of Cory and Doy Laurel spent the short time remaining before the final deadline, talking on the telephone and racing around the city. Just minutes before the deadline was reached, Cory and Doy registered as the presidential and vice-presidential candidates for Laurel's Unido Party.

"Before that moment," the cardinal remembered, "the whole nation was sad. They thought that Cory and Laurel would run against each other. Everybody knew that with the Marcos cheating already in place and the opposition divided, Cory and Doy would lose and the Philippines would face more years of Marcos terror. But at midnight when Cory and Doy signed together, there was singing and dancing in the streets."

On December 15, the Unido Party declared Cory Aquino to be their official candidate for president. On December 16, the campaign began with an informal interview with reporters from the *New York Times*. The interview proved to be a disaster.

"What on earth do I know about being president?" Cory admitted telling those who had urged her to run. "The only thing I can really offer the Filipino people is my sincerity."[1]

Cory thought she was talking "off the record." In fact, her words made headlines across the Philippines and around the world. Cory admitted that she had no specific programs to propose as yet. She also hoped for the eventual removal of the American military bases from Filipino soil. She even shared her convictions that most of the New People's Army were "not really communists" and that if she were elected she "would declare a truce and begin a dialogue" with them.

Ferdinand and Imelda were ecstatic. Their American allies in the White House and the State Department were puzzled. Even Cory's supporters were surprised and disappointed by the interview.

"See, look what's going to happen if she wins," the American critics warned. "She's not strong. She's not forceful. She's a housewife. She'll force us out of the bases, and she'll make a deal with the communists."[2]

It was the first salvo fired in a dirty and deadly campaign that lasted 45 days and saw more than 86 people killed in campaign violence.

Cory Aquino did not want to run for president. But she told her friend Senator Soc Rodrigo that accepting the will of God and the will of the people was "the cross I have to bear. It's a heavy cross," Cory told him at the beginning of their campaign, "and I can't drop it." Every day the cross grew heavier.

Cory Aquino and Doy Laurel traveled to every corner of the Philippines. Together they sounded Cory's Tagalog campaign cry: "*Tama na! Sobra na! Palitan na!*" "Too much! We've had enough! It's time for a change!"

In every village and town, enthusiastic Filipinos turned out to hear Cory restate her campaign themes: Honesty, sincerity, simplicity and faith in God. Like her, each of them had suffered under the Marcos regime. "I don't seek vengeance," Cory told them. "Only justice, not

only for Ninoy, but also for the suffering Filipino people. Here I am,"
she said quietly, her voice echoing over the portable speakers to the
excited crowds, "asking for your help to topple the Marcos regime."
To every election rally, Cory wore yellow, the color of protest. The
excited crowds responded in kind. The people wore yellow shirts and
dresses, yellow ribbons and armbands. They carried yellow "Cory for
President" signs. Yellow "Cory and Doy" banners hung from buildings, posts and tree tops. "Join me in my crusade for truth, justice and
freedom," she urged them. "Think less of ourselves," she exclaimed,
"and more of our country!"[3]

At first, Marcos and his cronies did not take the lady seriously. The
president called Cory a *"Walang alam 'yan!"* a "know nothing." With
a smile of derision he claimed that Filipino women belonged in the
bedroom and the kitchen and not in government. Imelda added her
own critique of Cory's presidential abilities. "She doesn't even wear
make up," the first lady claimed, "or put on nail polish."

The chauvinistic remarks about Filipino womanhood backfired
on Ferdinand and Imelda. Outraged women asked the president
why he had allowed his own first lady "out of the bedroom" to take
such positions of power and prominence as minister of Human
Settlements, governor of Metro Manila, ambassador plenipotentiary
as well as a member of the National Assembly. And Imelda's expensive jewelry and clothing, her heavy makeup and colored nails became a symbol of their corrupt regime.[4]

Marcos claimed that Cory and her supporters were communists
or communist sympathizers. "If they are communists they will be
wiped out," the president promised. "That is the objective of my
government anyway."[5]

The president tried to create fear and gain support by raising one
last time "the communist threat" but this time the people would not
be taken in. Cory was reaching out to all Filipinos. She offered forgiveness and reconciliation to all her people. "So long as the communists renounce all forms of violence," she promised, "we welcome
them. We will certainly need everybody's help."

When Marcos responded by accusing Cory of being a communist
as he had accused her husband, Cory replied, "I can't possibly be a
communist, because I am a very devout Catholic and, as we all know,
there is no God in communism."[6]

Marcos controlled the major media sources. Most of the television and radio stations, the newspapers and newsmagazines were
in his hands or the hands of his loyal cronies. Until the last days of
the campaign Cory had little access to the media. She had to take to
the people directly her answers to the half-truths, the exaggerations
and the lies that Marcos and his supporters were spreading.

"How do you deal with an inveterate liar?" she asked of Marcos in a speech before the Manila Rotary Club. "What do we do with the overgrown child struggling to lie his way to a reelection?"

When an American historian released his findings that Marcos had lied about his exploits in World War II and proved that his medals and honors were fake, Cory called Marcos a coward and asked him to "stand up like a woman and answer the charges of his cowardice with truth . . . if he dares."

When Marcos criticized Cory for having no experience in government, Cory answered, "I admit that I have no experience in cheating, stealing, lying or assassinating political opponents."[7] In every speech Cory returned to her campaign themes: honesty, sincerity, simplicity and faith in God—and with each of Cory's appearances, the crowds grew larger and more enthusiastic.

In his fascinating and yet unpublished manuscript, *The Real Hero of EDSA*, historian Rolando E. Villacorte summarized Cory's prophetic confrontation with Ferdinand Marcos ". . . as history will remember it." Villacorte paraphrases Cory's soft words and gentle manners in the style of the Old Testament prophet.

"You're coming against me with guns, goons and gold, but I come against you in the name of the Lord Almighty whom you've defied. Come February, the Lord will put you in my power; I'll defeat you and your arrogant head will roll. Then the whole world will know that our God's alive and is in full control of human affairs, and everyone will see that the Lord doesn't need guns, goons and gold to save His people. This battle is the Lord's and He'll put you and all of your KBL lapdogs in our People Power."[8]

Cory's campaign posters and banners were being torn down. Her volunteers were being terrorized, assaulted and even murdered. Her own life was threatened. On several occasions she barely escaped ambush when traveling through the countryside. The Marcos-dominated media mounted a hate campaign against her and the world's free press continued to question her qualifications for the presidency.

But Cory did not succumb to criticism or to fear. When grenades exploded at a rally for Cory in Zamboanga City, the people panicked and surged forward toward the platform. Cory remained calm. When reporters asked her if she had been frightened during the bloody attack, Cory answered, "I was too tired to care . . . . Anyway, if it's my time to go, it's my time to go."[9]

Cory saw every challenge in terms of spiritual not political realities. "We know by faith," she said, "that nothing happens by accident. Christ knows full well what He put into us and what He must put us through to make us what we must be."[10]

Cory's faith was genuine. But, so were her fears.

"Pray for me," Cory said quietly after announcing her candidacy and during the exhausting campaign that followed, "and pray for our nation."

Asking for their prayers was not a political tactic that Cory used to gain credibility with the Filipino people. She really needed them to pray. She knew and admitted her weaknesses, confident that only God could see them through the struggle. They were risking everything to challenge the absolute power of Ferdinand and Imelda Marcos. From the beginning there were death threats against Cory and against those who supported her. Cory's oldest daughters even asked their mother, "Why do you have to be a martyr like Dad?" When Cory asked for the people's prayers, she meant it.

Cory had good reasons to be afraid. During the martial law years the conjugal dictators had imprisoned, tortured, terrorized and even murdered to get their way. Marcos began his political career with a murder. Ninoy was just the latest in a long line of Marcos's victims. Cory's friends and family knew that by running against him, she was putting her life and theirs on the line.

Early in the campaign, while Cory was speaking to village rallies in Mindanao, one of her campaign chairmen was shot and killed. An eyewitness testified that the assassin was a member of Marcos's Civilian Home Defense Force (CHDF) and a bodyguard to the local mayor. That was the first of many assaults on Cory's volunteers and supporters who would be terrorized, attacked and even murdered by Marcos's goons.[11]

As the campaign heated up, Cory drew comfort from Ninoy's memory. She shared her fears and feelings with him in death as she had in life. Without ceasing Cory prayed for God's strength and guidance. The pressures were mounting. There were times she almost collapsed from exhaustion. She remembers praying on at least one occasion, "Lord, I am about to collapse. I've been taking all these trials. You better help me soon."[12]

And though it was a costly battle, as election day, 7 February 1986, approached, the tide had turned in Cory's favor. Marcos's campaign to discredit her had been a total failure. Cory had met the president's lies with truth. She answered every charge against her and she made countercharges of her own against his corruption, greed and cruelty. She had called for honesty, sincerity, simplicity and faith in God. And the people had answered "Cory . . . Cory . . . Cory . . . ."

To make matters worse for President Marcos, it was becoming more and more evident that his physical and mental health were deteriorating. The old campaigner was gone. And in his place, Imelda sang. She even made speeches. And she gave campaign balls and parties. But the president seldom appeared and when people did see him he looked weak and confused. On several occasions his guards had to carry Marcos on to the stage. Among his many maladies, Marcos had suffered kidney failure. There were rumors that he was incontinent and had to wear diapers. (Pampers® were his favorite and when the first family had to flee the country, Imelda used Pamper boxes to smuggle out of the Philippines valuable pieces of jewelry.)

But the Marcos family was determined to maintain their regime. "I don't intend to die," Marcos promised, "and I don't intend to resign." When Cory held a final rally in Manila with at least one million people shouting her name, it became clear to everyone that she really had a shot at it.

"I will approach government," she promised the cheering masses, "with the zeal of a crusading housewife let loose in a den of world-class thieves . . . ."[13]

Already, Marcos had henchmen in place to guarantee his victory. But as enthusiasm for Cory mounted, the president decided that more drastic measures should be taken. He had promised to keep his army in their barracks during election day. Then, early in February, the president changed his mind. Soldiers were assigned to police the local polling stations. Cory and her supporters prepared as best they could to protect the election process from fraud and violence. Many innocent volunteers would suffer and die in the process.

COMELEC (the Commission on Elections) was the official governmental agency assigned to guard the integrity of elections in the Philippines. Their representatives would supervise the 85,000 polling places where 26,000,000 Filipinos were registered to vote. But COMELEC officials were Marcos appointees. Given the president's record at stealing elections, a more neutral organization was needed to guard the polling and counting process.

NAMFREL (the National Citizens Movement for Free Elections) was an organization of volunteers created in 1950 to help monitor the election of President Ramon Magsaysay. When American Senators Lugar and Pell asked Marcos to allow NAMFREL volunteers to function freely with full access to the polling places, Marcos agreed.

On 7 February 1986, at 7:00 A.M. the polls opened. One eyewitness wrote later that those next hours generated "more excitement, more fraud, and more selfless commitment to democracy than any election in Philippine history."[14]

At 7:45 A.M., Cory Aquino cast her ballot in Precinct 44 at the Lourdes Elementary School in the little town of San Miguel in Tarlac Province. At 11:30 A.M. President Marcos voted in his native Batac, Ilocos Norte, at the school that bore his father's name, Mariano Marcos Memorial Elementary School.

By twelve noon evidence of massive election fraud was accumulating in NAMFREL headquarters and in the offices of Cardinal Sin. In a pastoral letter, three weeks earlier, the cardinal had warned of "a sinister plot" to steal the election. Teachers, campaign workers and ordinary citizens had informed their cardinal that Marcos's agents were paying out large sums of money to buy votes away from Cory. The cardinal reminded his large flock that it was immoral to buy or sell votes. But, since the money was stolen from the people and since the people risked their lives to refuse it, the cardinal encouraged the people to take the money but to vote their conscience. He told them that "money offered to you in no way obliges you to vote for a particular candidate."[15] He also warned the candidates that cheating was a serious sin that "can only be forgiven by God if he renounces the office he has obtained by fraud."[16]

On election day, Filipino and American journalists filmed voters lining up near polling stations to receive a fifty-peso bribe to vote for Marcos. One man rushed up to a Cory campaign worker, handed her the fifty-peso note and with a grin said, "Here's a donation from the president to Cory's campaign." According to Sterling Seagrave, author of *The Marcos Dynasty*, Ferdinand Marcos spent $430 million to buy votes that day.[17]

Squads of "flying voters" admitted they were paid by Marcos to cast multiple ballots in various precincts across the cities. Other voters were disenfranchised because Marcos's men removed voters who supported Cory from their precinct list or transferred those names to precincts across the town or city. Many registered voters who found themselves mysteriously disenfranchised spent the day going from precinct to precinct trying in vain to find their names. Polling places in pro-Cory neighborhoods were moved in the night. Other voting centers were never even opened.

Anti-Cory graffiti was sprayed on the windows and walls of select polling places. Many pro-Cory voters were assaulted as they approached the polls by Marcos's thugs. Threats and obscenities were hurled. Rocks and bottles followed. Guns were pointed threateningly by military and police. Voters were slapped, beaten, shot and even killed.

When the polls closed at 3:00 P.M., NAMFREL volunteers were responsible to guard the ballot boxes until their contents could be counted and reported to COMELEC and NAMFREL election night headquarters. NAMFREL volunteers had been given the right to do a quick count tabulation of the precinct totals. But even before the polls were closed, it was obvious that no accurate count would be possible.

Marcos's henchmen were busy all day trying to switch or stuff ballot boxes. When NAMFREL workers weren't looking, the president's men would substitute an identical ballot box stuffed with forged, pro-Marcos ballots. In some precincts, Marcos's agents arrived waving guns and clubs to steal ballot boxes or to destroy their contents. Television cameramen recorded several of these brazen, daylight attacks. Unarmed NAMFREL volunteers formed protective human chains around the ballot boxes. Six hundred nuns, nicknamed the NAMFREL marines, chained themselves to ballot boxes or joined with other volunteers to guard the boxes with their lives. Marcos's people tried to push or club them aside. Thousands of courageous Filipinos risked their lives to guard those ballot boxes and to deliver them safely to the counting centers.

The NAMFREL counting process proceeded quickly. In Metro Manila, Cory was leading Marcos, as had been anticipated, but when the slower COMELEC count was released, Marcos was in the lead. It became immediately apparent that the two counts were vastly different. By 10:30 P.M. the next evening, the COMELEC count gave Marcos 1,112,275 against Cory's 1,079,228. But Cory was ahead in the NAMFREL count 4,306,684 to 3,455,548.[18]

As the count continued into the weekend, more and more evidence of Marcos fraud began to surface. By Sunday night, February 9, even the CIA had "calculated and reported" Aquino's win by approximately 60 percent of the vote. And that, they said, was after "taking into account the intimidation of voters, the disenfranchisement of Aquino voters, the padding of the rolls with Marcos voters."[19]

By Tuesday, the nation was in an uproar. Even the American congressional team on hand to observe the elections reported that they had ". . . witnessed and heard disturbing reports to undermine the integrity of [the electoral] process . . . serious charges have been made in regard to the tabulation system."[20]

That same night, 38 government computer technicians risked their lives to protest Marcos fraud at the election headquarters where the final, official vote was being tabulated. A reporter from the New York Times captured that moment. "Weeping and fearful, the government computer workers arose from their terminals and, data disks in hand, darted from the Commission on Elections to make the charge that the Marcos Government was rigging the presidential vote."[21]

Cardinal Sin rushed personally to protect those courageous Filipino computer technicians. "Marcos was after them," Cardinal Sin told me in an interview. "I gave them outfits as nuns, and put them up in different houses for one month until they were safe."

The cardinal's fears for the workers' safety was well justified. Even after election day, the killings continued. On Tuesday, February 11,

Evelio Javier, the highly respected former governor of Antique Province and a leader of Cory's campaign, was chased through the streets of his provincial capital by six masked men who had been hired by Marcos warlord Arturo Pacificador. They shot and killed Governor Javier in broad daylight just outside the building where the votes were being counted.

Pictures of the bodies of Cory's campaign workers and supporters who had been murdered by Marcos loyalists were featured on the front pages of the world's press. The U.S. congressional team of observers, the NAMFREL volunteers, even the CIA were condemning Marcos fraud when President Reagan released his statement from the White House expressing his concern over "the possibility of fraud, although it could have been that all of that was occurring on both sides."

Mr. Reagan's statement was received in the Philippines with shock and anger. Once again, 52 million Filipinos had been effectively disenfranchised by Ferdinand Marcos. Democracy in the Philippines had suffered another massive blow and the United States government seemed not to care.

Cory replied in quiet dignity to the president's insensitive and uninformed remarks. "No Filipino president has ever received the overwhelming mandate at the polls that I have been given," she said. "I would wonder at the motives of a friend of democracy who chose to conspire with Mr. Marcos to cheat the Filipino people of their liberation."

Cory also appealed to the Marcos troops. She knew that many soldiers and policemen had used their weapons against her workers and supporters on election day "to silence our voices and steal our victory," but she praised those individual members of the army and the police who refused to participate in Marcos fraud and promised the others that it was not too late for them to return to "truth, courage and honor."[22]

Priests and nuns, bishops and lay leaders of the Catholic church had witnessed the election fraud in cities, towns and villages all across the Philippines. When President Marcos called upon the church to stand with him, they refused. One hundred and twenty members of the bishops conference came together in Manila. Cardinal Sin remembers that the spirit of joy and celebration that the bishops usually feel at their Conferences was missing.

"There was silence," a bishop told me. "We didn't even greet one another. Fear filled the room. So we went to our knees in prayer. 'Be careful we do not pray too long,' I told them. 'Something serious must be done.'"

After prayer, the bishops composed a letter that would help destroy the Marcos regime. The letter stated clearly that "the polls were unparalleled in the fraudulence of their conduct." The bishops condemned "the systematic disenfranchisement of voters," "widespread and massive vote-buying," "the deliberate tampering of election returns, intimidation, harassment, terrorism, and murder.

"According to moral principles," the Bishops continued, "a government that assumes or retains power through fraudulent means has no moral basis . . . . If such a government does not of itself freely correct the evil it has inflicted on the people, then it is our serious moral obligation as a people to make it do so."

The Bishops' letter condemned violence but advocated "active resistance of evil by peaceful means—in the manner of Christ." After praising NAMFREL workers, the COMELEC computer technicians, the poll officials who did their duty "without fear or favor," the millions of ordinary voters and Radio Veritas, the Bishops called the people to action.

"In a creative, imaginative way, under the guidance of Christ's Spirit, let us pray together, reason together, decide together, act together, always to the end that the truth prevail, that the will of the people be fully respected."[23]

Several times that week, Imelda Marcos visited Cardinal Sin to persuade him against releasing the strong, anti-Marcos statement. On one visit she brought him a cross covered in diamonds. (He told me that he took the cross, sold it and gave the money to a Catholic charity. "It was a chance to liberate some of the Marcos wealth," the cardinal explained with a grin.)

At approximately 3:00 A.M. on Friday, February 14, Imelda Marcos returned to the cardinal's official residence one last time hoping to stop the public release of the Bishops' letter. The Cardinal met the first lady at the door. "It isn't good for you to come to the house of Sin so late at night," the Cardinal said, trying to soften the occasion with his own unique brand of humor. Imelda wept bitterly and hurried back to the palace.

When several bishops hesitated to sign their letter, Cardinal Sin said, "All must sign because after one week Marcos will leave this country."

"I don't know why I said that," the cardinal told me. "I just felt in my heart that the president was going to leave. The bishops were looking back and forth at each other and saying, 'Is this cardinal with the CIA?' But they signed."

Even the papal nuncio, the official representative of Pope John Paul II in the Philippines, warned the Cardinal not to sign and then not to release the Bishops' strong letter. The cardinal signed anyway. Later, he went to Rome hoping that he had not offended his old friend and co-worker, John Paul II.

"Are you happy with what we are doing?" Sin asked the Pope during their face-to-face meeting in the Vatican. "I bless you," the Pope replied. "What you are doing is correct."

On Friday, Cory heard the Bishops' letter condemning Marcos at the funeral of her friend and campaign worker, Evelio Javier. On Saturday, figures were released that 86 people had died in election violence and on Sunday, just after midnight, the National Assembly declared Marcos the official "winner" of the February 7 election.

Cory answered with strong, courageous words: "No tinsel and celebration of the president's make-believe win can hide his loss of moral and political authority. He is beaten. When is he going to go?"[24]

At 4:00 P.M. on Sunday, February 16, more than a million Filipinos gathered in the Luneta to hear Cory's cry for nonviolent, civil disobedience to protest Marcos's illegal and immoral acts. Cory stood on the grandstand stage framed by its half-shell proscenium and looked out across Roxas Boulevard and Rizal Park at the huge crowd who had gathered to support her. The people cheered as Cory asked the people to boycott the "crony" press, to stop patronizing companies owned by Marcos and his friends, and to delay payment of their water and power bills. She asked police and military officers to quit obeying the orders of "a president who does not have the people's mandate."

As the crowd swelled to nearly two million people, Cory continued to lay out her plan of nonviolent protest. Radicals wanted Cory to order the people to march on Malacañang. Instead, she asked employees of the government and of privately held corporations to bombard the Social Security System and Government Service Insurance System with loan applications. She also called for work stoppage and class boycotts on every level the day after Marcos was scheduled to be inaugurated (February 25). She also asked the people to organize on neighborhood and community levels for concerted nonviolent protest.[25]

Monday, February 17, stocks in companies held by Marcos and his cronies plunged on the stock market. Stocks in San Miguel, the nation's largest corporation (owned by Marcos's crony Eduardo Cojuangco, Cory's first cousin), dropped twenty-one points after Cory's call to boycott San Miguel products including San Miguel beer, the nation's favorite. People rushed to sell their Marcos related stocks and to withdraw their funds from Marcos-controlled banks.

That same day, President Reagan issued a statement from his Santa Barbara ranch reversing his support for the Marcos regime:

". . . it has become widely evident," he said, "sadly, that the elections were marred by widespread fraud and violence perpetrated largely by the ruling party." On Wednesday, February 17, the United States Senate voted 85 to 9 to condemn the recent elections in the Philippines due to "widespread fraud." And on Thursday, the twelve-nation European parliament condemned Marcos's election fraud and issued a strong statement supporting Cory Aquino's claims to the presidency.

In the Philippines, as Cory continued to mobilize the people against him, President Marcos struggled to maintain his firm control of the Armed Forces. A group of young military officers united under RAM (Reform the Armed Forces Movement) accused their commander-in-chief of election fraud. They warned Marcos that military men were prepared to assassinate Marcos cronies who supported his illegal claims to the presidency. They urged military officers and men to disobey any "illegal orders" by the president if he commanded them to arrest protesters or opposition leaders. As rumors surfaced of a military coup planned to oust Ferdinand and Imelda, military insiders warned that General Ver was planning to reinstate martial law and arrest all opposition leaders including Cory Aquino on February 25, Marcos's inauguration day.

Cory and the president faced each other eye to eye and Cory didn't blink. "This is my message to Marcos and his puppets," she said. "Do not threaten Cory Aquino, because I am not alone. Many of my countrymen are ready to come to my help if Marcos and his puppets have any evil plan."[26]

For almost two decades, Marcos had ruled the Philippines with his iron fist. One historian, looking back over those Marcos years, called Filipinos, "a nation of cowards who cringed before one S.O.B." God used Ninoy and Cory Aquino to renew their nation's courage.

On Saturday, 22 February 1986, a People Power Revolution was launched that would sweep away a tyrant and open the doors for a new era of freedom and democracy in the Philippines. Months later, Cory would describe that moment when "the Filipino raised his head and turned a new face to the world, the face of faith and courage."[27]

10

Cory:
the Revolutionary
(21 February–25 February 1986)

I will never be able to forgive myself if I will have to live with
the knowledge that I could have done something and I did not
do anything. If I fail, okay . . . At least I can face my God and
say: I have tried everything I could do to the extent of sacri-
ficing my life and my family.

Senator Benigno Aquino, Jr.

In the letter of James . . . he says: "Consider it pure joy
whenever you face trials of many kinds: because you know that
the testing of your faith develops perseverance. Perseverance
must finish its work so that you may be mature and complete,
not lacking in anything."

A faith tempered by trials accepts that God has dignified us
to be the instruments of His will, not just the passive receivers
of His grace.

President Corazon C. Aquino

The People Power Revolution of 1986 (sometimes called the
Prayer Power Revolution) began on Saturday morning, February 22,
and ended four days later on Tuesday night, February 25. In less
than 100 hours, millions of courageous Filipinos took to the streets
to end the twenty-year reign of Ferdinand and Imelda Marcos.
Armed only with their love of freedom and their faith in God, the
Filipino people stood up against the military might of their oppres-
sors, regained their sacred freedom and installed Cory Aquino as the
seventh president of the Third Republic of the Philippines. When
the dust cleared, this nearly bloodless revolution was, by anybody's
standards, a modern miracle.

Since election day, 7 February 1986, rumors of military coups and countercoups had been raging around Manila and across the Philippines. Cory Aquino and other opposition leaders had been warned that President Marcos was about to declare martial law for the second time. There was ample evidence that Marcos and General Ver had drawn up a list of opposition leaders, including Cory and her advisors, government officials, businessmen, clerics, military officers and members of the press, whom they were planning to arrest, imprison and even execute.

On the other hand, Marcos and Ver were convinced that the National Minister of Defense, Juan Ponce Enrile, had approved a plot to assassinate Ferdinand Marcos (and to take control of the government) planned by members of RAM, the Armed Forces reform movement, with support from America's Central Intelligence Agency.

The four-day People Power Revolution began on Saturday morning, February 22. Cory was in Cebu, the second largest city in the Philippines, about to speak before a large, anti-Marcos rally. In Manila, Defense Minister Enrile was having coffee with friends at the Atrium Coffeeshop in Makati when he was summoned urgently to the telephone. Trade and Industry Minister Roberto V. Ongpin was calling to warn Enrile that General Ver was about to begin a massive crackdown on all people in or out of government who were suspected of opposing Marcos. It was time to act.

Enrile called Lt. General Fidel V. Ramos, vice chief of staff of the armed forces of the Philippines and chief of the Philippine national police. They had discussed the possibility of taking a stand against the excesses of the Marcos regime. "Are you with us, Eddie?" Enrile asked. "All the way," Ramos answered.

Minister Enrile returned home, armed himself with his favorite Uzi machine gun and drove with his security force to his offices in the National Defense Building located in Camp Aguinaldo, a military base in Quezon City, in the heart of Metro Manila. Immediately, Enrile ordered his chief security officers, Colonel Gregorio "Gringo" Honasan and Colonel Eduardo "Red" Kapunan, to barricade the Defense building against the possibilities of an attack by troops loyal to Marcos and General Ver.

Approximately 200 to 400 rebel officers and soldiers rushed to prepare machine-gun emplacements and sniper positions. Lookouts were posted. Guards stood ready. The handful of men loyal to Enrile were vastly outnumbered and outgunned by the more than 250,000 soldiers still under the command of Marcos and General Ver. Lieutenant General Ramos, a graduate of West Point, his security team and another handful of military officers affiliated with RAM, joined Minister Enrile behind the barricades at about 6:00 P.M.

By 6:30 P.M., television crews, newspaper and radio reporters had assembled in the Social Hall on the third floor of the National Defense Building for a press conference with Defense Minister Juan Ponce Enrile and Lieutenant General Fidel V. Ramos, the deputy chief of staff of the Armed Forces of the Philippines. That press conference would shock the nation and launch the People Power Revolution.

"As of now," Enrile said quietly, "I cannot in conscience recognize the President [Marcos] as the commander-in-chief of the Armed Forces."

While cameras and microphones carried his words live to the palace and to the people of the Philippines, Enrile charged that Marcos had cheated to win the election. Enrile himself admitted to contributing some 350,000 votes to assist the president in stealing the election from Cory and the people.

"I searched my conscience," Enrile said, "and I felt that I could not serve a government that is not expressive of the sovereign will."

It took four hours before President Marcos responded officially to the charges Enrile leveled against him. "I feel sad," the president said at a hastily called 10:30 P.M. press conference. "I did not know Enrile and Ramos could reach this height of treason and rebellion."

For the past twenty-four hours, General Ver had been transporting men and materials into Manila. Full battalions of combat-ready troops were already moving through the city in armored personnel carriers. Tanks, artillery units, heavily armed helicopters and jet bombers were prepared to support the president's ground forces. Naval ships under Ver's command patrolled Manila Harbor and the Pasig River which flowed to the bay past the presidential palace.

Marcos had little to fear from this handful of rebels barricaded into the National Defense Building. In just hours, before dawn on Sunday morning, General Ver and thousands of troops would be ready to launch a full-scale attack on Camp Aguinaldo. The rebellion by Enrile and Ramos and the officers of RAM could be put down in one quick, bloody battle.

But Marcos and Ver did not anticipate the power of the people or the power of the people's prayers. On Saturday afternoon, Minister Enrile's wife called Cardinal Sin to ask his help. An hour later, Enrile called the Cardinal from Camp Aguinaldo. "Cardinal," he said, "I will be dead within one hour . . . . But if it is possible, do something to help us."

Minister Enrile also called the *Inquirer*, an opposition newspaper, to ask for help. "Get opposition leaders to call Radio Veritas," Enrile asked urgently. "Have them broadcast live appeals for people to support us in the streets."

Betty Go Belmonte, an evangelical Protestant and co-chair of the *Philippine Daily Inquirer*, rushed to the telephone. Her first call was to former Justice Cecilia Muñoz Palma, one of the nation's most respected jurists and a devout Catholic lay leader. Justice Palma was the first to phone Radio Veritas and in a live broadcast urged her fellow Filipinos to support Enrile and Ramos by taking to the streets on their behalf.

Betty Go Belmonte also called the Cardinal begging his support for the rebels. Finally, Fidel Ramos, himself a Protestant, called the Catholic Cardinal. "Help us," he said, "by calling the people to support us."

Cardinal Sin faced an enormous predicament. He realized what might happen in the heart of the city when Marcos and Ver ordered out the tanks and helicopter gun ships to put down the rebellion. If the cardinal called the people to take to the streets in support of Enrile and Ramos, many thousands might die. But if he didn't call them, the rebellion would be crushed and democracy might be snuffed out forever.

"I walked quickly into the chapel," the Cardinal recalled. "'Help me,' I prayed. 'I am supposed to be their pastor. What am I to do?'"

The Cardinal stayed on his knees for more than an hour. He knew that what he said or did at that moment could make or break the revolution. Eighty-five percent of the nation's almost 60,000,000 people are Catholics, and Filipino Catholics are devout. They take their religion and their religious leaders seriously. At that moment, Cardinal Sin was potentially the most powerful person in the Philippines. He had only minutes to decide whether he would support the fledgling rebellion against Marcos—or remain silent. Either decision brought great risk to himself and to his people.

The cardinal had already angered the papal nuncio by releasing the bishops' strong letter calling the people to join in "a nonviolent struggle for justice." Minister Enrile had been convinced and convicted by the letter. Now, a contrite and obedient Catholic layman was asking for the Cardinal's support.

But the cardinal's boss, John Paul II, had carefully stated the official Catholic position for just such a moment. Cardinals, bishops, priests and nuns were to seek social change through spiritual, not political nor military means. If the cardinal supported the rebels, his actions might be seen by Rome as disobedience. And whether the rebels won or lost their struggle, Cardinal Sin could have been in deep trouble with the Pope and his fellow cardinals.

But if the cardinal didn't support the rebels, President Marcos might stay in power. That would be a disaster for the nation. Cardinal Sin had buried too many Catholics, lay and clergy alike, who had

been tortured and killed by the Marcos regime. Sin was determined to help stop the suffering and to help restore democracy
in the Philippines, but if the cardinal supported the rebels and
the rebels lost, Marcos and Ver would wreak a terrible vengeance
and the cardinal's actions would only increase the suffering of his
people.

"I got up from my knees," the cardinal told me, "and went
immediately to the telephone. I called the three convents of contemplative sisters. 'Get out from your cells,' I told them. 'Go immediately to your chapels. You are our power houses. Pray and fast
until I tell you to stop. We are in a battle and, like Moses, you have
to stretch out your arms.' When they asked me 'Why?' I promised
to tell them later."

Then Cardinal Sin called radio station Veritas ("Truth"). This
powerful Catholic station, founded by Cardinal Sin and heard as far
away as Beijing, China had courageously fought the Marcos regime
when Ferdinand and Imelda were controlling the other major media.
The engineer on duty hooked up the cardinal's telephone to broadcast live to the nation.

"I want you to pray," the cardinal told his people. "Only through
prayer can we resolve this problem."

But Cardinal Sin had decided to risk his life and the immediate
future of the Church in the Philippines against the Marcos tyranny.

"I am deeply concerned about the situation of General Ramos
and Minister Enrile," he continued. "I am calling on our people to
support our two good friends at the camp. Go to Aguinaldo and
show your solidarity with them in this crucial period. I would be
very happy if you would help them. I wish that bloodshed will
be avoided . . . ."

When the cardinal finished his broadcast he went back to his
chapel to pray and to wait. Would the people leave their warm
houses in the middle of the night and make the dangerous journey
to Camp Aguinaldo where a battle was about to rage? Would Filipinos risk their lives to join the rebellion against a dictator who had
ruled them for two painful decades?

In the palace, President Marcos sneered when he heard the cardinal's announcement. "I'll take care of him later," Marcos muttered as
he, General Ver and other loyalist officers planned their assault on
Camp Aguinaldo. By sunrise they would have their troops in place
to crush the rebellion. They didn't know that in the darkness the
people were already moving toward the Epifanio De Los Santos
Avenue, the wide boulevard that ran between Camp Aguinaldo and
Camp Crame in the heart of Metro Manila. By morning Marcos and

Ver would find their tanks and armored carriers bogged down in a sea of praying Filipinos.

Butz Aquino, Cory's brother-in-law, a leader in the recent "Parliament of the Streets" movement, heard Justice Palma's call over Radio Veritas. He was one of the first to arrive at the camp. He talked to Enrile and Ramos briefly, then Butz Aquino also broadcast live on Radio Veritas to challenge the people to join him in front of Camp Aguinaldo on Epifanio De Los Santos Avenue, the wide boulevard through the heart of Manila nicknamed EDSA.

By 10:30 P.M., only six curious people were milling about the gates. But in their convents, just as the cardinal had ordered, the contemplative nuns were praying. "Lord, have mercy," they sang together quietly. "Christ, have mercy." And within minutes of his broadcast, thousands of Filipinos, Protestants and Catholics alike, had joined in that prayer. And even as they prayed, the people were getting dressed, packing lunches, finding candles and flashlights, calling friends, flagging down cars, taxis and jeepneys or making their way on foot toward EDSA.

By midnight, at least ten thousand Filipinos were crowded onto EDSA between Camps Aguinaldo and Crame. At 1:30 A.M. a foreign reporter estimated that fifty thousand people had blocked all entrances to the Camp.

"God had heard our prayers," the cardinal remembers. "God was mobilizing his own army and the battle for our freedom was about to begin."

Cory Aquino was leading a protest rally in Cebu when she heard that Enrile and Ramos had taken their stand against the president. Their actions came as a total surprise. She had called for peaceful, nonviolent protest. A bloody civil war seemed imminent. Cory risked arrest or even assassination. Her friends urged her to go into hiding. The American Embassy called, offering her sanctuary. An American submarine was waiting nearby to transport her and her party to safety.

Cory refused. She called her children in Manila and instructed them to go immediately to a house where they would be safe. Then she called Enrile and Ramos, thanking them for their courage and offering them her support. "There is nothing you can do, madam," Enrile replied, "but pray." Cory went immediately to the Carmelite Monastery near Cebu where she could rest and pray. The nuns made it clear to Cory that they would die to protect her.

All night long in Manila the rebels smuggled arms and ammunition into Camp Crame. Enrile and Ramos were preparing to defend themselves against General Ver's troops. The rebels knew they were massively outnumbered by loyal Marcos forces. "So be it," Enrile replied. "After all, life is God's gift. It is only he who will take it. Even with all the guns arrayed against us, if God's will is to spare us, he will spare us."[1]

In Washington, D.C., the White House and the State Department were on alert. Philippine experts had gathered in the crises room on the seventh floor of the State Department. President Reagan, the Joint Chiefs of Staff and members of the Congress were involved in briefings and discussions. Everyone was afraid that a shooting war between the Marcos-Ver forces and the Enrile-Ramos rebels could lead to a disaster in the Philippines and a triumph for the communist insurgents.

In the middle of the night, in a news release, President Reagan finally acknowledged that Marcos and his cronies had perpetuated massive election fraud "so extreme as to undermine the credibility and legitimacy of the election . . . ." Americans in the Philippines had suffered confusion and some embarrassment from Reagan's earlier statements of support for the Marcos regime. But they feared his change of heart had come too late. Embassy officials called leaders of the American community, warning them to stay off the streets.

Just before dawn, the studios of Radio Veritas were attacked by thirty armed men who ransacked and destroyed the station. June Keithley, the young announcer who would win the nation's highest honor for her courageous broadcasts during the revolution, began her search for another broadcast station. All through that first night, June Keithley had mobilized Manila with her news of the rebellion, with her repeated calls to march on Camp Aguinaldo and with her continuous playing of inspiring music including "Onward Christian Soldiers" and the opposition's theme song, *Bayan Ko*" (My Native Land).

With Radio Veritas silenced, by morning the crowds of people around Camp Aguinaldo dwindled from 50,000 to 500 or less. General Ver and his officers knew that it was time to crush the rebels. Four battalions and two armored companies of Marines were poised to invade Camp Crame through a nearly unguarded gate. Helicopter gun ships and artillery fire from howitzers set up on a nearby university campus would launch the attack. Air Force and Naval Units would provide general support to the marines. Army troopers would be held in reserve to clear the city and reestablish order.

At daybreak, a priest gave Communion to the rebels waiting at Camp Crame. An ominous silence greeted the second day of the People Power revolution. The rebels waited inside Camp Crame. Ten miles away at Fort Bonifacio, Ver and his commanding generals were putting final touches on their plan of attack. Nobody knew exactly what would happen next. Suddenly, Radio Veritas and June Keithley were back on the air broadcasting from various secret locations about the city on a transmitter they had dubbed "Bandido Radio."

"Troops are on the move," Keithley warned. "Come to EDSA. We need you."

Once again Cardinal Sin broadcast an appeal for "brave Filipinos to return to the streets in love." He urged the people to protect the rebel soldiers, to bring them food, and to pray mightily for their safety and for a nonviolent resolution of the conflict.

With the contemplative nuns still fasting and praying in their chapels, the cardinal called his army of activist nuns out of their convents and into the streets, to pray and if need be, to risk their lives for freedom.

Once again, people by the thousands returned to form a human barricade around Camp Crame to protect the rebels from forces loyal to President Marcos. From Fort Bonifacio, approximately five miles south, General Ver assured the president that his troops were ready and waiting for his order to attack. But President Marcos hesitated. Just hours before, President Reagan had called Marcos to warn him against bloodshed. Financial aid to the Philippines would be terminated if Marcos allowed his troops to fire on the peaceful protestors regathering at the gates of Camp Aguinaldo.

That same morning, Cory held a press conference in Cebu. She was relieved that President Reagan had finally realized the truth about the elections and she praised him for his statement. Once again, she called the people to pray for Enrile, for Ramos and for their nation.

With crowds waving and cheering, Cory drove to the airport in Cebu and climbed into a small private Cessna for her flight back to the Capital. To avoid any military jets that might be called in to intercept them, Cory's pilot flew fast and very low. Early in the afternoon, Cory was back in Manila. She praised Enrile and Ramos and once again called on the president to resign.

Marcos had called a second press conference. Ver and his officers were ordered to attend. Once again Marcos was forcing them to delay their attack on the rebels. Angrily, they rushed from Fort Bonifacio to the heavily guarded Malacañang Palace to stand behind their president as he faced the nation.

After blaming Enrile and Ramos for "the aborted coup," President Marcos sneered. "We could finish this in one hour," he claimed, "but it would be a bloody mess and I don't want that."[2] Marcos denied being ill. Reporters asked him if he were about to resign. "Of course not," the president answered with a tired laugh. He reminded them of his own days in the military. He bragged that it would be easy for him to retake Camp Crame. "The first thing you must do," he explained to the press, "is cordon off the area from civilians."

That remark broadcast live was a costly blunder. Hundreds of thousands of people rushed to frustrate the president's plan. Every major street or highway in the city was clogged with Filipinos traveling toward EDSA. By the end of the president's press conference, at least 250,000 Filipinos were blocking every entrance to Camp Aguinaldo (where Enrile was headquartered) and Camp Crame (where Ramos had gathered his men).

General Ver knew that time was running out. He had to order an attack before more civilians could gather. Preparing for his attack, Ramos and Enrile consolidated their forces in Camp Crame directly across EDSA from Camp Aguinaldo. Finally, at 2:15 P.M., Marine General Tadiar led a column of Marines from Fort Bonifacio toward the Crame, Aguinaldo area. The long, heavily armed procession included six tanks, ten armored personnel carriers, eight jeeps, and thirteen six-by-six trucks loaded with Marines, their ammunition and supplies.

Immediately, volunteer spotters called June Keithley. Over Radio Bandido she announced that tanks had been seen leaving Fort Bonifacio. She named the streets they would pass and urged people to block the column's way. General Tadiar managed to lead his Marines around the first human barricades they encountered. To avoid the crowded boulevards, tanks rumbled across sidewalks and empty lots. They even crashed through cement walls trying to get around the people in their way. But upon approaching Camp Crame, the general found every possible highway, sidestreet and empty lot jammed with men, women and children praying, singing and calling out to them.

"Turn back!" the people shouted. "Join us!"

The general rushed to a waiting helicopter to make an aerial reconnaissance of the scene. He was staggered by the sea of faces staring up at him. EDSA was jammed by more than one million people! The general could see that his tanks and troop carriers were surrounded by tens of thousands of determined Filipinos. A distinguished old Filipino woman sat in a wheelchair directly in the path of a giant armored personnel carrier. Young people sat or lay on the pavement in front of the large military vehicles poised above them with their engines running. Other unarmed, nonviolent protestors were kneeling in prayer or trying to hand flowers to the soldiers. Many were crying.

"We are Filipinos, like you," the people shouted to the heavily armed Marines. "Would you kill us? We are trying to stop Marcos and win back our freedom. Join us!"

The general had been ordered to make his way through the crowds, whatever the cost in life or property. His armored personnel carriers could have forced a bloody trail through the people. Instead he ordered his column of Marines to return to Bonifacio.

Tears formed in Enrile's eyes when he heard of that encounter. "We, the army, are supposed to be protecting the people," he said. "Instead, they are protecting us." On the streets of Manila, Filipinos were discovering the power of the people, but most who were there would tell you that God was the source of that power. Millions of Filipinos had been praying for the nation's healing. In the streets of Manila, God was answering those prayers.

Darrell Johnson, the American pastor of the Union Protestant Church in Makati, was in the crowd that day with hundreds of his parishioners. "There were four dominant symbols of the revolution," he explained to me in an interview, "the Eucharist, the cross, the Virgin Mary and the child Jesus. Until you understand those symbols," he said, "you can't really understand the People Power revolution in the Philippines."

Pastor Johnson went on to describe the incredible scene as he remembers it:

Helicopter gunships were roaring overhead. Tanks were making their way toward us from the distance. Troops poised to fire tear gas and brandished their automatic weapons. But on key street corners near the scene of the battle, priests were giving communion. That was the first symbol of the revolution. The power and the presence of Christ's body and blood gave people the courage to stay out there.

The crucifix was the second symbol of the revolution. Young seminarians had taken down crosses from their chapel walls. Thousands of Filipino families took crosses from their living rooms and bedrooms into the streets. Everywhere you looked people were wearing or waving crosses. Jesus died on a cross and through his death eternal life was brought to the world. The cross was a sign to the people that God makes us strong in our weakness. What looks like death in fact is the beginning of life.

A third symbol you saw lifted above the people's heads were thousands of statues of the Virgin Mary. Protestant Americans have trouble relating to Mary, but once you have lived and worked in the Philippines you begin to understand why the people love this woman who submitted her will to the will of God and through her submission gave birth to our Savior. On the streets that day Mary was the symbol of the power of women who submit themselves to the will of God. Cory Aquino, the nuns, the young Filipino girls and old Filipino women were about to end a dictator's regime with their simple, faithful prayers and the Virgin Mary was a symbol of their power.

And last the little statues and pictures of the baby Jesus were a fourth symbol of the revolution. Freedom in the Philippines was regained through the childlike faith of the Filipino people. Against the military might of Marcos and his men, it was a "child's crusade." Like children, the Filipino people entered into battle armed only with their trust in God, but it was enough.[3]

There were hundreds of thousands of Protestants in the streets that day, standing side by side with their Catholic brothers and sisters. Although there are approximately 45,000,000 Catholics in the Philippines, there are at least 5,000,000 Protestants whose churches are affiliated with the National Council of Churches in the Philippines and an estimated 500,000 Protestants in churches associated with the Philippine Council of Evangelical Churches.

The NCCP, often called the umbrella organization of mainline Protestant churches, had opposed President Marcos's martial law from the beginning. While Catholic and Evangelical churches waited for years to take a stand against Marcos, NCCP pastors and leaders were "harassed by the Marcos government and many were jailed, are missing or have been killed."[4]

When Marcos was declared winner of the fraudulent elections of 7 February 1986, the executive committee of the Philippine Council of Evangelical Churches issued its "Call to Sobriety," urging Filipinos "to uphold and respect the resulting declaration of winners" by the Marcos-controlled National Assembly. Ten days later, on February 24, one day before the People Power revolution, the PCEC executive committee issued its new statement announcing:

> Where Caesar conflicts with Christ, we declare that Jesus is Lord. Divine Law supersedes human law. Therefore our obedience is not absolute. Whenever government rules contrary to the will of God, then civil disobedience becomes a Christian duty . . . . After much prayer we have arrived at the moral conclusion that the legitimacy of the present administration should be questioned.[5]

At the first call from Cardinal Sin on Saturday evening, February 22, both liberal and conservative Protestants rushed to the streets to pray and to act alongside their Catholic brothers and sisters.

Protestants were also included among the revolution's leaders. Lieutenant General Ramos, his sister, Senator Leticia Ramos-Shahani, Senator Jovito Salonga, attorney Sonny Belmonte, now president and general manager of the Government Service Agency and his wife, Betty Go Belmonte, a respected Filipino publisher, columnist, vice-chairperson of the *Philippine Daily Inquirer* and a founder of the *Philippine Star*, are all members of the same Protestant church, the Cosmopolitan Church (affiliated with the United Churches of Christ in the Philippines).

Richard L. Schwenk's wonderful little book, *Onward Christians: Protestants in the Philippine Revolution*,[6] tells dramatic true stories of Protestant Christians who swelled the ranks of the People Power revolution. Some 150 members of the United Methodist Youth Fellowship from the East Manila District were leaving a concert on Saturday night, February 22, when they heard Cardinal Sin's broadcast. They rushed directly to EDSA and were one of the first large groups to arrive on the scene. The Faith Baptist Church van delivered dozens of evangelical young people to the streets near Camp Crame. The Christian Youth Fellowship of Faith Bible Church brought bags of rice and vitamins to the rebel soldiers. The pastor and members of Kamuning Bible Church rushed to join other Filipinos guarding television Channel 4 while snipers were still firing.

By Sunday evening, Catholic, Protestant and Moslem Filipinos had united at the barricades. (Early Sunday morning when the crowds had dwindled temporarily, a small group of Moslem young people remained faithfully on watch at the gates of Camp Aguinaldo. Throughout the revolution, Moslems had joined with Catholics and Protestants to protest the Marcos regime and to help protect the rebel forces.)

At 7:00 Sunday night, Enrile and Ramos called another press conference. They named the officers and the military units from around Metro Manila and across the Philippines who had called to denounce Marcos and to promise their loyalty to the revolution. Marcos called Enrile, promising the rebels a full pardon if they would surrender. Enrile stalled. When Marcos sent two members of his Parliament to negotiate, Enrile answered them with "the bottom line demand—which is nonnegotiable—is for him [the president] to step down!"

All night long Filipinos by the hundreds of thousands milled about Camp Crame. The People Power revolution had become a revolution of "milling about." When a new wave of soldiers or marines threatened the rebels, June Keithley would sound the warning over Radio Bandido and tens of thousands of people would surge into their new positions.

Cardinal Sin had appealed to the people to bring food for the soldiers and for the protestors in the streets. Men, women, and children, hundreds of thousands of them, responded immediately. Much of Manila became a ghost town, silent, empty; while on EDSA and on the streets and boulevards leading to the Camps, the capital took on a carnival atmosphere. Bonfires blazed. Guitars played. People sat or lay in great clusters on the streets and sidewalks singing and praying through the night.

At 4:14 on Monday morning, February 24, the third day of the People Power revolution, General Ver ordered the Fourth Marine Regiment to move on Camp Aguinaldo. Using tear gas, the first marines breached the human barricades, and assault forces moved quickly into the Camp.

From her secret broadcast location, June Keithley could hear the cries of the people being tear-gassed. She began to pray into her Radio Bandido microphone:

> Lord, You know that there are many people out there. You know what they are going through . . . . You teach us to always turn the other cheek . . . . Please take care of all who are out there. Protect them and save them from harm. There are children out there, young girls and boys, parents, brothers and sisters, husbands and wives. Who knows what they may have to face this morning? . . . We add our prayers to the prayers of the people in our country. Lord, I am not very good at this, but I just ask You, please, in Jesus' name, please save our people. Amen.[7]

Across the street in Camp Crame, Enrile and Ramos knew that Ver was positioning his troops for a full-scale assault on their positions. Broadcasting live, Ramos warned the nation that "an overwhelming military force has been assembled and directed to move against us." June Keithley's spotters reported from the scene. She continued exhorting the people to take courage and to block the troops with their lives.

To end the stalemate and to blast a way into Camp Crame, General Ver called in helicopter gunships from the Air Force's Fifth Strike Wing. Colonel Antonio E. Sotelo, the wing commander, briefed his battle-trained pilots. The five Sikorsky gunships roared into the skies above Camp Crame at 5:55 A.M. The camp defenders and thousands of people in the street knew that these American-made machines could blast their way through those human barricades like a hot knife slicing through melted butter. Rebels and civilians alike expected to die at any moment as the helicopters maneuvered noisily above them.

At that moment, Radio Veritas broadcast Cardinal Sin's strong voice. "May we come to a peaceful solution to our crisis," he said. "I will bless the men in uniforms, but only those who are for peace."

Behind their barricades, Enrile and Ramos had just heard a reading of Psalm 91. "I will say of the Lord, He is my refuge and my fortress: my God, in Him will I trust . . . ."

A million Filipinos, many of them kneeling and in prayer, waited while the helicopters circled menacingly overhead and then suddenly landed on the parade ground at Camp Crame. Sixteen pilots jumped out waving white handkerchiefs and grinning at the people. The crowds went wild, cheering the courageous defectors and thanking God for their deliverance.

At 6:27 A.M. June Keithley announced that the Marcos family had just departed the Philippines from the Manila International Airport. Cory broadcast her own message of thanks to the people. Enrile and Ramos came down from their headquarters and joined the excited crowd. "Democracy has been restored to us," Enrile said. "From this moment on, the armed forces are your armed forces, loyal to you, the people, the nation, and the Constitution, and not to any one man."

The victory announcement proved premature. The rumor was false. Marcos and his family were still in the palace. The Fourth Marine Provisional Brigade had taken its position in the Secretariat building at Camp Aguinaldo. Men of the Third Marine Battalion were in place on the Camp golf course. The Fifth Marine Battalion was lined up nearby. Mortars and recoilless rifles were being trained on rebel positions in Camp Crame. Thousands of Filipinos stood in harm's way between the forces of General Ver in Camp Aguinaldo and the rebels in Camp Crame. At 9:00 A.M. the order was given to fire on Camp Crame. Colonel Braulio Balbas, the commanding officer, looked out on thousands of Filipino faces. He stalled. The order was repeated. He stalled again. Finally, word came directly from the palace to fire. "Sir," he answered, "I just cannot fire. We will be killing thousands of civilians."

"I understand that," his commanding officer replied. "You can use your discretion."

At that moment, President Marcos began another live press conference to prove that he and his family were still in the Philippines. He declared a national state of emergency and promised to take his oath of office the next day as scheduled. As Marcos addressed the cameras, General Ver interrupted the president, asking for permission to use force against the rebels.

"We are ready to destroy them and annihilate them at your command," Ver said, his voice trembling.

"My order is not to attack," Marcos replied looking away from the cameras just long enough to silence the agitated general.

The two men argued back and forth. Ver pushed Marcos to let him attack. Marcos continued to stall.

"They are massing civilians near our troops," Ver said anxiously. "And we cannot keep on withdrawing."

"My order is to disperse without shooting them," Marcos replied.

"We cannot withdraw all the time," Ver answered defensively.

"No, no, no," Marcos said again. "Hold on. You disperse the crowds without shooting them. You may use any other weapons."

Finally, Ver quit trying. "We will carry out your order, sir."

No one can say for certain whether the scene was real or staged. On videotape the confrontation looks real enough! But the question remains: Was Ver really trying to get permission to fire on the crowds or was Marcos using this media event to prove that he was a man of peace to Filipinos and especially to his old friend, Ronald Reagan, who had threatened to shut off aid if shots were fired?

The press conference ended in confusion when at 9:56 A.M. the television picture went blank. Rebels had taken Channel 4 from its Marcos defenders. Moments later, a lone Sikorsky gunship attacked the palace. The first family, reporters and the room full of generals dove for cover. The sudden surprise attack damaged cars and two presidential helicopters. No one was killed, but several palace personnel were wounded, none seriously.

This isolated and almost harmless use of fire power against the president accomplished its goal. Ferdinand and Imelda were frightened. Already, the first lady had packed more than 300 large wooden crates with clothing and jewelry, art pieces and gold. The crates had been removed secretly from the palace to a barge in the Pasig River. President Marcos had determined to stay on as President of the Philippines, but Imelda Marcos was hedging his bet.

When Ver and his forces could not control the growing crowds, the president was furious. "If you are going to be frightened by 2,000 civilians," he shouted at his generals, "then let's not talk about running a government."

In fact, there were at least one million people blocking all routes in and out of Camp Crame and another million Filipinos guarding roads, bases, television and radio stations across Manila. Ver's forces were still poised to attack. One shot fired by either side could have led to the deaths of thousands. And yet Cory insisted on visiting EDSA to encourage the people. "This is my doing," she argued when her security guards refused to take her to EDSA. "With or without you," she added, "I am going."

At 3:00 P.M. Cory Aquino arrived at the corner of EDSA and Ortigas. A huge crowd was waiting to greet her. She spoke briefly and then issued this written message:

"We have recovered our freedom, our rights and our dignity with much courage, and, we thank God, with little blood. I enjoin the people to keep the spirit of peace as we remove the last vestiges of tyranny, to be firm and compassionate. Let us not, now that we have won, descend to the level of the evil forces we have defeated.

"I have always said I can be magnanimous in victory, no more hate, no more fighting. I appeal to all Filipinos of both sides of the struggle. This is now the time for peace, the time for healing."[8]

The revolution was reaching its successful conclusion. Roughly 90 percent of the 250,000-man Armed Forces had joined Enrile and Ramos in opposing Marcos. Cory Aquino's inauguration had been scheduled for early Tuesday morning. And though President Marcos had called a 6:00-P.M.-to-6:00-A.M. curfew, no one paid attention to it. The Filipino people stayed in the streets that last night to celebrate their victory and to guarantee that General Ver would not try any last-minute military move to oust the rebels.

By 6:00 P.M. Monday, the White House appealed to Marcos to step down. At 1:00 A.M. on Tuesday, February 25, Marcos called President Reagan's friend, Senator Paul Laxalt, in the United States suggesting that Marcos and Cory share power. Laxalt consulted with State Department officials and then telephoned Marcos to oppose his suggestion. When Laxalt offered President Marcos sanctuary in the United States, Marcos replied, "But the Philippines is my home. I want to stay and die here."

About the same time, Imelda called Nancy Reagan, begging her to intervene with President Reagan on her husband's behalf. Nancy repeated the official sanctuary offer.

At 3:00 A.M. Marcos placed one last call to Senator Laxalt.

"What should I do?" Marcos asked.

"I think you should cut. And cut cleanly," Laxalt answered. "I think the time has come."

A long silence followed.

"Mr. President," Laxalt asked, "are you still there?"

"Yes," Marcos replied softly. "I'm so very, very disappointed."[9]

Throughout the last night and day of the People Power Revolution, Filipinos rushed to areas where conflict threatened. Cory had called for peace and the people used their own bodies to keep loyalist and rebel soldiers from further confrontation and bloodshed. In spite of everything, blood was shed. At 8:00 A.M. loyalist snipers were spotted on a television transmission tower near Cory's home. In the fire fight that followed, three snipers and one civilian were killed. For this, those miraculous days of People Power in the Philippines had to be called "the nearly bloodless revolution."

At 10:50 A.M., Tuesday, 25 February 1986, Cory Aquino was inaugurated President of the Philippines before a crowd of about 800 people jammed into the Club Filipino. Senior Associate Justice Claudio Teehankee of the Supreme Court administered the oath of office. Ninoy's mother, Doña Aurora Aquino, held the family Bible.

"I felt that Ninoy was between Cory and me," Doña Aurora remembers. "After the oath taking, I asked: 'Cory, did you feel the presence of the invisible President?' Cory laughed. 'Yes, I felt the presence of the invisible President. I felt that he was around.'"[10]

In her short speech, Cory reminded the nation that "Ninoy believed that only the united strength of a people would suffice to overturn a tyranny so evil and so well organized. It took the brutal murder of Ninoy to bring about the unity, the strength, and the phenomenon of People Power . . . . As I always did during the campaign," Cory concluded, "I would like to end with an appeal for you to continue praying. Let us pray for God's help especially during these days."[11]

Cory wore a simple yellow dress. She led the people in singing the "Lord's Prayer," *"Bayan Ko,"* the theme song of the revolution and *"Bayan Magiliw"* (Cherished Land), the Philippine national anthem. Outside, thousands of exhausted and jubilant Filipinos joined in the singing. Millions of Filipinos still clogging the streets heard the ceremony broadcast live.

At the close of the inaugural festivities, President Corazon Aquino issued Proclamation No. 1 mandating the new president to reorganize the government and to appoint key Cabinet officials. Juan Ponce Enrile was appointed Minister of National Defense. Lieutenant General Fidel V. Ramos was promoted to full General and appointed Chief of Staff of the New Armed Forces of the Philippines.

President Marcos took his oath of office just an hour and ten minutes later in the Ceremonial Hall at Malacañang Palace. Even Marcos's vice president, Arturo Tolentino, didn't bother to attend. And during Marcos's short inaugural address, his last hold on the media was broken as Channel 9 went off the air.

Just before 9:00 P.M. two U.S. helicopters landed on the palace golf course. Ferdinand Marcos and his family boarded one helicopter. General Ver and his son boarded the second. As they lifted up off the grass, thousands of cheering Filipinos charged the gates of Malacañang. A few of Marcos's guards tried to turn the crowd away. Heads were bloodied in the brief skirmish before the guards gave up and sneaked away. For the first time since martial law was declared, the Filipino people had access to the palace.

During those next chaotic hours, as thousands of Filipinos poured through the palace grounds, only the pictures and artifacts of Ferdinand and Imelda Marcos were vandalized. "Don't ruin anything," the people shouted to each other. "Cory may need it."

The Air Force Pilot of the plane that flew President Marcos and his first lady to Hawaii remembers hearing Imelda singing the popular show tune, "New York, New York." Already she was planning her return to power and prominence, this time in the Big Apple,

12,000 miles from her island home. "If I can make it there, I'll make it anywhere. New York, New York!"

After the inauguration, Cory Aquino began her drive back through the streets of Manila to her home on Times Avenue. Less than three years earlier she had ridden through these same streets behind Ninoy's casket. On that sad day, she wore black and sat with her children in the back seat of a funeral hearse. On 25 February 1986, she was wearing yellow and riding in her white Chevrolet van. On this ride, motorcycle officers and armed guards accompanied Cory Aquino while helicopters whirred overhead. The grieving widow had become the president of her nation and the people cheered her as she passed. Cory sat at the window waving and smiling. Tears streamed down the faces of the people who were waving back. Cory was thinking of the courage of these people and of Ninoy whose example they had followed:

> I cannot resist comparing his death to Good Friday, she said later, and our liberation to Easter Sunday. I am sure that Ninoy is smiling at us now from the life after, for truly we have proved him correct: the Filipino is worth dying for.
>
> In the dark days before liberation, I said that I believe God is on our side and that we have nothing to fear. I truly believe that he is not only on our side, he actively intervened and fought on our side. How else can we explain many of the events in the days that just passed?
>
> I pray that he will continue to be by our side in the difficult yet challenging days to come. I am confident that he will not fail us: our cause is just. God is beside us. We can face the coming trials.[12]

Just five days after being an eyewitness to the People Power revolution, Darrell Johnson stood up before his large congregation in the Union Church of Manila and began his sermon.

"How does one speak about a modern-day miracle?" he began. "How does one speak of that gracious and mighty Hand which intervened in the crisis? You saw it, didn't you? The hand of God preventing civil war, the hand of God keeping the streets of Manila from flowing with blood, the hand of God restraining and protecting . . . . The Filipino people gave Jesus' way a try—and they demonstrated that it works—it really works!"[13]

11

Cory's First Year as President
(26 February 1986–25 February 1987)

This blood-letting must stop! This madness must cease! I think it can be stopped if all Filipinos can get together as true brothers and sisters and search for a healing solution, in a genuine spirit of give and take. We must transcend our petty selves, forget our hurts and bitterness, cast aside thoughts of revenge and let sanity, reason, and above all, love to country prevail during our gravest hours.

Senator Benigno Aquino, Jr.

In Saint Paul's letter to Timothy, he writes: "I urge then, first of all, that requests, prayers, intercession and thanksgiving be made for everyone—for kings and for all those in authority, that we may live peaceful and quiet lives." If we pray and claim the promise with faith, and if we lend ourselves as instruments for its fulfillment, then we are already destined for times of quiet and peace.

President Corazon C. Aquino

The First Ten Days

On the night of Ferdinand and Imelda's departure and Cory's inauguration, Manila went berserk. In its cover story for 10 March 1986, *Time* magazine called the happy celebration a "fiesta of freedom." Hundreds of thousands of Filipinos took to the streets. Fireworks exploded overhead. Yellow confetti rained down from high rise buildings upon a sea of yellow T-shirts, yellow "Cory" dresses, yellow flags and banners bearing Cory and Ninoy's names. One man carried a sign reading "Rebellion against tyrants is obedience to God." Another said, "Thank God almighty, we are free at last!" Cars and buses honked their horns. Sirens sounded noisily. Church bells

176

rang. Fathers held waving children on their shoulders. All across the city, nuns and teenagers, wealthy businessmen and squatters, old people and seminarians, greeted each other with the Laban sign and spontaneous, tearful hugs of joy.

The revolution had ended. Now the hard part would begin. Cory asked Rene Saguisag to be her official spokesman. "We are a government," he told the media, "that doesn't even have a typewriter." Cory refused to move into the palace. Instead, she opened Malacañang to the public and established her offices in a nearby guest house.

During her first day in office, Cory appointed seventeen cabinet members. Her vice-president, Doy Laurel, Ninoy's boyhood friend, was named prime minister and foreign minister as well. Juan Ponce Enrile, a long-time Marcos crony and the signer of the order to imprison Senator Ninoy Aquino, was appointed Minister of Defense. His critics knew that Enrile's break with Marcos had helped to launch the People Power revolution, but they also knew Enrile's presidential ambitions and they feared that in the long haul he might try to undermine Cory's administration.

Enrile tried to assure everyone that he and Cory could work together. "Do you think we would have laid down our lives for a corrupt purpose?" he said. "If these [skeptics] will give me time to show them what kind of person I am, I will show them."[1]

At her first press conference, Cory asked for resignations from Marcos's appointees but assured tens of thousands of loyal civil servants that most of their jobs were safe. "I can be magnanimous in victory," she said again. "It is time to heal wounds and to forget the past."

On February 27, Cory released 39 political prisoners who had been detained by Marcos for their political beliefs, as Ninoy had been detained. But Cory's new executive secretary, Joker Arroyo, a human rights lawyer and another old friend of the Aquino family, warned that thousands of political prisoners might not be coming home from Marcos's jails. In a television interview Arroyo compared the Philippines to Argentina where an estimated 9,000 political detainees mysteriously disappeared forever from their homes and offices between 1976 and 1982. "When the history of the Philippines is known," Arroyo said somberly, "perhaps we will beat the record of Argentina in magnitude and torture."[2]

Soon after Arroyo's warning, Task Force Detainees, a Philippine religious organization that investigated political arrest, torture and murder, announced that under Marcos in 1985 alone, there were at least "602 reported disappearances, 1,326 cases of torture and almost 300 political executions."[3] The next day Cory promised to release all political detainees "without exception."

On March 2, Cardinal Sin presided at a thanksgiving mass in the Luneta. Tears glistened in Cory's eyes as she stood before the massive crowd. Waving, cheering, applauding Filipinos stretched as far as she could see in all directions. They roared their approval as Cory restored the writ of habeas corpus and promised to retire the old army generals who had backed the Marcos regime.

A young Air Force officer with an automatic pistol tucked away stood with reporters and cameramen just fourteen feet from Cory as she addressed the crowd. He had come to assassinate the president and had managed to get within easy killing range when suddenly he froze and walked quickly from the scene. When he was captured on April 9, Romualdo Mercado, 30, confessed that he had been promised 500,000 pesos by an Air Force colonel to kill the president. He had used a forged "Cory Press Card" to pass through presidential security. At the last moment he just could not pull the trigger.

It would be the first of many attempts to end Cory's presidency. "I am a fatalist," President Aquino told the press when the first assassination attempt was announced. "I know that when my time is up, there is nothing I can do about it." In the next few months, many conspiracies would be launched against her and her government. "My life is in God's hands," Cory would tell the press. "Every day is an act of faith."

The Communist Insurgents

On March 4 Cory retired 22 "overstaying generals" as she had promised that vast audience at the Thanksgiving rally. By March 5 the new president had released from prison 517 detainees including Jose Ma. Sison, the founder of the new Communist Party of the Philippines (CPP), and Bernabe Buscayno, known as "Commander Dante," the supreme commander of the New People's Army, the military arm of the CPP.

On March 20, Commander-in-Chief Corazon Aquino addressed the graduating class of the Philippine Military Academy. After congratulating the military for mingling their khaki green colors with "the yellow shirts of our followers, the white frocks of our priests, and the gray habits of our nuns" in the People Power Revolution, she issued this challenge to the communists:

"To our brothers and sisters in the hills and the underground we have this to say: You waged war against Mr. Marcos because he was the embodiment of the worst injustice, greed and cruelty. I fought Marcos for the same reasons. We had a common stand and an overriding purpose: the end of tyranny and shame and the beginning of hope and pride. This is why I ordered the immediate release of political prisoners. Now that evil has fled from the land, I shall soon call on you to come out and rejoin your people in rebuilding our country. There should be no more reasons to continue fighting. Our other differences can be settled through participation in peaceful process."[4]

President Aquino was taking a calculated risk. She was both praised and condemned for releasing the communist leaders from their prison cells. Her decision was based on the teachings of Jesus. "Blessed are the peacemakers," he said, "for they shall be called the children of God." The release of political detainees was for Cory an act of faith in God and in her people. The immediate results seemed promising.

One by one, communist insurgents left their mountain camps and surrendered their weapons to representatives of Cory's new government. On March 24, 1,000 communist fighters surrendered on the same day to military representatives on the island of Negros. Over the next weeks and months, Cory's offer trickled down to hundreds of members of the New People's Army who took their own leap of faith and bet their lives on Cory's words. "I know," she promised them, "that the roots of insurgency are in the economic conditions of the people and the social structures that oppress them. We must address ourselves to these conditions vigorously if we are to hope reasonably for a lasting peace."[5]

The Search for Stolen Treasure

On March 12, Cory signed an order freezing all the assets and properties of Marcos, his family and his cronies. She used her second executive order to authorize the Presidential Commission on Good Government to work with governments and banks around the world to prevent Marcos from selling or transferring his assets until the Philippines could reclaim what he and Imelda and their friends had stolen from the people.

In its first report, the Presidential Commission on Good Government announced it had discovered corporations belonging to Marcos or his cronies with 10.7 billion pesos in equity, 310 million pesos in Imelda's jewelry, private aircraft worth 779 million pesos, ships and yachts valued at 748 million pesos and Marcos properties in New York alone worth over $500 million.[6] As the PCGG investigation continued, it became painfully clear that the Marcos crowd had stolen literally billions of pesos from their country. As a result, the Philippine treasury was nearly bankrupt. The economy was sliding toward disaster. Cory was determined to find and reclaim the missing Marcos monies.

Human Rights

On March 18, Cory appointed the Presidential Commission on Human Rights. For too long, the nation's fifty-five million people had been victims of violence. The Commission, chaired by Pepe Diokno, was given the responsibility to investigate kidnappings, killings, tortures, disappearances, hamletting (refusing to let residents of suspected NPA villages leave their towns) and food blockades (refusing to allow the shipment of food to such towns).

The communist and Moslem insurgents had committed their share of the human rights abuses, but the Armed Forces of the Philippines, the national police and the security forces of wealthy businessmen and private armies of the provincial warlords were also to blame. On March 22, Cory appointed a special panel to investigate the excesses of the military under Marcos. There were critics who complained about Cory insisting on cracking down on military human rights abuses as well as on abuses by the insurgents. "This revolution began with a bullet," she reminded the people, "a bullet fired by a soldier into the head of my husband."[7]

A New Constitution and a New Government

On March 25, Cory abolished the Marcos Constitution of 1973. At the same time the president announced her "Freedom Constitution," written by Father Joaquin Bernas. The president authorized this temporary charter to guide the nation back to democracy while a brand new constitution for the Philippines was being drafted by a constitutional commission which she would soon appoint. "No right provided under the unratified 1973 Constitution is absent from the Freedom Constitution,"[8] she assured the people.

At the same time, Cory dissolved the Marcos National Assembly (the Parliament or Batasan Pambansa) calling it "a cancer in our political system which must be cut out." Because the government was in chaos, Cory would take onto herself extraordinary (though temporary) power "to pass or change all laws, reorganize the government, revoke or alter agreements on the use of natural resources made by Marcos, and select or remove all elected or appointed officials."[9]

Soon after assuming her new power, the president fired more than 70 provincial governors, 1,600 mayors and 10,000 council members formerly associated with the Marcos regime. To replace them until local and provincial elections could be held, Cory appointed her own OIC's, Officers in Charge.

Cory's critics charged her with creating an Aquino dictatorship to replace Ferdinand and Imelda's reign. And it was true that some experienced, trustworthy public figures were ousted alongside Marcos cronies. President Aquino's decision to start her government with "a clean slate," even if good people were thrown out with the bad, was greeted by howls of protest from Cory's friends and her foes alike. They took to the streets to protest Cory's actions. A few violent confrontations followed. Cory would not be dissuaded.

"Let the handful murmur," she said. "They are within their rights under our covenant of freedom. But let them not stand in the way of our passage to lasting peace." Then she added this warning in a front page story labeled "Cory gets tough": "Remember," she said to Marcos supporters, insurgents, paramilitary organizations from the left wing or the right, and to anyone else who might stand in the way of her quest for peace and prosperity for the Philippines, "this government of peace is not unarmed."[10]

The Economy

The White House and the State Department noticed Cory's "new muscle" and praised her "sound, market-oriented economic policies." President Reagan's spokesman lauded the Aquino government for clearly demonstrating ". . . its intention to carry out needed economic and military reforms."

The State Department had known all along that Marcos was bankrupting the Philippines. American officials had estimated that Cory would face a budget deficit of 6.9 billion pesos ($336.6 million) in 1986 and a national debt of more than $20 billion. But that was even before Marcos tried to buy his election against Cory. "Marcos went through that annual deficit in just two months," one U.S. official said. Cory had inherited a budget deficit for her first year in office of 30–34 billion pesos (more than $1.5 billion) and a national debt of almost $30 billion.

In his first call to President Aquino, Mr. Reagan announced the release of $400 million that had been committed to the Philippines by Congress in economic loans and aid, and he promised to request immediately from the Congress an additional $150 million in emergency economic and military aid.[11]

From her first day in office, Cory struggled to bring economic recovery to the Philippines. She blamed poverty and hunger for the growth of the insurgencies. She knew, too, that her government had a limited time to get people jobs, houses, education and health care. The nation's infrastructure—roads, bridges, railroads, communication systems, water and power—was in terrible disrepair. Everything required money and money required business and business couldn't prosper in a nation hounded by fear.

On 23 May 1986, President Aquino flew to Davao City in the southern Philippines to hold dialogue with communist insurgents. The streets of the third largest city in the Philippines were lined with cheering crowds wearing Cory's color and waving yellow banners welcoming their new president. Cory met with rebel leaders in a convent and promised amnesty to a group of 168 insurgents who had decided to surrender their weapons and end their loyalty to the 16,000-member communist-led New People's Army.

"I believe in the power of prayer to work miracles," she told the leaders of Davao City and Eastern Mindanao. "For we prayed not for freedom, but for the strength to persevere in the fight for it without hate or rancor until freedom came . . . . And we found the strength and the courage to face down a dictatorship . . . . What am I saying? That we pray to God and then we work so that deliverance from our tribulations will come through our efforts and singularly to our labor . . . ."

Cory didn't end her speech here, however. She went on to share frankly what must happen before their goals of peace and prosperity could be realized in the Philippines.

"Knowing that poverty is a main cause of insurgency," Cory offered forgiveness, rehabilitation and skills training to the insurgents who would surrender their guns. Knowing that peasants needed land to live on and to plant, Cory announced that she had learned there were 33,000 hectares of military reservations in the Davao area "which could be used for land reform and rehabilitation." She also promised that all human rights abuses, "whether committed by the armed forces or the communists, will be prosecuted equally vigorously. For on a par with basic material needs, is the hunger for justice."

Knowing that a handful of rich landowners and businessmen had recruited their own private armies to keep the peasants and workers in servitude, President Aquino also directed the minister of defense to implement immediately "a disarmament campaign against warlords in the countryside and the criminal syndicates in the cities." She promised local elections "as soon as the new constitution had been written and ratified." She begged the people to give the officers in charge a chance "to prove themselves." To the charges of inexperience that critics were leveling against them, Cory answered, "Only Marcos men had experience. I had no experience. If I had had experience it would have been in Marcos politics and I would not have led you to freedom." But she also promised that their grievances would "be acted upon with dispatch."

Cory promised that she would soon call for a national ceasefire and she begged her listeners to be patient while she and her government set about to solve the overwhelming problems that the nation shared.

While Cory addressed the problems of the people in violence-torn Mindanao, back in Manila, military units were placed on full alert "to control any untoward incidents while the president is out of town." While she was gone, Vice President Laurel, in a speech before a Rotary Club Convention, warned what might happen if the government failed in its attempts at financial recovery, "the communists will take over . . . . In the end," he said, "it will be your future and the future of your children that will suffer."[12]

The First 100 Days

Cory had to find a way to convince the insurgents to lay down their arms and at the same time to get business and agriculture on their feet again. She had to pay interest on a mounting national debt and at the same time find cash to pay the costs of national recovery. It was a difficult tightwire to walk. She was caught between warring factions and embroiled in controversy and criticism.

Thousands of officials appointed or elected during the Marcos regime protested when President Aquino fired them. The officers in charge (OIC's), whom Cory had appointed in their place, were often inexperienced and had to work without their constituencies' support or cooperation. Military leaders, including Enrile, criticized Cory for granting herself these "extraordinary" powers. The Armed Forces of the Philippines and police representatives complained that the appointment of these officers in charge was leading to unrest and even violence in towns and villages across the islands. Army and police officials were also angry that Cory insisted on their being investigated for human rights abuses alongside the insurgents. Businessmen complained about strikes and the insurgencies. The poor complained about graft and corruption, unemployment, the lack of food, housing, education and medical care. Everyone complained about the garbage, about potholes in the highways, about rising food and fuel prices and about crime and terrorism in the streets.

Just before her hundredth day in office, Cory addressed 30,000 members of the Catholic Charismatic Movement in the archdiocese of Manila on Pentecost Sunday at the Araneta Coliseum. In her address she shared a personal conversation she'd had with Ninoy just before his assassination. Ninoy confessed to Cory that whoever would take over from President Marcos would have a hard time. "The country is in such a mess," he had told her, "that anyone who might succeed Marcos would have to be crazy." Of course neither of them dreamed that Cory would be that "crazy" person whom the people would choose to clean up the Marcos mess.

"Ninoy never dreamed it was his wife who would take over," she told the people, "but he also never envisioned that there would be more Filipinos who would be awakened and would no longer be apathetic but would help themselves and their country."

The revolution had worked because of the prayers of the people, Cory said again. "I believe God has helped me in my most difficult moments," she told them, "and God will continue to help me and the country if we pray."[13]

At the close of her address, the leaders of the convention surrounded Cory, anointed her with oil, and prayed that God would bless, strengthen and guide their president. Cory stood before them in her simple yellow dress. Her head was bowed. Her eyes were closed. Cory's daughter, Viel, stood nearby also bowing in prayer. The bishop had explained that they were anointing Cory as David had been anointed by the prophet Samuel. Both had been chosen by God to lead their people in times of trouble. Both had been chosen for their faithfulness.

As Cory and her daughter turned to leave the Coliseum, 30,000 people began to pray. Hands were lifted up to God. Faces strained heavenward. Eyes filled with tears. Lips moved in silent prayer for Cory and for the difficult days ahead.

In an interview published later, Doña Aurora Aquino, Ninoy's mother, joined Cory in asking the people of the Philippines to pray for their new president. "Ninoy must be having the last laugh now on us," Doña Aurora concluded. "Look who has to lead the country out of the mess of the past."[14]

On May 25, just three months after coming into power, President Aquino appointed a constitutional commission to replace the previous 1973 document within six months of assuming office. On June 2, Cory addressed the opening ceremonies of the 1986 Constitutional Convention in the elegant hall that once housed Marcos's National Assembly (the Batasang Pambansa).

Doña Aurora watched her daughter-in-law receive a standing ovation as she walked up through the cheering delegates to take her place beside the Commission's elected president, retired Supreme Court Justice Cecilia Muñoz Palma, one of Cory's closest advisors during the February "snap" elections. Justice Palma had been responsible for the unification of the opposition political parties on Cory's behalf. The two women stood side-by-side before the applauding delegates. Doña Aurora remembered that moment when she was suddenly struck by the realization that her "little Cory" was indeed the President of the Country.

"I guess things have just moved so fast," Doña Aurora said, "and I have not had time to ponder over events; but when the Con-Con [Constitutional Convention] opened and everyone stood up and applauded—all those justices, diplomats, officials, Con-Con members—for that woman who walked in, I shed tears. Our little Cory is indeed the new President."[15]

In spite of her critics, President Cory was receiving high marks from the people on her first months in office. The newspaper *Malaya* conducted a poll in Metro Manila to determine public response to the president's controversial actions. A great majority approved the resignation of the members of the judiciary and the resignation of all local officials and appointment of new ones. A majority also favored the dissolution of the National Assembly and the calling of a constitutional convention.

When the same organization polled the people to find their priorities for the new president's first year in office, a majority agreed with Cory that economic recovery should be the president's top priority. The list included, in order, the investigation and prosecution of human rights violations, the recovery of hidden or ill-gotten wealth, the reorganization of local government, peace and reconciliation talks with the communists and Moslem insurgents, and the drafting of a new Constitution.[16]

On June 12 Cory and her cabinet led the people in their first meaningful celebration of Filipino Independence Day in the fourteen years since Marcos had declared martial law. Eighty-eight years before, the new national flag of the Philippines was raised in Kawit, Cavite to signal the victory of Filipino forces over the Spanish colonizers. Almost 400 years of Spanish reign ended on that day.

In her Independence Day speech before tens of thousands of celebrating Filipinos, once again Cory thanked God for delivering them from the colonizers and dictators of the past, including Ferdinand Marcos. On that same Independence Day, the U.S. delegation which monitored the February elections announced that they had determined that "the true winner was President Corazon Aquino." Their five-month investigation proved to the American delegation "that Corazon Aquino was democratically elected" to be president of the Philippines.

The Manila Hotel Incident

But opposition leaders still loyal to Ferdinand Marcos continued to demonstrate against Cory in the streets. They wrote editorials, picketed the palace, used occasional violence and terror and even plotted to overthrow her. On July 6, after their weekly Sunday pro-Marcos rally in Manila's Luneta Park, opposition leaders tried to persuade Arturo Tolentino, Marcos's vice-presidential candidate in the February elections, that he and Ferdinand were the rightful rulers of the Philippines.

As Tolentino moved from the Luneta grandstand to the nearby Manila Hotel, they urged him to grab power in Marcos's name. In a suite in the hotel, Tolentino was sworn into office. He even appointed a cabinet. Several hundred pro-Marcos soldiers armed with assault rifles rushed to support Tolentino and at least 5,000 Marcos backers responded to Tolentino's call for a new revolution.

Cory was in Mindanao. Vice-President Laurel was in Europe. Two radio stations announced quite falsely that Defense Secretary Enrile had broken with Cory and had joined with Tolentino. "I am still a member of the cabinet of President Aquino," Enrile responded. "I am not looking for another job," he said.

With that announcement, Enrile closed temporarily the radio stations that had broadcast the false reports and he ordered troops to seal off the Manila Hotel. Tolentino and his followers were trapped in the five-star hotel. Throughout the night, the crowd of Tolentino sympathizers diminished as they began to realize that there would be no popular support for this new revolution. By noon the next day, an exhausted and emotional Tolentino addressed approximately 3,000 supporters in the lobby. He condemned Cory for her "undemocratic rule." Claiming that he had moved to restore "a constitutional democracy," he waved a letter from Marcos authorizing him "to be the legitimate head of the country until such time that I return." Then he surrendered to authorities thus ending the Manila Hotel's "room with a coup."[17]

Cory had been in constant communication with Enrile. Insisting on a nonviolent solution to the crisis, she gave amnesty to soldiers and civilians who participated in the failed coup, promising that next time she would not be so lenient. She reminded her critics that the people had defeated a dictator through nonviolence and that nonviolence would remain one of the cornerstones of her administration in dealing with antigovernment forces.

"Had we not given them a chance to go out peacefully," she said, "and instead pushed them against the wall, a bloodbath would have been certain." President Aquino believed that the aborted coup had helped show the nation that pro-Marcos forces, civilian and military, were far outnumbered by Filipinos loyal to Cory's government. But the president warned that she "would not allow them [pro-Marcos forces] to work against the government by misusing the right to free assembly and by noising their anticommunist hysteria."[18]

In fact, the communists were about to accept Cory's invitation to join her in a time of cease-fire and negotiation. The CPP, the Communist Party of the Philippines, had boycotted the 1986 elections. With good reason they had assumed that once again Marcos would misuse his power to stay in office. But the communists were stunned when the People Power revolution unseated Marcos and propelled Cory Aquino into the presidency.

For seventeen years communist leadership had condemned the "U.S.-Marcos dictatorship" and its "enforcer," the Armed Forces of the Philippines. They couldn't believe that the revolution had been launched by top army officials turning against President Marcos or that America had at last ended its support for the Marcos regime. Cory held out the branch of peace. After months of discussion, the communists agreed to meet her at the bargaining table.

The Anniversary of Ninoy's Death

On 21 August 1986, 8,000 people crowded into the Santo Domingo Church to celebrate the life and to recall the death of Senator Ninoy Aquino. In his sermon, Cardinal Sin condemned "the factionalism, the rumor-mongering, the political maneuvering, and the inordinate search for personal security going on around us." He said that Ninoy's legacy lay in jarring the nation back to a sense of reality, the reality of "self-sacrificing love, unconquerable optimism about people and surrender to faith in God."[19]

In her address, Cory remembered Jesus' words that a seed must first fall and die before the plant can grow and be fruitful. "A new life rises from a martyr's death," she said, recalling the story of Ninoy's assassination. "One man sprawled on the tarmac. One seed fallen to the ground watered with blood. Tyranny had sowed a bullet and reaped a revolution. One man had worked the reluctant field of his people to finally throw in his blood and brought us hope and a harvest of freedom."[20]

In the afternoon, a granite marker was unveiled at the Manila International Airport: "On this spot, Benigno Ninoy Aquino, Jr., was assassinated on 21 August 1983. It is eternally enshrined, for wherever a martyr has shed his blood for truth, justice, peace, and freedom, there is sacred ground. The sun cannot bleach, the wind cannot blow, the rain cannot wash away that sanctity. From ground like this springs that which forever makes the Filipino great."

Coretta Scott King, wife of the assassinated civil rights leader, Martin Luther King, Jr., was a special guest of the Aquino family at the dedication ceremony. Ninoy's only son, Noynoy Aquino, read the speech that his father planned to read upon his return. Cardinal Sin and two Moslem leaders blessed the marker.

Nur Misuari and Conrad Balweg

Of the more than 55 million Filipino people, there are five to seven million Muslims, most of them living in the south. In December 1976, a Marcos emissary had signed the "Tripoli Agreement" granting local autonomy to Muslims living in the thirteen southern provinces. Marcos never delivered on his promise. For eighteen years, Muslim insurgents had waged a bloody war to gain their independence. At least 100,000 Filipinos had died and another 300,000 had been displaced in the violence.

On September 5 Cory Aquino traveled to Jolo island in the heart of Muslim territory to meet with Nur Misuari, the exiled chairman of the Moro National Liberation Front (MNLF). They agreed on continuing their "cessation of hostilities" and beginning talks to end the conflict permanently. The president's brother-in-law, Agapito "Butz" Aquino, was selected as the civilian coordinator of the talks.

On September 13 President Aquino traveled into the Cordillera Mountains of northern Luzon to negotiate peace with a former Roman Catholic priest, Conrado Balweg, the leader of a small antigovernment force called the Cordillera People's Liberation Army. As a priest, Balweg had ministered within the system to "the forgotten people of the Cordillera." But as Marcos continued to exploit the region, leaving the people in even greater poverty and despair, Balweg committed himself to a more violent form of protest. He exchanged peace promises with Cory and she agreed to halt government projects or actions opposed by tribal leaders.

President Aquino Visits the United States

On September 15, Cory Aquino left on her first official visit to the United States as president of the Philippines. Everywhere she appeared, Americans greeted her with standing ovations. This small, rather fragile looking woman, wearing her trademark yellow dress and her stark, gold rimmed glasses, spoke softly and barely gestured. But each time she spoke, lumps formed in the throats of those who listened and eyes glistened with tears. The public and the press were equally inspired and impressed.

In her address to a joint session of the United States Congress, Cory retold the story of Ninoy's life and death. She moved and impressed the legislators with her own account of the bloody, rigged elections and the People Power Revolution. Cory reaffirmed her commitment to the ways of democracy and promised that the new Constitution, which would be submitted later that year to a free vote of the people, would give full respect to the Bill of Rights.

She promised to honor the nation's $26 billion foreign debt, but she called on the Congress to assist her fledgling democracy in economic recovery. "Ours must have been the cheapest revolution ever," she reminded them. "With little help from others, we Filipinos fulfilled the first and most difficult condition of the debt negotiation: the full restoration of democracy and responsible government. Elsewhere, and in other times of more stringent world economic conditions, Marshall Plans and their like were felt to be necessary companions of returning democracy."

Cory spoke frankly. "Half our export earnings, $2 billion out of $4 billion . . . [in 1986] went to pay just the interest on a debt whose benefit the Filipino people never received . . . . Still we fought for honor, and, if only for honor, we shall pay . . . . Yet to all Americans . . . I address this question: Has there been a greater test of national commitment to the ideals you hold dear than that my people have gone through? You have spent many lives and much treasure to bring freedom to many lands that were reluctant to receive it. And here you have a people who won it by themselves and need only the help to preserve it.

"Three years ago, I said, thank you, America, for the haven from oppression, and the home you gave Ninoy, myself, and our children, and for the three happiest years of our lives together. Today, I say, join us, America, as we build a new home for democracy, another haven for the oppressed, so it may stand as a shining testament of our two nations' commitment to freedom."[21]

The members of the House and Senate stood to their feet applauding as President Aquino turned to wave one last time and then was gone. Less than two hours later, members of the House of Representatives voted a supplementary aid package to the Philippines of $200 million.

During her nine-day visit to America, Cory persuaded those who doubted that she could be trusted. She obtained $150 million in additional economic and military aid, $20 million in medical supplies from the government and from other private agencies, plus the House promise of $200 million in supplementary aid. She secured a promise for a $508 million standby loan from the International Monetary Fund, a $300 million credit from the World Bank and a pledge of favorable repayment terms on Philippine debt from commercial banks.

In the Oval Office, Cory and President Reagan seemed to patch up their differences. He told her about his own dealings with communists when he was president of the Actors' Guild in Hollywood. Aquino shared her own strategy for dealing with the insurgents. "By offering a cease-fire and reconciliation she was building her moral authority to use military might against the communist New People's Army if they did not respond." Apparently, Reagan replied, "I accept all that, but be careful."[22]

Tension and Terror in Manila

President Reagan wasn't the only person who liked and respected Cory but who questioned her peaceful approach to the communist insurgents. Her own cabinet was divided about the issue. Defense Secretary Enrile had turned against the president. He attacked her "soft approach" to the insurgency problem and claimed that the communists were even making headway in the cabinet.

Cory tried to negotiate a peaceful settlement with Enrile. She arranged to meet him in a private home in Manila. "Johnny," she said to him at that meeting, "I don't know if I have offended you in any way, but if I have I'm sorry." Stunned by the president's simple, straightforward approach, the defense minister answered, "No, no, Ma'am, it's not you. You have not offended me." But to regain his support, Enrile demanded that Cory do the following: call a new presidential election; scrap the draft of the new Constitution; reconvene the National Assembly; remove the incompetent OIC's, adopt a stronger, clear-cut counter-insurgency program; and fire from the Cabinet ministers Enrile thought to be communist dupes or sympathizers.[23]

Cory refused Enrile's demands. The defense minister continued his attacks on the president and members of her cabinet. The coalition of parties that had supported Cory had dissolved into warring camps. On October 8, Cory's friends and advisors announced the creation of a new party called Lakas ng Bansa or People's Power. The sign of the party would be the acronym, Laban, or fight, the party that grew out of "Chino" Roces' Cory-For-President movement.

"I am not in favor of creating a new political party," Cory said again. "I would like for all the different parties to get together, the same coalition that got us where we are now."[24]

On October 15 the draft Constitution was submitted. "With this Constitution," the president said upon that occasion, "we have the framework of the house of democracy that we hope to build, a house worthy of the great collective act that made it possible: the rising of the Filipino people to vindicate their voice, a rising that continues to be the wonder of the world."[25]

Opposition leaders from the right and from the left stepped up their attacks on the "house of democracy" that Cory was trying to build. They seemed to want another kind of house altogether; and they did their best to undermine and destroy what she had already built. While Cory was negotiating for a cease-fire with the communists, the Armed Forces of the Philippines—without Cory's knowledge—arrested Rodolfo Salas, alleged to be the top military commander of the New People's Army. At the same time, insurgent forces were stepping up their terrorist attacks against army and police units who often retaliated in kind.

[Note: "Insurgent" is the common word for those forces in the Philippines working to overthrow the elected government. Most ordinarily, communist (NPA) and Muslim (MNLF) guerrillas are labeled "insurgent forces" while their political movements are called "insurgencies."]

During the last weeks of October and the first weeks of November, bombs and grenades had exploded in several Manila theaters, shopping centers and restaurants. Anticommunist politicians were blaming the communists for the rash of terrorist acts. The communists denied the charges. A dark and dangerous mood was settling down on the capital. On November 10, Cory was leaving for an important state visit to Japan. Rumors that there would be another coup against her government while the president was away were circulating in Manila.

General Fidel Ramos, the AFP (Armed Forces of the Philippines) chief of staff, was trying to act as a middleman between Cory's friends and advisors and Enrile and his supporters. But a plot code named "God Save the Queen" was in the works "to save the government from the communist threat." Because Cory maintained her popularity with the people, the plot was designed not to appear as a threat to Cory herself, but the "left-leaning" members of Cory's cabinet would be arrested.

After conferring with almost all of his commanders in the twelve military regions, Ramos warned that any coup attempts would be "destabilizing and bloody." On November 9 Cory predicted that the people of the Philippines would not follow a "few self-appointed messiahs." She also warned the people that "if it should be necessary, I shall once more ask you to take to the streets."[26]

On November 12, the president left on her state visit to Japan. From the Manila International Airport, Cory spoke again of "the rumored threats to the security of my government and the rights and liberties of our people." After urging the people to decide for themselves, she added, "In plain terms, any coup or other military action by misguided elements must contend with my opposition, which means with the power of the people, in order to succeed."[27]

The Assassination of Rolando Olalia

Soon after her departure from Manila, Rolando Olalia, the president of a trades-union federation and the leader of a new leftwing party, and his driver, were abducted in the outskirts of Manila. The next day, their bodies were discovered. Olalia's eyes had been shot out. His driver's head was split from top to bottom.[28]

After two brief days of meetings with the Japanese, Cory rushed home to Manila. At her arrival she announced to the press that Japan "came through with unequivocal expressions of support for the Aquino government." She announced a Japanese assistance package of "at least one hundred billion yen."

Then quickly she got down to the real business at hand. "I mourn the death of Lando Olalia," the angry president began, "as well as the other victims of violence, like his driver, Leonoro Alaya." Then Cory expressed her sincere grief and sympathy for others who had died in the past few months of her administration. She named just two of them: Patrolman Ernesto Gutierrez, who was killed in the insurgent raid in Calumpit, and Rex Baquiran, a Philippine Constabulary colonel well known for his contacts with the right and the left and a man, Cory noted, like Olalia who would be remembered ". . . for their gentleness of manner, their commitment to certain ideals of justice." She promised to find their killers and to bring justice to their families. "I can only pray and hope," Cory added, "that in time the sufferings of widows and children will be mitigated. I understand the hurt and pain they feel and that, although justice will not make up for the loss, it will be given. Our nation is shamed by this brutal tragedy."[29]

Later, in an emergency meeting with the president, General Ramos revealed that he had uncovered seven plots to take over the government by military officials loyal to Defense Minister Enrile.[30] After their meeting, Ramos issued orders that no officer in the Armed Forces of the Philippines should obey an order issued by Minister Enrile or the Ministry of Defense. Cory in turn asked all her cabinet members to submit resignations. Minister Enrile's resignation was accepted immediately. Newspaper headlines read: "Cory Fires Enrile!"

Cory Gets Tough

President Aquino acted quickly and with strength. The nation sighed with relief. On November 27 a cease-fire was signed with the communist insurgents. In her address to the National Prayer Breakfast shortly after, Cory spoke eloquently of her gratitude to God for intervening in those past months of conflict on behalf of the Filipino people:

"In the past months, in times of danger and crisis, we have prayed for our Lord's mercy, intervention, blessing, and grace. Despite our failing, He has always answered. As the Prophets would marvel: The Lord's loving kindnesses indeed never cease; His compassion never fails; they are new every morning . . . ."

"I therefore would like to take this opportunity to thank our Lord Jesus Christ, who is our Savior and our strength, our guide, and the true leader of our nation. His compassion—throughout our bondage, our struggle, our attainment of freedom, and our battle to keep and give it meaning—has been new every morning. As we suffered, He called to us: Come to me, all of you who are heavily laden, and I will give you rest."[31]

Two weeks later, in her Christmas address to the nation, Cory added, "For the first time in fourteen years, we celebrate Christmas in freedom. . . . Years ago, Jesus Christ, our Savior and Lord, came to join the family of men and give them peace, forgiveness and life. How can we, who are so much less, choose to give less of ourselves? Let us take to heart His earnest message: Let us love one another as He loved us."[32]

Cory celebrated the New Year at home quietly with her family. The first year of her presidency would end in less than eight short weeks. Her government had survived another coup attempt. Her trips to the United States and Japan had reaped a bountiful harvest. On February 2, the new Constitution would be judged by the nation's 20,000,000 voters. And on February 25, the nation would celebrate the first anniversary of the People Power revolution. No one dreamed that during the next eight weeks tragedy would strike or that Cory's government would face its greatest crisis.

Tragedy at the Mendiola Bridge

On January 22, 10,000 angry Filipino farmers marched toward Malacañang Palace demanding land reform. Already they had camped for seven days in front of the offices of Agrarian Reform Minister Heherson Alvarez. The protestors wanted some of the land that had been sequestered from Marcos and his cronies to be distributed to poor, landless farmers like themselves. When Minister Alvarez urged that they wait to press their demands upon the new Congress, which would be elected not long after the anticipated February 2 ratification of the Constitution, the farmers refused. They were convinced that the new Congress (like Marcos's National Assembly) would be made up of wealthy businessmen and landlords who wouldn't carry out Cory's promises of land reform any better than the officials of her Ministry of Agrarian Reform.

When Minister Alvarez would not agree to their demands, the farmers marched toward the palace to take their protest directly to Cory. As they crossed over the Mendiola Bridge, which links the palace area to central Manila, they were met by 1,000 marines and police carrying shields who attempted to push them back across the bridge. Demonstrators hurled rocks and charged directly into the ranks of the policemen. The riot forces panicked. Back-up troops behind the lines began to fire their automatic rifles. In just a few seconds, twelve farmers were killed and ninety more were wounded.[33]

"I am shocked over the bloody incident at Mendiola," the President admitted, "and deeply saddened at the lives that were lost. I commiserate with the families of the dead. I grieve equally over what this does to the ideals we stood for in the struggle to bring freedom and peace to our land, ideals we continue to cherish." Cory ordered a complete investigation of the tragedy and placed the police officer in charge on leave.

"In the meantime," she added, "I urge our people to maintain calm and sobriety." Cory warned that there would be those who tried to exploit the tragedy to "derail our efforts to bring about full democracy in the coming plebiscite." She also admitted her fears that before the February 2 national referendum to approve/disapprove the new Constitution there would be more "attempts to destablize the government and defeat our democratic aim."[34]

Early the next day, thousands of angry Filipinos gathered near the Mendiola Bridge to protest the massacre. The protestors were enraged by the farmers' violent deaths at the hands of Cory's troops. Once again a bloody confrontation seemed inevitable. Then, suddenly, members of Cory's own cabinet walked arm-in-arm to meet the protestors.

These men and women, now high government officials, had marched those same streets to protest the excesses of the Marcos regime. They had been the backbone of the "Parliament of the Streets" movement that had eventually helped depose the former president. Their presence on the Mendiola Bridge helped defuse the violence and, together, farmers and cabinet members walked across the bridge toward the Malacañang Palace to signal their mutual goals for the nation and their shared grief for the farmers who had died.

Cory spent that same day visiting the hospital rooms where the wounded farmers were being treated. Her eyes reflected the nation's anger, shock and sadness.

A Mutiny in the Armed Forces

Early on the morning of January 27, Cory's worst fears were realized. As many as 500 Marcos loyalists in the military staged the fourth military "coup d'etat" against Cory's eleven-month-old government. Simultaneously, mutinous troops who were members of secret organizations within the armed forces attacked military and civilian targets around Manila, including Camp Aguinaldo, Fort Bonifacio, Villamor Air Base, Sangley Air Station and television Channel 7.

Troops loyal to Cory and General Ramos managed to secure the military installations, but Marcos forces occupied and held Channel 7 for fifty hours. General Ramos circled the station with 1,000 of his soldiers. As he was about to order them to attack, 78 of Ramos's own officers reportedly threatened a rebellion "if any military blood was shed." And though the general denied later that his officers had issued him an ultimatum, Ramos canceled the attack and worked out an "honorable" surrender with the rebel forces.[35]

President Aquino was pleased "with the peaceful, nonviolent resolution of the GMA-TV incident," but she angrily confronted the leaders of this new coup attempt. She accused them of trying one more time "to derail our effort to establish full constitutional democracy in the coming plebiscite. Let me make myself clear on this matter: We shall not treat this like the Manila Hotel incident." President Aquino announced full court martial proceedings against the officers and warned everyone involved, civilian and military alike, that the full force of the law would be applied against them. "I have ordered their arrest and detention," Cory announced. "There is a time for reconciliation and a time for justice and retribution. That time has come."[36]

Two days later, in a speech of installation for the new president of the Far Eastern University, Cory referred to "the darkened minds of the perpetrators of the last coup attempt. How they can explain an assault on democracy as an attempt to save it can only be explained and perhaps, after justice is done, forgiven, as a struggling remnant of the dark age from which we emerged last February 25."[37]

A Vote of Confidence

Less than one week after the fourth coup attempt against Cory's government, 20 million Filipino voters would go to the polls to approve or disapprove the nation's new Constitution. For the past weeks, while Cory urged a massive "yes" vote, forces opposed to the Constitution had mounted an anti-Constitution propaganda barrage, terrorist tactics and coup attempts to defeat it.

"Go out and get the vote," Cory urged the people. "Get this constitution ratified by an overwhelming majority, so we can get on with the challenge I described . . . ."

In her campaign speeches on behalf of the new Constitution, Cory summed up its message in the following way:

"Energy to the executive, wisdom and control to the legislature, justice to the courts, integrity to the public servant, civic responsibility to the people, dynamism to the economy, equity to the poor, and dignity to all Filipinos under a democratic government of laws.

"And," she added, "running as a constant thread through all of it will be the principle of accountability: of government of the people, and the people to God, their conscience, and their history . . . .

"Weekend coups are mere distractions," Cory warned, "poor excuses to delay our confrontation with history. I believe the Filipino is eager to take on the challenge of achieving Philippine greatness. Let us stop bickering and guessing about the future and instead go for it."[38]

Millions of Filipinos went to the polls as Cory had urged them. Some waited for two or three hours in long lines to mark their "yes" or "no" ballot. When the votes were counted, 76.36 percent had voted "yes." The polling and the counting had been carefully monitored by COMELEC and NAMFREL workers. And though the high percentage of "yes" votes decreased in the home provinces of former President Marcos and former defense chief Juan Ponce Enrile, even there the fairness of the election was generally acknowledged. Enrile lost graciously. "We accept the verdict of the people," he said. "We must now join hands in addressing the serious problems of our country."[39] The Constitution had been ratified and Cory had been given an overwhelming vote of confidence.

President Corazon Aquino proclaimed the new Constitution and then placed her left hand on the Bible and her right hand in the air swearing to preserve and defend it. That same day, in the Ebenezer Baptist Church in Atlanta, Georgia, Coretta Scott King awarded President Corazon C. Aquino the 1987 Martin Luther King, Jr., Nonviolent Peace Prize.

The Cease-fire Ends

On February 8, the sixty-day cease-fire ran out between Cory's government and the communist rebels. Attempts to negotiate a truce had failed. "The truce is over," Cory announced sadly. "History will decide who is to blame for its end . . . but all hope of peace is not lost."

Cory went on to promise that her government would continue "to explore the possibilities of regional and provincial negotiations with the insurgents." She shared her hope that their attempts to bring economic recovery would, over the long haul, "significantly reduce the root causes of the insurgency." She commanded the new armed forces of the Philippines "to resume operations against the insurgents," but insisted that they "conduct themselves with honor and humanity against the enemy . . . . Even as we prepare for the struggle to come," Cory concluded, "let us continue to pray that God may yet snatch us from the brink of war and set us gently down in peace."[40]

The First Anniversary of the Revolution

At sunrise, on 25 February 1987, church bells began to ring across Manila and up and down the Philippine island chain. Before dawn the people were gathering in the streets of the capital to celebrate the first anniversary of the People Power Revolution. By mid-morning millions thronged to EDSA, that great street that leads to Camp Aguinaldo and Camp Crame, where freedom had been reborn in the Philippines. People surged through the open gates. Civilians hugged soldiers. Helicopters hovered overhead dropping yellow flower petals on the cheering crowds below. People had their pictures taken in front of a tank parked nearby. Yellow T-shirts announced "I am proud to be a Filipino" or "Ninoy, we remember!" or "Unarmed Forces of the Philippines."[41]

Cory was driven through the crowds into Camp Aguinaldo. She waved and smiled as the people cheered. At the flag-raising ceremony inside the camp, Cory addressed the soldiers: "Many of you resisted, and for that we thank you. In the moment of truth, when you were ordered to fire on the marchers for peace, for once in your life, you disobeyed. You disobeyed the dictator in obedience to the higher call of freedom. And for that you will be rewarded."[42]

After the bands had played and the fireworks had lit up the darkness, Cory returned to her home on Arlequi near the presidential palace. She had survived the first year in office. The new constitution determined that she would spend five more years as president of the nation. The first year had been exhausting. What would the next five years bring? Before the president slept that night, she spent time in prayer thanking God for his mercies.

"It is my fervent hope," she had told a prayer rally just a few days earlier, "that as we face each other and all the difficulties the future brings, we will not waver in our faith in Him who continually showers us with His blessings."[43]

12

Cory's Second Year as President
(26 February 1987–25 February 1988)

We claim to be a Christian nation, and we point to the February Revolution as a marvelous manifestation of our deep faith. Well, those who claim to have faith, but whose deeds do not manifest it, are really not of the faith at all.

According to James: "If a brother or a sister is naked and short of daily nourishment and one of you says to them: Go in peace, keep warm and eat, but you do not give them what they need for their bodies, what good does it do? So even faith, if it does not have the acts of faith, is a dead thing in itself."

We should show our faith from our actions.

President Corazon C. Aquino

Life at best is a perpetual compromise between the ideal and the possible. Through effort and difficulty, ideals sometimes struggle to realization. We have struggled hard for our ideas through endless difficulties and I have no doubt, soon, these ideals will become realities.

Senator Benigno Aquino, Jr.

A Year of Death and New Life

President Aquino walked quickly from her office to the nearby Malacañang Park in the shadow of the palace. Her guards, wearing dark slacks and simple blue barong tagologs, the traditional Filipino dress shirt, walked with her. The five men and one woman wore security passes and carried portable phones and hidden automatic weapons. In the park, the men and women of Cory's full Presidential Security Group snapped to attention. Cory stepped up to a small podium bearing the national seal. She smiled.

"Good morning," she said quietly.

For a moment she stood looking out at the crowd of young men and women who had risked their lives to protect her during the past year of death threats, failed coup t'etats, and assassination attempts. Twenty-four hours a day they had guarded their president from her enemies and even from the masses of enthusiastic Filipinos who often mobbed her entourage and, by their very love for her, endangered Cory's life. As she stood before them, Cory's security group could see in her eyes the respect and the gratitude she felt toward them.

"To our people goes the credit for the restoration of democracy in our country," Cory began. "But to the armed forces go the credit for its immediate defense against its armed foes. Within the armed forces, however, a special force is charged with the difficult task of protecting the seat of government and the person of its leader. That force is the Palace Guard which in our country today is called the Presidential Security Group."

When Cory mentioned the name of their proud unit, the men and women before her cheered. The president looked up from her manuscript and smiled. Through it all they had been by her side. In the good times and the bad they had accompanied her. They had steered her safely through millions of people gathered to see her at the Luneta. On journeys to the United States, to Japan and throughout South East Asia they had accompanied her. They had flown with her to Jolo Island and Davao City in the southern islands and into the rugged Cordillera Mountains to meet with leaders of the various insurgencies. Their bodies had stood between her and the would-be assassins who threatened her life. They had succeeded in keeping her alive and well, and they could see the love in her eyes.

In her short speech that day, President Corazon C. Aquino expressed her "deep appreciation and gratitude." She praised the armed forces as a whole, "the shield and sword of the Republic," but to her Presidential Security Group she added that they had been "the buttress protecting the heart of the Republic."

Before she dismissed them, she added one last word of advice concerning the year to come:

"Oliver Cromwell told his soldiers to put their faith in God but to keep their powder dry."

During the first six months of Cory's second year in office, the young men and women standing before her would be put to the ultimate test. It would be another year of tragic deaths for Cory and the nation. There would be more assassination attempts and more aborted coups. Terrorists would invade the palace grounds. Cory's son, Noynoy, would be shot, but thanks to the brave security forces who died protecting him, the president's only son would survive his wounds.

The Legacy of Senator Jose W. Diokno

Cory's second year in office began with the death of Senator Jose W. "Pepe" Diokno, whom Ninoy had called "the most brilliant Filipino, the one man I would unquestioningly follow to the ends of the earth." In her eulogy, 3 March 1987, President Aquino lauded the human rights lawyer who had been imprisoned by Marcos with Ninoy at the declaration of martial law.

"When the guns speak, the laws fall silent," Cory said, referring directly to the Marcos dictatorship, "until Pepe Diokno stood up, a black toga draped over his shoulders. Immediately, one felt the cause of law and justice pass from [Marcos's] Supreme Court to the accused standing before them."

Just one year before his death, Cory had appointed Senator Diokno as Chairman of the Presidential Commission on Human Rights. She had depended on their old friend's "tremendous intellect and his unshakable integrity" to bring justice to the victims of human-rights abuses throughout the Philippines. How she would miss him!

"We have learned a lot from Pepe Diokno," Cory said. Then she paused to paraphrase three of the great truths that this brilliant human rights advocate had left as his legacy to the Filipino people and to the world:

> Why should we fight against impossible odds? Because being in the right is its own justification and reward.
>
> Why should we be nationalistic? Because no other people will really ever see things from the standpoint of the Filipino.
>
> Why should we put such a premium on our personal integrity, when it is so ill-rewarded in this world? Because we cannot avoid seeing our own faces and living with ourselves. Because if we cannot do right by ourselves, by our souls, we cannot do justice to others . . . .

Death at the Philippine Military Academy

On March 22, Cory addressed the 1987 graduating class of the Philippine Military Academy in Baguio City. Once again she spoke of death, this time the death of Lt. Edgardo Dizon, a member of the graduating class of 1986 who heard Cory explain at his graduating exercise, ". . . the difficulty of waging war for a democracy, of fighting for its honor and integrity without violating its principles."

Before her speech, Cory had visited the place where Lt. Dizon was killed in a battle with the insurgents. "As I came to power peacefully," Cory said to the young officers, "so had I hoped to keep it. God knows, I have tried. But my offers of peace and reconciliation have been met with the most bloody and insolent rejections by the left and the right. It is clear that the forces of the extremes will not leave us in peace to achieve the recovery and progress we so badly need."

Those young graduates knew first hand the bloody results of a terrorist attack. On March 18, just four days before Cory was scheduled to address them, a terrorist bomb had exploded near the speakers' stand at their own school, the Philippine Military Academy in Baguio City. Young soldiers and civilians were killed and mangled by its force.

"March 18, 1987, will live in our memory as the most treacherous act committed against [the PMA] by the enemies of democracy," Cory began. "Here, even before your graduation, you had your first encounter with the enemy. Now you know his methods and the evil he can do. You have seen the fate he intends for us, for your president and your people, if he prevails . . . ."

Tears formed in the eyes of the young graduates, their parents and their teachers as they remembered the four students and civilians who had died and the more than forty others who had been seriously wounded in the attack.

"The enemies of democracy will not play by any rule," Cory reminded them. "And yet we who stand for the truth can only fight with honor and humanity. That is the difficult challenge at fighting a democratic war . . . . Let us pledge to defeat the ambitions of the left and the right to enslave this nation again and bring down our newfound pride . . . .

"To our enemies, let me say that nothing will intimidate this President. Death holds no fear for us, neither for the commander in chief nor for the soldier in the line . . . . Our enemies have delayed the peace and progress for which we have worked so hard. The battle has only begun. But the victory will certainly be ours."[1]

Cory Declares War against Communist Insurgents

Cory had entered her first year in office filled with hope that the same nonviolent revolution which swept out a dictator and carried her into office could prevail over the forces of violence and bloodshed. She had released political detainees; she had offered pardons; she had negotiated cease-fires; she had risked her life to meet with the opposition in their strongholds, all to bring a just and lasting peace to the Philippines. But nonviolent means had failed.

In a more intimate speech before the PMA Alumni Association Cory defined her new policy. She sat at the head table surrounded by military brass and their civilian advisors. It was a day of celebration. The officers and their wives had come to dine with the president. But

Cory was angry. She had just learned that another nineteen of her men were killed in an ambush in Quezon Province.

"These are terrorist acts," she said softly as she stood to address them. "The insurgency of the communists and the treachery of the Right, the [Marcos] loyalists and others, may have deep-rooted causes that may take a long time to remove. Economic development will probably cure both sicknesses. Government efficiency in the delivery of basic services, particularly speedy justice, should speed the cure.

"But the answer to the terrorism of the left and the right need not wait on total solutions. To a terrorist act the *immediate* answer is not social and economic reforms but police and military action."

The officers and advisors sensed Cory's call to battle. They leaned forward in their chairs as their president continued to address them. It was immediately clear that the lady had not come to entertain them with a clever after-dinner speech. She was their commander in chief and she was issuing their orders.

> I told you when we were discussing the peace initiatives that when they fail, as we feared they would, and when it becomes necessary to take up the sword of war, that I want a string of honorable military victories to follow my proclamation of war. Victories of which we can all be proud. Clean victories, aimed straight at the core of the enemy, be it Left or Right, with a minimum of collateral damage to the civilians we are supposed to protect and avenge.
>
> I want these victories. I want justice for the PMA . . . . I want an end to these ambushes, and victories in the field as positive proof to our people that you, the Armed Forces, and I, the Commander-in-Chief, can protect them . . . .
>
> "Gentlemen, let us enjoy the rest of this occasion. But tomorrow it is down to business. Carry on.[2]

Digging Up the Roots of Insurgency

In her speech to the military officers, Cory expressed her two-part agenda for her next year as President of the Philippines: First, she would work on digging up the roots of insurgency, poverty, hunger, despair, government waste and inefficiency, human-rights abuses, graft, corruption and the terrible national debt; but second, she was ordering the Armed Forces of the Philippines to cut off the branches and destroy the fruit of the insurgencies with all the fire power at their command.

Cory knew that members of the AFP in their desire to destroy the insurgents had at times overreacted. Villages suspected of harboring or aiding insurgent forces had been burned. Innocent villagers had been murdered. Captured insurgents had been tortured or killed on the spot before proven innocent or guilty in a court of law. In remote areas, homes, shops, little factories, farms, crops, supplies, and livestock had been pillaged by the military during their search for insurgent forces. Innocent people had been harassed, terrorized, raped, tortured and even killed by members of the AFP or the constabulary forces.

At the beginning of Cory's second year in office, she assigned AFP chief of staff, General Fidel Ramos, to begin a rigorous indoctrination of the military. Immediately, he introduced values formation courses as "a major new component of civil-military operations." Ramos hoped that his seminars, discussion groups and values courses would lead to the end of human-rights abuses by the 180,000 strong AFP and the 60,000 members of the Philippine Constabulary.

These courses were geared to "seek the internal transformation of the soldier into a professional, God-centered, people-oriented, nation-focused individual." And though there was some criticism that Ramos, himself a Protestant, was introducing Christian fundamentalism into the military ranks, most agreed that the General's "Life of the Spirit" seminars and his twelve-session "Christian Life" program that followed was at least an attempt to help bring about a spiritual renewal in the military.[3]

The Muslim Insurgents

Cory was deeply committed to the teachings of Christ. She was convinced that knowing more about Jesus would help end the rash of human rights abuses in the Philippines. But the President was also determined to serve the 5–7 million Muslim Filipinos in her charge. In May, Cory called all Filipinos to join with their Muslim brothers and sisters in the celebration of *Eid-Ul-Fitr*, the culmination of the Muslim holy month of Ramadan.

"To Filipinos of whatever creed or belief," the president said, "the solemn observance of this Muslim holiday serves as a reminder of the diversity of religions and cultures which enriches our national life. For Islam stands side by side with any religion or culture as one of our nation's proud legacies."

The president noted that this Muslim holiday marked the end of a month "of prayer and fasting, of atonement and sacrifice." She reminded all Filipinos that "the goals we seek, particularly peace and progress, can only be won through sacrifice and hard work, patience and perseverance.

"On this holy day," she concluded, "let us join our hands in prayer that Allah may bless our efforts and give us the strength to keep the nation together and bring peace and prosperity to our communities and our people."[4]

In fact, negotiations with the leaders of the Moro National Liberation Front (MNLF), the largest Muslim separatist group in the Philippines, had been going slowly. It appeared that much "sacrifice and hard work, patience and perseverance" would be required by both sides before peace could be won.

On May 9, the cease-fire Cory had negotiated with MNLF chairman Nur Misuari, would come to an end. His representatives had promised a new outbreak of insurgent violence against the government if Muslims were not given autonomy over at least thirteen southern Philippine provinces with Muslim majorities. The Organization of Islamic Countries supported Cory's attempts at a negotiated settlement. Islamic leaders around the world were pressuring Misuari to continue the cease-fire and the talks. Cory promised the Muslim provinces an immediate one billion-peso ($48.8 million) development grant as a kind of motivation to continue the cease-fire dialogue. Misuari threatened military action, but agreed to stay at least temporarily at the negotiating table.[5]

The First National Elections

National elections for the new two-house legislature of the Philippines, established by the nation's new Constitution, were scheduled for May 11. Twenty-four senators would be selected in a national contest and 200 representatives would be chosen from the Provinces for the 250-member House of Representatives. (In establishing this first Congress, President Aquino was ordered to appoint the other 50 members from lists submitted by political parties and "sectoral groups" such as women, tribal minorities and labor unions.)[6]

Once again COMELEC, the government elections agency, and NAMFREL, the citizens election-policing group, would monitor the vote-taking and counting process. And once again, American congressional officials were invited to observe and report their own views about election honesty.

When the votes were counted, representatives of the pro-Cory party, Lakas ng Bayan, held 22 of the 24 Senate seats and an overwhelming majority in the House of Representatives. (Former Defense Minister Juan Ponce Enrile was one of two opposition candidates elected to the Senate.) Once again Cory had received a resounding vote of confidence from the people.

"No one in our delegation saw any serious violations," Senator Al Graham told the president as he spoke for the American team of election observers. "You are a shining example to the whole world and a genuine hero."

Cory Aquino called the May 11 elections "the most peaceful since [Philippine] independence." But she admitted there had been abuses. Terrorist bombs went off in Davao, killing voters and election workers. Military operations against the New People's Army led to ill-timed village evacuations that must have influenced local ballot counts. Opposition party workers were killed. There was some tampering with ballot boxes. At least 20,000 people blocked streets near the AFP and Philippine Constabulary headquarters for 24 hours protesting "election fraud," but the 20 million Filipino voters had been heard. By anybody's standards, Cory's first election had been a vast improvement over the Marcos days when one man's power determined everything.

"During the campaign," Cory announced, "I have often stressed that more important than winning were peaceful and orderly elections . . . . The result was a record 90 percent turnout . . . I challenge any country to match this record. We may be a poor country, but we are very rich when it comes to people power . . . . Where charges of cheating are concerned we have a free press . . . . I hope in the next few days emotions will die down and that the opposition will accept the people's will . . . . This is what a democracy is all about."[7]

Two weeks later, when the emotions had died down and the president had a chance to really celebrate the people's victory, she thanked God for it.

"We thank God for the victory of those who have always stood by democracy," she said nearly three weeks after the election. "We thank God for those who will strengthen and defend democracy in the months and years to come. We thank God for a people who defied the experts again by rising early, patiently awaiting their turn at the polls, and filling out their ballots completely. We thank God for a people whose powers and achievements have been prodigies and miracles. We thank God for our answered prayers, and for miracles yet to come from Him . . . .

"For it is written in Corinthians: 'No eye has seen, no ear has heard, no mind has conceived what God has prepared for those who love Him.'"[8]

On June 12, Cory led the eighty-seventh celebration of Philippine independence from Spain. In the majestic Ceremonial Hall in Malacañang, once again Cory praised the people. "Against rightwing coups and leftwing terrorists, in the plebiscite [to approve the Constitution] and in the recent elections, they gave one astonishing demonstration after another of their deep sense of responsibility and commitment to democracy—as if to underscore what the rest of the world refused to believe, that a people so poor could be so proud and jealous of their freedom."

On 19 July 1987, President Aquino joined with her people in celebrating the bicentennial of the United States Constitution. "The light of freedom that first shone forth in Philadelphia," Cory proclaimed, "now shines as well . . . across the Pacific in Manila."

The lights in Cory's office burned late during the last two weeks of July. On July 27, her extraordinary powers would end. Since abolishing the Marcos parliament, President Aquino had held the nation's legislative power to make laws as well as the executive power to execute them. Her critics called that year and a half of Cory's extraordinary power "the 478 days of one-woman rule."

During that time President Aquino was responsible for the writing of more than 300 laws (executive orders) as well as the new Constitution of the Republic.[9] During those last few weeks before the Congress convened Cory spent long days and late nights in her office taking advantage of her last days of extraordinary power to create and sign laws that she felt were "establishing the framework and climate wherein our people can work in freedom for progress and with a reasonable expectation of a just and lasting peace."

Land Reform

On July 21, "the blizzard of decrees blowing out of Malacañang"[10] included President Aquino's recommendations for land reform in the Philippines. From the beginning of her administration, Cory had struggled with the awful problem of poverty and landlessness. Her Comprehensive Agrarian Reform Program (CARP) was a presidential decree giving the congress a ninety-day deadline to complete legislation to advance the cause of land reform in the Philippines.

In 1981, the government announced that 10 percent of all Filipinos owned 90 percent of the land. And though approximately 35,000,000 Filipinos lived in the rural areas, most of them didn't even own the land on which their little houses stood, let alone land to plant and plow.

In 1985, the Philippine National Census and Statistics Office announced that of the 21.6 million Filipinos in the labor force, 10 million were employed in agriculture. Of these, 5 million were landless workers, 2 million were tenant farmers, 1.5 million worked public lands illegally and only the remaining 1.5 million owned the land they worked.[11]

Cory's family, the Cojuangcos, still owned one of the nation's largest plantations, Hacienda Luisita in Tarlac, Luzon. Ninoy Aquino had been chosen by the Cojuangco family to manage Hacienda Luisita shortly after he and Cory were married. Ninoy had gained farm-management experience while developing his own little farm with his grandfather Servillano Aquino. During the same time he and Cory experienced firsthand the plight and poverty of the landless workers.

Because of their new sensitivities to the problems of landlessness, Ninoy and Cory had begun to pioneer their own kind of land reform. They gave their tenant farmers full title to the plantation land on which their houses stood. Seventy percent of their harvests was shared with their tenant farmers. They provided health care and education to their workers, and they encouraged workers to organize and govern themselves. Eventually they sold their own farm to their workers.

Cory knew that poverty was the underlying cause of insurgencies and terrorism. According to the National Economic and Development Authority, the average six-month family income of the bottom 30 percent of farm families was 5,151 pesos (approximately $250.00). Those same families living in poverty needed at least 5,931 pesos to survive. That meant every six months these families were 780 pesos deeper in debt just trying to meet their basic needs.

"We must raise up the seven million families below the poverty line," the president urged members of the new Congress when she released CARP, her land reform decree, "so they can see the future we want for us all. We look to agrarian reform to bring this about."

President Aquino was well aware that simply dividing up the working farms or plantations and giving little parcels to the people would not end poverty, but she was convinced that some kind of serious land reform was her government's responsibility ". . . to give the vast body of our people a real and rightful stake in the land." Believing that the ultimate goal was worth the conflict and the sacrifice, President Aquino launched CARP, ". . . making this democratic country of ours truly the land of all our people, of the few who are rich and of the multitudes who remain poor."[12]

Another of her unilateral acts just days before the new Congress was convened was to make one last, secret attempt to end the government's long struggle with the Muslim insurgents. On July 21, she offered to create a Muslim Mindanao Autonomous Region under the supervision of an eleven-member Muslim council. Council members would exercise wide power to govern the region under the general supervision of the nation's President. The 15,000 Muslim guerrilla fighters would be converted into a regional security force.

Moro National Liberation Front (MNLF) leader Nur Misuari rejected Cory's plan. Christians living in Muslim-dominated provinces condemned it. In the region fighting broke out again between MNLF and AFP. It was another lost opportunity for peace.

The State of the Nation

On July 27, Cory stood before the first joint session of the nation's new Congress to deliver her State of the Nation address. In her dramatic opening remarks, President Aquino reminded her listeners that fifteen years before, her husband, Senator Ninoy Aquino, had stood in the Senate "and delivered what turned out to be the valedictory of Philippine democracy." Her very presence helped them remember that "the route to these Chambers was long and difficult, fraught with danger and paved with sacrifice."

Cory looked back over her short 17 months in office. When she took power the nation's production had fallen by 11 percent for two consecutive years; unemployment had reached double-digit levels; 2.6 million workers (12 percent) of the labor force were unemployed; real per capita income had been set back 10 years; and interest payments on the $26.3 billion external debt took almost half of the nation's export earnings.

"Poverty blighted the land," she continued. "Five million families (59 percent of the total) lived below the poverty line, as compared to 45 percent in 1971. Dictatorship had done nothing but make more of our people poorer."

The president reviewed her government's goals and achievements. Recession had bottomed out in 1986. The gross national product had posted a modest 1.5 percent growth. And Cory's projections for the first quarter of 1987 included a 5.5 percent growth of the GNP. Exports had grown 21.7 percent. Unemployment had already gone down a full percentage point (even though 750,000 new workers joined the labor force every year). Investments in the Philippines had increased 23 percent. Nearly 7 million people had received food assistance. More than 5 million poor had taken advantage of vital services, including job placement and family planning.

Once again Cory renewed her commitment to dig up "the roots of insurgency" by measures of "economic improvement and equitable distribution." At the same time she admitted that such measures "need time to bear fruit, time that only feats of arms and negotiating from strength can buy us."

She confessed that she was glad to be surrendering power and responsibility to the congress. And the audience applauded enthusiastically when she used the words of Gandhi to describe how all branches of government must work together: ". . . the people will not judge us by the creed we confess or the label we wear or the slogans we shout, but by our work, industry, sacrifice, honesty and purity of character."

In Manila's daily papers the next morning, critics and supporters had a field day in praising and condemning the president. They admitted that key indicators in the first quarter gave hope that Cory's economic program was taking off. But they blamed her for not using her powers more aggressively in solving the economic and social ills, in disciplining and controlling the army, in negotiating lower debt payment with foreign creditors and in winning the war against the 26,000-member New People's Army.

The Assassination of Jaime Ferrer

Three days later, Jaime N. Ferrer, 71, the oldest member of Cory's cabinet and a long-time family friend, was on the way to an early evening mass at a church near his home. Suddenly, heavily armed gunmen using automatic weapons attacked Minister Ferrer and his driver. As local government secretary, Jaime Ferrer had been responsible for replacing local mayors, councilmen and provincial governors with Cory's officers-in-charge. He was accused by his critics of organizing anticommunist vigilante groups in the countryside. Ferrer, the first full-ranking cabinet member assassinated in the history of the Philippines, was fatally wounded by gunshots to the head. He died as he was rushed to the hospital bathed in his own blood.

When told of her friend's death, President Aquino rushed to the San Juan de Dios Hospital to express her condolences to the Ferrer family. "Democracy can survive the death of Jimmy Ferrer," the president said in her eulogy, "as it can survive the deaths that may follow . . . . But democracy cannot survive the adoption of the ways of its enemies."

Because of Ferrer's strong anticommunist views, it was first believed that he was a victim of an NPA "sparrow unit," one of many small squads of assassins believed to be active in the Manila area. Later, suspicion focused on powerful members of the political opposition who wanted to end Ferrer's influence in the coming local and provincial elections.

A week after Ferrer's death, Cory called again for an end to the killing. In the first nine months of 1987, already 600 soldiers and policemen, uncounted insurgents and dozens of local officials had been killed. Cory blamed no one for Ferrer's death or for this rash of politically motivated attacks, firefights, ambushes and murders. But she issued several clear directives to the military, police

and civilian authorities to adopt "sweeping measures aimed at eliminating the alarming proliferation of firearms and impunity of crimes
in our society."

That same day, August 6, in the Hall of Heroes Malacañang
Palace, President Aquino was inducted into the Women's Hall of
Fame by the International Women's Forum. In her response, Cory
expressed her personal feelings about the Ferrer killing and about
the continuing complaint from her critics that she was a weak and
vacillating president.

"People accuse me of being weak because I do not resort to acts of
violence," she said. "Just before I came here I was asked if I were not
disappointed that things are going too slowly in the solution of the
Ferrer murder. And I think this is what democracy is all about. We
cannot just arrest a person or detain a person unless we have all the
sufficient evidence necessary. And perhaps this is what I would like
to tell you today. While we would like to do things instantly or to
bring reforms today or yesterday, sometimes it is necessary to go
through this step by step."[13]

On May 17, in a speech at the opening of National Laity Week in
the Manila Hotel, President Aquino pointed once more to Jesus,
her strength and her guide, ". . . One who chose humiliation,
suffering, and death for Himself to overcome humiliation, suffering
and death for us all." Then she reminded those who would have
her fight violence with violence that Christ's ". . . one solitary life
continues to change our lives today—as one poet wrote—more
than 'all the armies that ever marched, all the navies that ever
sailed, all the parliaments that ever sat, and all the kings that ever
reigned.'"

On August 21 Cory and her family commemorated the fourth
anniversary of Ninoy's death at a mass in the Santo Domingo
Church celebrated by Jaime Cardinal Sin and thirty co-celebrating
priests. Ninoy's assassins had yet to be punished. Three separate
commissions had held hearings. No one doubted the military's direct involvement in the killing. But few believed that the military,
regardless of the presiding chief of staff, would ever be willing to
concede guilt.

One editor wrote, "The inefficiency of the police and the intelligence office is well known, their loyalty to the Aquino government
doubted and even their involvement in some crimes held suspect."[14]
There was growing evidence that powerful military and police officials had the president intimidated. If President Aquino couldn't
even bring justice to her martyred husband, how could she promise
justice to the people?

The Mutiny of 28 August 1987

On August 28, the nation's worst fears were almost realized. Just after midnight, 16 trucks, buses and armored vehicles loaded with more than 1,000 heavily armed troops rolled into Manila. Two of the trucks headed toward Malacañang Palace and the nearby Guest House where Cory and her family lay sleeping. Just after 1:00 A.M., 50 soldiers wearing black ski masks opened fire on the president's security forces with automatic weapons, mortars and grenades.

Just after the attack began, Cory's son, Noynoy, 26, and his four Presidential Security Guards drove into the area from Makati. Noynoy had heard that his mother was under attack. When his driver slowed at the checkpoint in front of St. Jude's Church, mutinous soldiers opened fire. One of Noynoy's guards threw the young man down on the floor of the car covering Noynoy with his own body. Three guards were killed instantly. The fourth was seriously wounded. Noynoy was shot in the neck and left hand.

Civilians and reporters rushed to the scene. Several were caught and killed in the murderous crossfire between rebel troops and presidential security guards. Because the president was scheduled to begin a three-city trip that same day, many of her guards had already departed Manila to set up travel security. Marines were called to help defend the palace; across the city other key targets were simultaneously under siege.

Rebel forces had targeted Channel 4, the government communications center, the headquarters of the Minister of Defense at Camp Aguinaldo, and the Villamor Air Base, adjoining the Manila International Airport. As far away as Cebu, the nation's second largest city, military and civilian targets were under attack. The mutiny was commanded by Colonel Gregory "Gringo" Honasan, a leader of RAM (Reform the Armed Forces Movement) and once the security chief of former Defense Minister Juan Ponce Enrile. The mutineers had planned to overthrow President Aquino and install a military junta as ruling head of the nation.

As Honasan led 300 heavily armed troops into Camp Aguinaldo he told a reporter that the operation was "not a coup" but was aimed at "unification of the people, the concept of justice and true freedom . . . . We've been blamed and ignored so much," he added. "It's time to hear the voice of your soldiers."[15]

"Gringo" Honasan, a dashing soldier-of-fortune type who helped Ramos and Enrile take their stand against Marcos during the People Power revolution, talked his way past guards into the offices of General Fidel Ramos, the AFP chief of staff. Once again he barricaded the building, hoping for popular support for his latest coup t'etat attempt but preparing his rebel soldiers to fight until death if a battle followed.

All across Manila, battles raged. At Channel 4, rebel soldiers fought for nearly six hours to capture the nation's communication's center from its defenders. At 7:30 A.M. they ended their attack and hundreds of Filipino civilians, many wearing Cory T-shirts and waving Philippine flags, rushed to the scene waving and cheering.

By sunrise, Honasan's rebels who had taken Camp Olivas, 35 miles south of Manila, surrendered to government forces. Near the Manila International Airport, renegade troops who had taken Villamor Air Base also gave up the fight. In Cebu, a Brigadier General who had flown the Philippine flag upside down as a sign of support for Colonel Honasan's military coup, surrendered his forces to General Ramos.

But the battle to regain Camp Aguinaldo had just begun. Thousands of civilians gathered on EDSA, the avenue of the People Power revolution, to watch and to cheer loyal government forces as they arrived in armored personnel carriers to begin their assault. One eyewitness described the scene more like a fiesta than a battlefield with vendors selling peanuts, T-shirts, cigarettes and cold drinks to the excited crowd.

In a nationwide address, President Aquino reminded the people not to forget the sacrifices that they made for the return of freedom and democracy during the People Power Revolution. She said the rebels had claimed they were trying to protect "our" children and "our" democracy. "But look what they have done," she replied. "They shot my only son and killed three of his companions and seriously wounded another.

"Speaking as your President," Cory told the nation, "let me assure our people that the government is firmly in control of the situation. We shall defeat and punish these traitors. The Armed Forces and the police, true to their pledge of loyalty to flag, country and Commander-in-Chief, are at this very moment moving to destroy this threat. I commend their bravery."

The attack on the Defense Ministry headquarters at Camp Aguinaldo began in early afternoon. A rebel mortar shell exploded in the crowd of spectators. Two civilians were killed instantly. Dozens more were wounded and thousands scrambled for safety. Intense firing between government and rebel forces continued until two vintage World War II fighter-bombers suddenly appeared in the sky. They bombed and strafed Honasan's positions in the Ministry of Defense until the three-story building was destroyed by flames. The rebellious Colonel Honasan escaped in a waiting helicopter and was flown into hiding with twelve of his officers. The rest of the renegade troops surrendered to General Ramos. Fifty-three soldiers, civilians and mutineers were killed and another three hundred wounded in this fifth and bloodiest coup attempt by rebellious military forces against President Aquino.

In a second nationwide television address Cory insisted that most of the more than 1,000 troops who had joined in this latest coup attempt were tricked by their officers into joining Honasan's rebellion. But there was no way to minimize the seriousness of the threat to her government. According to eyewitness reports, at least another four battalions of rebel infantry (each consisting of 640 armed soldiers) had been turned back at heavily manned roadblocks outside Manila. AFP officers admitted that after Honasan's coup had failed, another 500 to 13,000 suspected rebel sympathizers went AWOL and even military guards outside the Filipino House of Representatives were dismissed for expressing sympathy with the mutineers.

To make matters worse, the Speaker of the House, Ramon Mitra, Jr., and the Senate President, Jovita Salonga, both demanded investigations of the U.S. role in Honasan's coup. During the mutiny, an American military attaché (with long and friendly ties to "Gringo" Honasan) had met with rebel leaders who had taken the Villamor Air Base. An Embassy spokesman explained that the American army officer was just doing his job in staying informed of the military situation in the Philippines. Critics of America's powerful long-term influence in Philippine affairs insisted it was another case of "meddling."

After a flurry of charges and countercharges, the new American Ambassador, Nicholas Platt, who just thirty-six hours before the coup attempt had presented his credentials to President Aquino, relieved the attaché of his post. In Washington, Secretary of State George Shultz warned that "a military takeover would encounter stiff resistance from the U.S." And in Manila, U.S. Assistant Secretary of State Gaston Sigur delivered President Reagan's message of "solid, total and complete support" for President Aquino and her government.

A Government in Chaos

The coup attempt and the storm of charges that followed left Cory's government in disarray. Vice President Laurel resigned his cabinet post as foreign secretary and joined the ranks of President Aquino's opposition. Cory fired her friend, the highly respected finance secretary, Jaime Ongpin. Ongpin had been an outspoken critic of Joker Arroyo, another friend and advisor to the president.

The Manila stockmarket responded to Ongpin's departure from the cabinet with a one-day, ten-point drop. Soon after firing Ongpin, the president was also forced to accept the resignation of Arroyo, who had been severely critical of the nation's military and business leaders.

As Cory struggled to preserve her civilian government, General Ramos rushed to shore up military defenses in Manila and across the country. Cory had praised her loyal troops for teaching rebel forces "their most bitter lesson." But it was growing more apparent that the Armed Forces of the Philippines was divided in its loyalties and fearfully ineffectual in its battle against the insurgents.

Coup leader Honasan remained at large with at least 2,000 of his followers. After the coup, in a brief television appearance from an unknown location, Honasan accused the president of being soft on communist guerrilla forces. He blamed the government for neglecting the common Filipino soldier who earned only $75 a month with a meager food allowance of 60 cents per day. He reminded the nation that even while fighting communist insurgents, Filipino soldiers "must also endure inadequate equipment, medical supplies and even death benefits."[16]

General Ramos was the first to admit that loyal government troops deserved better. But he said that while the nation's "unsung heroes" in the Army had fought and died on the front lines, Honasan—whom Ramos described sarcastically as "everybody's darling"—had spent most of his active service sitting behind a desk. Ramos also denied charges that the AFP was weak or divided and promised that less than 3–4 percent of the 160,000 army regulars would support Honasan in any future coup attempt.

Political and military chaos in Manila brought delight to the 26,000 communist insurgents all across the Philippines. An unprecedented number of NPA attacks on government and civilian targets followed the aborted August 28 coup. In the Bicol peninsula south of Manila, communist forces damaged four key bridges isolating the region. One American official on the scene claimed that communist forces were competing with Cory's government for popular support in 63 of the 73 Philippine provinces.

The President moved quickly to maintain the support and confidence of her people. She made an unscheduled visit to Bicol and ordered the military to launch an all-out offensive "to crush the communist rebel movement in the region." She released scarce government funds to rebuild bridges that the communists had just destroyed to isolate the area.

In a nationwide television and radio address, the president moved to rally the nation against the communist insurgents ". . . who have directed their attacks against the people themselves, affecting their livelihood." And she ordered the military ". . . to stop its defensive posture and carry the war to the rebels."[17]

While President Aquino was besieged by rebel forces from the right and the left, her political enemies in the Philippines and the United States rushed to join the attack. A systematic and well-funded disinformation drive was launched against Cory and her government. Criticism against the president ranged from political weakness to corruption and graft. A barrage of half-truths, exaggerations and lies about Cory and her government was carefully fed the media in both nations. Honasan was described as a modern-day Robin Hood while Cory was described as a weakling and a traitor.

At the same time, Cory was voted, with British Prime Minister Margaret Thatcher, the most important woman in the world. And in Oslo, Norway, the Nobel Peace Prize committee was seriously considering the nomination of Corazon Aquino.

"Unless the Lord Builds the City . . . "

In a satellite telecast upon the public announcement of the first Filipino saint, Lorenzo Ruiz, President Aquino spoke directly to the current conflict and to her continuing faith that God would not desert her or the nation in these times of stress.

> In many ways, the Philippines right now is like Lorenzo Ruiz. It looks like the odds are all against us . . . . Trouble from the right, the threat of a coup, every day . . . . Trouble from the left, the threat of violence from the hills. Trouble in the center, misunderstanding, quarrels, division . . . . But we are safe in the hand of God.
> Unless the Lord builds the city, they labor in vain who build it . . . .
> Unless the Lord guards the city, they labor in vain who guard it . . . .
> Unless the Lord watches over this nation, we labor in vain who govern it . . . .
> If God is with us, who can be against us? We will survive. The ship of state is rocked by waves, but God will bring it to shore.[18]

A New Beginning

On October 20, Cory stepped out of her white government van and walked into the elegant lobby of the Manila Hotel. Cameras flashed and people applauded as she walked through the marble lobby and into the massive ballroom where 1,300 of the nation's leading businessmen were waiting to hear her speak.

The wealthy and powerful Filipinos assembled in that historic place knew that their nation was living through troubled times. They supported the president but they had wondered privately and in public if "the little woman in yellow" could handle the growing crisis. The standing-room-only crowd applauded politely as the president rose to speak. Cory knew that in some ways the People Power Revolution was on trial. She had to convince the leaders of the Philippine business community that the people had not erred in electing her the chief executive of the land.

"You invited me here because you are concerned about the presidency," Cory began quietly, "about the way things are going—or not going—in the economy, in the labor front, in politics, in the war against the communists. Above all," she added with a slight smile, "I am told, you are concerned about me and my leadership."

The room grew silent. Nobody even whispered. Not even a waiter dared to move.

"But first," Cory said, breaking into a relaxed smile, "the formalities. Let me say it is a pleasure to meet with businessmen, 'the engines of economic growth,' as you are referred to in all our economic plans. In the next twenty months, I hope to see many more of you, together with those who work with you, on the shop floor and in the fields of your businesses. Because it is there, where Filipinos put their shoulders to the wheel of our national economy, that our future is made."

Cory explained that she had to mention work at the beginning of her speech because "there has been more talk than work in our country today. That is a pity," she explained, "because recovery and progress won't come through talking."

The businessmen smiled and nodded. There was a quiet ripple of applause. Then step by step Cory proceeded to answer their difficult questions:

About the economy: "We have a detailed plan. We are following the plan to the letter. If you don't like the direction, let us know. We can reopen the debate. This is a democracy . . . ."

About the August 28 coup attempt: "The coup was roundly defeated. The perpetrators are swaying in LST's [prison ships] awaiting trial, and their leaders are in hiding . . . ."

About the government: "The blueprint called for a restoration of democracy, respect for its processes, adoption of a democratic constitution, the establishment of its necessary institutions, an independent and honorable judiciary, an accountable Executive, and a representative legislature . . . and I carried it out to the letter and in record time . . . ."

As Cory spoke frankly and openly to the issues that concerned them, her audience grew even more attentive. A new President Aquino stood before them. The once quiet, bashful Cory had found a new voice. It was strong, sure and convincing.

About the military: "There are groups still resisting their personal and permanent loss of power and prestige, but the military as a whole demonstrated that it is firmly with, not against, the new democracy. I retain full confidence in the professional leadership of the Armed Forces . . . ."

About the insurgency: "First talk, in keeping with my pledge to negotiate a peace that respects law and democracy. And then fight, should it fail . . . ."

About labor: "I believe we must establish a decent, daily wage for all and a flexible bargaining system . . . . [labor and management] must accept the same values that drive our democracy: tolerance, fairness, respect for the law, and a shared commitment to bring progress not chaos to our nation . . . ."

President Aquino did not back away from the issues that troubled them. There was something about her new resolve which made them feel confident that even the impossible tasks could be accomplished.

About foreign debt: "The debt is growing even without fresh borrowing. Servicing the debt alone takes up over 40 percent of the budget and over 45 percent of our export earnings. In the next six years we shall have to pay $20 billion to our official and private creditors, while we shall be getting only $4 billion in additional loans. That means we shall pay out $16 billion more than we will be getting . . . .

"Our [debt] policy has been clear from the start: growth must take priority, for the plain and simple reason that if we have no money to pay, we can't. And if we starve the nation of essential services, there may be no one around willing to honor the debt . . . ."

About Cory: "Can she hack it? Isn't she weak? . . . The honeymoon is over, isn't it? It didn't last very long. By mid-1986, my Cabinet was getting it. By August, the attacks were hitting closer to the presidency. And now, it is out openly against me. The Cory who could do no wrong in those early invigorating months after February, 1986, is seen as having done nothing at all. Nothing, in spite of a constitution, a Congress, and a well-thought-out body of legislation that sets the direction of this nation to progress if you have the courage to follow . . . .

"Still you ask, is she weak? Let my scattered enemies answer that. Still you have reason to ask. For the style of government, by consultation, which I hoped would get your understanding and support, has disappointed you, has given you a sense of drift. It is time again to simplify.

"Henceforth I shall rule directly as president. To the ad hoc committees and commissions created to inform me on their special areas, I now add one more: an action committee with a single member: me! . . ."

After speaking to the practical problems of filling potholes in the nation's streets and highways, collecting the garbage piling high in the streets of Manila and keeping the electrical power flowing to homes and factories across the nation, Cory ended her speech with these words:

"I expect sniping from yesterday's men, passed over as they are, by the march of history. To all other Filipinos I say the tide is with us. Together our future can be as bright as we choose to make it. So judge my leadership as the sum of all our strengths. What sets me apart is that I bring us together where others would divide us . . . ."

That speech marked a new beginning for Cory and her government. The businessmen stood to their feet cheering and applauding as the president walked among them. She had emerged from coup attempts and political chaos with the apparent makings of a tough, no-nonsense chief executive.

Before her second year in office had ended, President Aquino reorganized her cabinet and the nation's military command. She cracked down on *jueteng* and other forms of illegal gambling saying, "Nobody is above the law." She increased her determination to privatize "the non-producing assets and properties of the government."

On December 10, President Aquino announced the capture and imprisonment of Colonel Honasan, the country's most wanted fugitive, with eight of his officers. Fifty soldiers had raided their secret residence in Pasig, an exclusive area of Metro Manila. Honasan did not resist. No shots were fired. Immediately, the rebel colonel denied leading the August 28 coup, declaring the rebellion a spontaneous action by certain dissatisfied military officers. Against the pressure to pardon him, Cory promised that Honasan would face trial for his crimes and be given justice through the due process of law.

On December 12–14, in spite of security jitters, the president hosted a successful summit conference of South East Asian heads of state in Manila. As 1987 drew to a close, Cory refused to fold to pressures for or against the continuation of American bases on Philippine soil. She insisted that all the options be kept open until official negotiations would conclude. Early in 1988 Cory resolved again for all government officials to cut through all unnecessary red tape to deliver necessary services in rapid time.

In January and February of 1988, Cory continued her drive

against terrorism from the right and left and ordered the military to use all necessary force against the insurgents. And she directed all law enforcement agencies not to spare anyone, including her relatives, from lawful arrest if found to be using her name to get away with illegal activity. "No favors, no excuses, no special treatment," shall be extended to anyone found to be violating the law because, she repeated, "Nobody is above the law."

More Tragedy

There were more tragedies during those last months of Cory's second year in office. On December 7 her friend and former Finance Secretary, Jaime V. Ongpin, was found shot to death in his Makati office. At first foul play was suspected. Ongpin had been a man of courage and of controversy. He had left his high salaried position as President of the Benguet Corporation to join Cory's Cabinet. In their debt negotiations with foreign banks he had represented well the Philippines. He had helped bring down inflation and stabilize the peso. Even before the revolution Jimmy Ongpin had served Cory as chief fundraiser and economic speech writer.

Police investigators concluded that former Minister Ongpin had taken his own life. After leaving Cory's cabinet he had suffered from depression. He had worked so hard for the nation's economic growth. It was difficult for him to understand the politics that led to his firing. When at last Jimmy Ongpin's wife released the suicide note her husband had written, it said simply, "I beg your forgiveness for the unforgivable act of taking my own life." At his funeral mass President Aquino delivered an eloquent eulogy for her old friend and supporter.

The 1987 calendar year, plagued with so many deaths, would end for Cory with one more tragic announcement. On December 22, the passenger liner *Doña Paz* collided with an oil tanker off Marinduque. Over 2,000 Filipinos died when the liner turned over and sank.

"I grieve with our people as we mourn this heart-rending loss of so many lives," Cory said on a nationwide telecast. "Our sadness is all the more painful because the tragedy struck with the approach of Christmas."

Four Christmas Wishes

At Christmas, Cory called a moratorium on military offensives. The guns were temporarily quiet. The president and her family worshiped together and then sat down for the traditional *noche buena* like millions of other Filipino families.

Cory had four Christmas wishes that year. First, "that there be peace." Second, "a better quality of life for all Filipinos, especially the poor." And third, that "God will always guide me in all my decisions."

She also had a fourth, she told a reporter, but that, she said with a smile, will remain a private wish.[19]

On 15 January 1988, a survey of a wide cross section of Filipino adults found that Cory's popularity with the people had risen from 57 percent in October, 1987, just before she spoke to the city's leading businessmen, to 66 percent in 1988. A Gallup International Research Institute poll found that Cory's rating in Manila had increased to 77 percent approval. Those who expressed their approval were citing Cory for her good administrative leadership, for her integrity, for the country's economic recovery, for restoration of democracy and for the improved peace and order situation.

The First Local Elections

Cory didn't have much time to bask in the warmth of her standings in the newest popularity polls. On 18 January 1988, Filipinos would elect 17,000 provincial and municipal officials. On that day roughly 80 percent of the 27.6 million registered Filipino voters would select 73 provincial governors and vice-governors, 60 mayors and vice-mayors of the country's smaller towns and 446 provincial board members.

Election day was fairly peaceful, but the eight weeks of campaigning before election day were marred with violence and death. The AFP reported 91 pre-election shootings. Fifty-seven candidates, their aides or key supporters, had died by January 9. Local feuds between the political parties caused most of the deaths.

Cory urged the candidates to "conduct their campaigns with more sobriety and respect for the democratic process." The president asked that the "wave of electoral violence and killings must stop at the very least." It was the president's sincere wish "that the New Year will usher in a period where our citizens will have a little more compassionate attitude for one another."[20]

On 25 February 1988, President Aquino ended her second year in office. It was a year marred by violence and tragic death. Nevertheless, it was a year of victory for Cory and her government. She was selected by the world's press as "Newsmaker of the Year." Stories depicting her presidency were headlined: "One Tough Cory" or "Aquino, Woman of Steel." The Filipino economy was on the rise. Cory's promises to the Manila businessmen were coming to pass.

The Second Anniversary of the People Power Revolution

On the second anniversary of the People Power Revolution, Cory arrived by helicopter at Camp Aguinaldo at exactly 7:00 A.M. Already, the streets and boulevards of Manila were crowded with Filipino men, women and children making their way to EDSA and the second celebration of their freedom from the Marcos regime.

Cory trooped the honor guard from four major military services and then received a twenty-one-gun salute. At the flag-raising ceremonies at Camp Aguinaldo, Cory stood alongside June Keithley, the radio announcer who became the voice of Radio Veritas during the People Power Revolution.

Then as the crowds descended on the celebration, President Aquino stood between Fidel Ramos, her minister of defense, and General Renato de Villa, her new chief of the AFP. They grasped hands with thousands of others in a huge human chain to pray for peace. As church bells rang, prayers for peace were recited in various Filipino dialects. Cory's guards struggled to keep the crowds away as Cory prayed for fifteen minutes with her head bowed and her eyes closed. Before the human chain was broken, the people all joined in singing, "Let there be peace on earth and let it begin with me."

By mid-morning hundreds of thousands of Filipinos filled EDSA and the Rizal Park for the second anniversary celebration of the People Power Revolution. Once again bands played, horns honked, church bells pealed and helicopters whirled overhead, dropping flower petals on the crowd.

In the afternoon Cory returned to the celebration, this time accompanied by her daughters, Ballsy, Pinky, Viel and Kris, her son, Noynoy, her two sons-in-law, Manny Abeleda and Eldon Cruz, and her two grandsons, Jiggy and Miguel. They worshiped at the corner of EDSA and Ortigas Avenues where earlier in the year Cory had dedicated a monument to peace with these enduring words:

"We thank God for the peace we now celebrate and seek to sustain," she said, "not only here in this intersection that was the crossroads of our destiny, but everywhere in this country that seeks His wisdom, mercy and strength."

The president closed her dedication remarks with a passage from the New Testament that must mean more and more to Cory as the years passed by.

"Christ said, 'My peace I leave with you; my peace I give you. I do not give to you as the world gives. Do not let your hearts be troubled and do not be afraid.'"

13

Cory's Third Year as President
(26 February 1988–25 February 1989)

I have worked with all my might and prayed with all my heart. The rest I leave to God and to you, my people. Let us not hold our breath for total answers coming from anywhere but our own efforts by which we won our freedom. The main effort is ours to do, so the greater honor will be ours again.

Let us get on with it then for what else is there to wait for? The time of talk and hesitation and criticism is over. The time for action is now.

President Corazon C. Aquino

We humans can make things better, but we can never make them perfect. "Better, yes; perfect, never."

Senator Benigno Aquino, Jr.

The Muslim Insurgents

One day after celebrating the second anniversary of the People Power revolution, on 26 February 1988, President Corazon Aquino stepped off her airplane onto Tawi-Tawi soil. Television cameras recorded the historic scene. No Philippine president had ever bothered to make an official visit to this beautiful island group in the southern tip of the Philippine archipelago.

Tawi-Tawi had become a two-edged symbol to Cory. For too long Filipinos living in these southern islands felt far away from the heart of power and patronage in Manila. But President Aquino had been elected to serve 55 million Filipinos and to Cory that meant all of them, even those in faraway Tawi-Tawi just north of Borneo. And secondly, this southern area, including Mindanao, Palawan and the Sulu Islands, is the home of most of the 5–7 million Filipino Muslims. These Muslim Filipinos were Cory's people, too.

222

The president's security guards looked nervously in all directions as she shook hands with local officials and spoke words of greeting to the hundreds of islanders who had assembled to welcome her to this isolated region of the nation.

"Let my presence this morning convey a clear and compelling message," the president began. "Tawi-Tawi is part and parcel of the Philippines and Cory Aquino is as much the president of Tawi-Tawi as she is of Tarlac."

Cory knew that the basic needs of these southern island areas had been sadly and shamefully neglected, even as its resources had been exploited. She also knew that the rights and the needs of the southern Muslim minority had too long been neglected by Catholic and Protestant Christians to the north. For almost two decades the Moro National Liberation Front (MNLF) had been fighting an insurgent war to gain Muslim autonomy in the region. In that time some 100,000 Muslims and Christians had been killed in the fighting between the MNLF and the Armed Forces of the Philippines; another one million had been rendered homeless.

As a senator, Ninoy Aquino had struggled for the rights of the Muslim minority. After his heart surgery in America, Ninoy traveled to Saudi Arabia to confer with Nur Misuari, the exiled Chairman of the MNLF, to help mediate between the Philippine government and the MNLF. In her first months in office, Cory traveled to Jolo Island to begin another round of talks with Nur Misuari on their shared concerns. Misuari, a former university professor, presided over perhaps 15,000 well-armed, well-trained guerrilla fighters. The president had traveled to Tawi-Tawi to show her concern for the Muslim peoples in practical and political ways.

"In the name of God the most merciful, the most kind," Cory concluded, ". . . let us work out a genuine autonomy law for Mindanao—one that stems from the wellsprings of our people and one that is not imposed upon them."

The Communist Insurgents

After addressing the problem of the Muslim insurgency, Cory rushed back to Manila to discuss with the newly elected governors and mayors her government's battle plan in the on-going war with the communist NPA. Cory seemed genuinely committed to the fact that communist insurgency would not be defeated by arms alone. Time and time again, the president warned the nation that poverty, hunger, homelessness, unemployment, inadequate medical care, inequality and injustice were the roots of insurgency.

"Until our nation's poor have an appreciably better life," Cory said in her new year's address, "we will be plagued by insurgencies."

At first Cory gave communist leaders the benefit of the doubt. She knew their ranks were filled with sincere Filipino men and women who wanted to end the suffering of the poor. From her first day in office, Cory had reached out to the insurgents. She had freed their leaders from military prisons and met with them face-to-face in hopes of negotiating a lasting peace.

But from the beginning, the insurgents didn't trust the government, not even Cory Aquino's. And the military replied in kind. Although Cory was sincere, negotiators from both sides seemed to negotiate in bad faith. Both the communist NPA and the Armed Forces of the Philippines used Cory's temporary cease-fire to prepare for renewed battle. Even before the cease-fire ended, the insurgent war broke out again. And in spite of all the rhetoric, there was nothing noble or principled about the conflict. The "war against the insurgents" had become a bloody fight for turf with the poor once again caught in the middle.

The president was trying to control her military and police, but there seemed to be no "democratic" let alone a "Christian" way to fight the war. Human rights atrocities were being committed by both sides on combatants and innocent civilians alike. Insurgent and government forces confiscated priceless foodstuffs and local supplies. Irreplaceable farming implements, manufacturing equipment, transportation and communication systems and prized personal possessions were damaged or destroyed. Women and children were raped and abused. Towns and villages were burned. Whole provinces were terrorized and held hostage. Innocent bystanders were kidnapped, tortured and killed. The people's dreams at EDSA in 1986 were never really given a chance to come true before the Philippines became a bloody war zone once again.

Money to support the NPA insurgents came from a variety of Philippine sources. The National Democratic Front, a communist-led umbrella organization made up of 13 illegal Philippine revolutionary groups, collected taxes in their areas of influence. Small businessmen, farmers and individuals were taxed by the "Provisional Revolutionary Government" which described itself as having "a growing ability to function as a government" which will encourage Filipino businesses "neglected [by the government in Manila] whose national economic policy is one of enslavement to big foreign capital."[1] Corporations operating plantations, mines, logging operations and other enterprises in N.D.F. areas often had to pay to avoid harassment by the insurgents—and even to say in business.

There was a time when Cory Aquino's leadership had threatened the future of communism in the Philippines. After the People Power revolution, insurgent leaders had reason to believe that Cory's presidency would be different from the others. At first, the communists had no real excuse to continue their operations. Even Cory's enemies had to admit that their new president was saying all the right things. She seemed genuinely interested in those who suffered and sincerely determined to use her power to help end the suffering. It was obvious that Cory meant well, but everyone began to wonder if she had the necessary power or resolve to bring lasting change.

After all, President Aquino was a member of one of the nation's richest families, the Cojuangcos. She might be sincere, but what about the members of her wider family? After Ferdinand and Imelda fled the country, Aquinos and Cojuangcos seemed to be taking over the businesses and the powerful political offices that the Marcos and Romualdez families had left behind.

During her first two years in office, insurgent leaders began to doubt Cory's long-term commitment to radical social change. Raised in wealth and comfort, she was part owner of one of the largest farms in the nation. She had politicians on both sides of her family all the way back to Spanish colonial rule. Though she spoke the right words, the actions didn't seem to follow.

Besides, the insurgents believed that greed, graft and corruption were historic forces in the Philippines that no one, not even Cory, could overcome. The insurgents were also afraid that Philippine military and business interests aided by the Americans were using Cory's popularity with the public to maintain their own private control of the nation and its resources. They would let her dream, but the forces working against her had the power to guarantee that Cory's dreams would never really come true.

So, right or wrong, the communists refused to join in Cory's democratic revolution. The Communist Party of the Philippines continued to advocate the violent overthrow of Cory's elected government. And while she worked to dig up the roots of the insurgency, Cory saw no other choice but to order her troops to launch a full-scale war against the insurgents.

Death and destruction followed in towns and villages across the Philippines. The president grieved for the innocent Filipinos who were dying in the cross fire. She had tried to make peace with the insurgents. She continued to speak out against the excess use of force by military and police alike. But communist strength had steadily grown. The threat to national security was real. Her advisors told her that there were more than 25,000 armed guerrilla fighters based in approximately 8,000 of the nation's 42,000 barangays (local districts). Cory had tried to end the war; instead, it was spreading from the isolated countryside into towns and cities, including Metro Manila.

Communist cadres were using their secret neighborhood centers for terrorist attacks and sabotage on vital public facilities, military and police stations and town halls. In 1987 alone, communist guerrillas were responsible for 3,118 reported acts of violence in the Philippines, more than eight violent acts every day.

And to make matters worse, President Aquino faced the continuing threat by ultra-rightist groups to local and provisional security. She was relieved when government forces finally captured Colonel Honasan, the leader of the bloody August 28 coup attempt and she felt confident that the coup attempts were over; but vigilante groups, private "security forces," insurgent guerrillas and errant soldiers and police posed a real threat to the nation's peace and security. During the January 18 election alone there had been a total of 286 election-related violent incidents resulting in 157 persons killed (43 candidates), 215 wounded and 22 others missing.

Cory's Insurgency Policy

At a meeting on 4 March 1988, with the nation's newly elected governors and mayors, President Aquino announced her government's "three pronged strategy for reconciliation, security and development."

First, ". . . the military is responsible for security to allay the fear of the people;"

Second, ". . . the police will be responsible to maintain peace and order;"

Third, "the civil side of government, supported by the military and the private sector, will accelerate economic developments to lessen if not totally eliminate poverty, give emphasis to spiritual and moral values to correct injustices and make education available to all to eradicate ignorance."[2]

It was President Aquino's goal that 1988 would be "the year the insurgency was broken." And late in March, her government's planning showed at least one impressive result in that direction. Cory's "Special Operations Team" captured a communist communications center on the outskirts of Manila. On March 28, computer disks were seized, including a full list of foreign reporters who were in regular contact with the insurgents.

Unfortunately, the data also revealed that communist insurgents were increasing their acts of violence in the two largest cities of the Philippines and across the nation. Communist assassins, called "sparrow units" by the press, had killed 120 persons in Manila in 1987 (a figure that matched the AFP estimates). In Cebu, the second largest city in the Philippines, "sparrow units" accounted for 337 violent acts during that same year.[3]

Colonel Honasan Escapes

Unfortunately, for Cory and the Philippines, the problems of violent communist, Muslim, or ultra-rightist insurgencies continued to be a headache that refused to go away. The president's problem with "insurgent" forces in her own military continued as well. On April 2, Colonel Honasan, the leader of the bloody coup attempt, escaped from a prison ship in Manila Bay. Fourteen of his military guards conspired to free Honasan in two rubber boats equipped with outboard motors. Cory and the Congress demanded immediate probes of the "Black Saturday" escape. The president was furious. She ordered Honasan's immediate capture and imprisonment. But to the president's embarrassment, the colonel and his associates continued to avoid arrest.

The AFP was proving itself ineffectual at policing itself, let alone at winning the war against the insurgents. However, during the president's state visit to China in April, 1988, Cory got support in her anti-insurgency campaign from one totally unexpected source.

President Aquino in the People's Republic of China

On April 15, in the Great Hall of the People in Beijing, President Corazon Aquino was the first head of state to visit with Yang Shangkun, the new President of the People's Republic of China, and with his Premier, Li Peng of the State Council.

On that occasion, China vowed to support the Philippines in its battle with the communist insurgents. After giving the Philippine president "a modest gift" of 10,000 metric tons of rice, the Chinese leaders promised that their government ". . . will not interfere in the internal affairs [of the Philippines]." Yang reiterated that "It is our firm policy to develop long-term and steady good neighborly and friendly relations with your country . . . ."[4]

Economic Reform

On May 1, Cory stood before the television cameras and radio microphones to deliver her nationwide Labor Day address. While she fought the insurgents with one hand, Cory continued to fight the cause of insurgencies with the other. On Labor Day she announced both victories and defeats in her battle to improve the conditions of the working people in the Philippines and those who would like to work but could not find employment.

"There is a widespread notion that Labor Day is the one day of the year where government pays attention to labor," the president began. "That day is regarded as the day of the laborers as opposed to the 364 days of the capitalists and managers. That was true under the dictatorship," she declared. "It is not true in this democracy. For me, every day is Labor Day—because it is the daily labor of the workman that sustains our economy and society, and brings us closer to the national strength and prosperity we seek."

Cory seemed sincere in her efforts to improve life for Filipino workers. And there were signs that her government was making a difference. Unemployment rates fell from 11.8 percent in 1987 to 9.2 percent in 1988. And programs were initiated to improve education in literacy, mathematics and science, those fields of study that Cory knew had been responsible for the remarkable productivity and inventiveness of Japanese, Korean and Taiwanese labor.

The president was building new job-training centers and she had commissioned a more effective population-control program. Price rollbacks were ordered on gasoline, kerosene and diesel fuels to help reduce the cost of living. Government expenditures for public health and nutrition were increased. By June, free secondary education would finally be available. Expenditures for education had been increased from 15 to 18 billion pesos. Funding for housing had been increased to 4.4 billion pesos to build 32,800 new low cost housing units. The president ordered mortgage rates lowered from the current 13 percent to 9 percent.

During her short term, Cory had managed to limit the number of strikes that might cripple industry and further depress the nation's economy. And she had managed to build a close working relationship with the Japanese who had become the nation's number one benefactor. Japan had far surpassed the United States in financial and technical aid to the Philippines during this critical time of economic renewal.[5]

Land Reform

At 4:00 P.M. on June 10 the churches around the presidential palace rang their bells as President Aquino signed the land reform bill into law. Gathered around Cory were the leaders of the nation: Senate President Jovito Salonga, Speaker Ramon Mitra, cabinet secretaries, other senators and congressmen, special dignitaries and guests.

President Aquino had first proposed her land reform legislation to Congress on 21 July 1987. She had given them a ninety-day deadline to write a comprehensive law that would advance the cause of land reform. The debate in both houses raged for 210 days before Cardinal Sin, in his sermon during the People Power celebration on 25 February 1988, chided the legislators for dragging their feet on land reform.

In his sermon that day (with Cory and the Congress present), Sin called on the people "to beg the Lord for the grace of a second miracle—a genuine, far-reaching, effective land reform."[6] Cardinal Sin declared that "ownership of land in the hands of a few is not in God's plan." Using the Scriptures as his evidence, the Cardinal informed his flock that "land reform is about the human dignity of those who till the soil." He said, "It is a matter of justice for them, and for Christians it is a matter of God's preferential love for the poor."

It had taken sixteen months of careful scrutiny and compromise to develop Cory's Comprehensive Agrarian Reform Program (CARP) into law. With the nation's press looking on, Cory signed the measure saying, "I hope this act will end all the acrimony and misgivings of the contending parties and unite the nation behind the effort to make agrarian reform a success in our country."

Thirty-five million Filipinos who lived in rural areas were landless. Of the nation's 10 million farmers, 8.5 million didn't own a share in the land they tilled while a handful of wealthy absentee landlords owned most of the nation's tillable soil. President Aquino and her Congress were taking steps to remedy hundreds of years of injustice and poverty.

In some cases, the government would buy land from its owners with cash and government bonds and extend to landless tillers and farmworkers the right of directly or collectively owning the land they tilled. Beneficiaries would pay for the land in 30 yearly payments at 6 percent interest to the Land Bank of the Philippines.

In other cases, owners would keep the lands but workers, managers, technicians and supervisory staff would be included in fair profit-sharing plans. Approximately 7 million hectares (more than 17 million acres) of land would be distributed by the government nationwide to landless tenants and other qualified farmers under CARP.

The cost in pesos would be high. Even using lands sequestered from former President Marcos and his cronies, foreclosed lands in government ownership, idle and voluntarily offered lands, and publicly owned lands, the land reform package would ultimately cost the government approximately 170 billion pesos over its ten-year duration. Funding would come from sales of government assets at home and abroad, from heavy foreign and domestic borrowing by the government and from the anticipated return of the ill-gotten wealth of Marcos and his cronies.

In spite of the cost and the criticism rising up from land owners (who said it was too much) and from radical farm organizations (who said it was too little), Cory pressed forward with her plan.

"I remain firm in my conviction," she said, "that agrarian reform is the key to lasting peace and certain progress in our country. I am appealing to all our countrymen to give the program all their support and encouragement. I am appealing to the landowners, do not look at agrarian reform as a taking of your land but as an opportunity for wider partnership of all our people toward progress and peace."

When reporters asked the president about Hacienda Luisita, the Cojuangco family's 14,000-acre farm in Tarlac employing over 7,000 farmworkers, Cory replied:

"Hacienda Luisita will, I repeat, will comply . . . ."[7]

When the president was questioned about the farmlands owned by other members of her cabinet and staff, she answered with a confident nod of affirmation.

"We are a team," she said. "We will work as a team for agrarian reform for our people and for our future."

On June 11, Cardinal Sin responded to the critics of Cory's land-reform legislation. In a sermon that he preached in the Central Bank Building on A. Mabini Street, where the Senate-House conference committee debated the CARP measure, the cardinal urged the nation to unite in prayer for its success.

"We are seeing another miracle unfold," the Cardinal announced. "CARP is to be our common undertaking as a people; its success, our common success. If we are not, in fact, one in heart and mind, as the first disciples were, no CARP legislation, no matter how well debated and finalized will work.

"If we believe that it is truly God's will that every person has the right to possess a sufficient amount of the Earth, goods for himself and his family . . . then we must also believe that if we do what we understand to be His will, God will reward our efforts with the results which would be best for each one of us . . . ."

The archbishop of Manila and the most powerful churchman in the Philippines went on to mourn the realities that made CARP "absolutely necessary . . . ."

> . . . seventy percent of our people live below the poverty line; one out of every four children born in our country dies before he reaches his first birthday. We see beggars on the streets; we see sick people unattended to; we see people who have no homes; we see people scavenging through garbage piles, and we ask ourselves: Why?

Even the poor pray the "Our Father." Why do they not have their "daily bread"? How can it be that in this country, often referred to as the only Christian country in this part of the world, there be such a big gap between the rich and the poor? How can this be if the 45 million or so Filipino Christians, particularly the rich among them, were truly living their daily lives aware of Jesus' teachings and words, "I was hungry and you gave me to eat . . .", "Love one another as I have loved you . . . ."

Might it be that such a sad situation exists because we stand in the way of God's goodness, and fail to cooperate in His will for his children? CARP . . . calls for unity in prayer: not for the victory of landlords over landless, nor of landless over landlords. Rather what is called for is unity in the prayer that there come to be the miracle of sharing with one another the gifts which God has given to each one of us . . . .

The landowners are to share not only their lands, but also concern for the future of those who will receive land from them. The landless are not only to receive land but also share in the task of drawing from the land the maximum it can yield from their labor.[8]

Cory Visits Europe

Early in the summer, President Aquino made her first state visit to Europe. In Berne, Switzerland, Cory accepted a gift-loan assistance package of 60 million francs (900 million pesos) to help finance her development programs in the Philippines.

In Italy, Cory was met at the Ciampino Military Airport with a twenty-one-gun salute and driven through the ancient streets of Rome to the Quirinale Palace where she was welcomed by President Francesco Cossiga and representatives of the 70,000 Filipinos who live in Italy. She thanked the Italians for their long-time friendship with the Philippines and for importing in the past year more than $35 million worth of Filipino products.

In Rome, Cory was escorted into the Vatican by Swiss guards and papal officials. She exchanged gifts with John Paul II in his private study and discussed the urgency of her development program in the Philippines with the Pope and Augustino Cassaroli, the Vatican Secretary of State. In her papal address, Cory described the People Power Revolution as that day ". . . when God's hand, working through the multitude of men, women and children, snatched my country from the edge of calamity and gently set it down in peace and freedom."

Cory's Goals for the Philippines

After acknowledging the contribution of Catholic missionaries "and our Muslim brothers" to the shaping of "the general character of the Filipino nation," the president described the five principles of development she had followed in her brief two years and three months in office. According to Cory, "development must:

. . . enhance the well-being and dignity of Filipinos from every walk of life, so that the nation's material progress must be matched by the Filipino's spiritual development . . .

. . . promote the unity of the nation and solidarity among the people; [not accepting] exploitation and class hatred as a necessary price. Fair to all, yet lean in favor of the poor who need to be helped . . .

. . . restore and preserve the values that distinguish the Filipino nation: faith in God and in the power of prayer, industry and honesty, love of country, respect for the unity of the family . . .

. . . increase our capability to stand on our own, to be self-reliant and autonomous in the world, so that we can be useful and helpful members of the community of nations . . .

. . . promote private enterprise and initiative, consistent with the common good and our democratic institutions . . .

Cory concluded with her belief that ". . . peace will come only through authentic development that fosters justice and solidarity. Development by any other path will lead only to violence and tyranny, of the left or of the right.

"In the midst of great difficulties, we tread our way to the future with a certain assurance drawn from our conviction that God walks with us, and guides us in the darkness with the teachings of His Church."[9]

Human Rights and the National Debt

In Geneva, Cory thanked banking officials for providing the Philippine government with the records of Ferdinand and Imelda Marcos's secret Swiss bank accounts filled "with their ill-gotten wealth stolen from the Filipino people."

President Aquino also addressed the 75th International Labor Conference in Geneva. Speaking in fluent French, Cory reiterated her commitment to human rights in the Philippines. "The first duty of democratic institutions is the protection of human rights." But Cory went on to warn them that "Chronic underdevelopment is the systematic abuse of human rights."

President Aquino made it clear that the present restraints on human freedom are "imposed by poverty and underdevelopment." Human liberation "must be economic," Cory declared, "which includes a fair resolution of the debt problem. For the tightening grip of its austerities threatens to strangle the life out of the new democracies of the Third World, even as it threatens to upset the stability of the international economic order . . . . The linkage of debt, development and democracy is undeniable and is the most pressing issue this body must address."[10]

International labor leaders praised President Aquino's impressive speech. Blas F. Ople, a Filipino and the first Asian to be elected president of the International Labor Organization, said that Cory's address would help trigger action with the International Monetary Fund (IMFF) and the World Bank (WB) to lighten the foreign debt crisis, "which has become a specter threatening the lives of workers all over the world." He praised Cory for her determination to repay her nation's debt, but supported her efforts to negotiate debt and interest reductions and new low-interest loans to assist in the repayment process.

He reminded the world's banking community that the Philippines had to pay $2 billion of its meager foreign currency earnings that year just to service the $29 billion foreign debt it inherited from the Marcos regime.

"In the Philippines," Ople said, "the workers, farmers and the common men bear the burden" of that debt. Cory could not improve the lives of her people or end the problems of violence and terror unless she could reduce the debt load and free up needed monies to develop the programs that would produce jobs and reduce poverty, hunger, homelessness and despair.[11]

After a sixteen-hour flight from Geneva and a three-hour layover in Thailand, President Aquino arrived at the Ninoy Aquino International Airport and was driven across Manila to her home near the Malacañang Palace. Through the window of her white government van, Cory must have been stunned again by the evidence staring up at her that the Philippines is truly a nation in life-and-death struggle against "poverty, hunger, homelessness and despair."

The Problem of Poverty

Along the president's route of travel were thousands of squatter huts built on the beaches and seawalls facing scenic Manila Bay and in empty lots or abandoned buildings on Manila's streets and boulevards. She could see children and women in rags carrying babies, thrusting outstretched hands into open windows. Among the professional beggars, she could see Filipinos who were obviously hungry and ill, the wives and children of unemployed farmers and workers from the countryside who had poured into Manila hoping to find food, jobs, education and medical aid.

Housing had become an overwhelming problem to Cory and her government. In the actual incorporated area of Manila alone, there were an estimated 2.5 million squatters, about a third of the city's total population. In 1987, Cory's National Housing Authority advised the president that there were more than 3.5 million squatters in the greater Metro Manila area alone.[12]

Cory struggled to mobilize national, provincial and local forces on behalf of the poor in Manila, a city *Newsweek* called, "a frightening showcase of a nation's suicidal instincts." The editors reported that "the four cities and 13 municipalities of the metropolitan area contain some of the biggest and most squalid slums in Southeast Asia."[13]

Cory had agonized over Tondo, a barrio just minutes from downtown Manila, where 16,000 squatters lived on a mammoth pile of the city's garbage known as Smokey Mountain. She ordered her bureaucrats to find ways to end the shame and suffering of the cities' slums, but not much seemed to happen.

There were those who advised the president to bulldoze the squatter cities that were springing up across Metro Manila. But she knew those tiny shacks, ("barong barongs") put together from scraps of wood, cloth and tin, were the only homes for thousands of desperate and destitute Filipinos. Somehow they had managed to buy or salvage sheets of plastic or tin for a roof and wood or cardboard for their walls and flooring. The president knew that many of the squatters had exchanged what little money they had for the "ownership" to their ten-foot square of land, only to discover when the police chased them away or, when their little home was bulldozed, that their "broker" was just another crook.

Cory continued to struggle with small budgets and sluggish bureaucracies as thousands of new squatters moved into Manila every day and the population of the Philippines continued to grow, plunging the nation even deeper into poverty. The president's population control programs showed some signs of working. The growth rate had decreased from an annual rate of 3.1 percent (almost 1.5 million births yearly) to about 2.3 percent. Still, after subtracting mortality rates, 3,750 more Filipinos were being born daily and almost 100,000 new births were recorded every month.[14]

The president was personally committed to population control programs but the Catholic hierarchy continued to oppose them. Just during her drive across the city, approximately 24 new Filipino babies had been born. By 1989, there would be approximately 60 million people in the Philippines. By the year 2,000 there would be 84 million Filipinos and just 16 years after that, the population of the Philippines could double to 116 million.[15]

Working with the private sector, Cory's government had already been responsible for the creation of hundreds of thousands of new jobs. Still, the unemployment rate staggered the president and her advisors. With at least 6 million underemployed or unemployed Filipinos already searching for work, at least 700,000 new job-seekers joined the workforce every 12 months.

Cory had worked to raise the minimum wage, but those Filipinos with jobs were still earning barely enough to survive. The average low-income wage-earner received less than 60 pesos ($3) a day. The average poor family had to spend at least 120 pesos ($6) a day just to survive.[16] And real wages had dropped by almost 30 percent in what they could actually buy since 1960.[17]

Cory knew that to make up the difference between what a father earns and what the family actually needs, each member of the poor Filipino family had to hustle. She was angry that so many young Filipino women had to accept employment as barmaids, call-girls and massage parlor attendants for the "sex tours" conducted for foreign tourists and the bustling communities just outside the American military bases. She worried about the thousands of young Filipino women who departed from their homeland every year for jobs abroad as maids and "companions." And Cory protested vigorously when she heard it rumored that a well-known European dictionary recently defined "Filipina" as "a domestic servant."

And though she fought it, President Aquino was aware that child labor had become a "necessary evil" in the Philippines, with youngsters doing piecework in the garment and embroidery industries, getting day jobs as private maids and janitors, doing household chores and running errands for the rich. She knew that for these demanding and often demeaning jobs, children as young as seven and eight years old toiled twelve hours a day for the equivalent of seventy-five cents to ten dollars a week.

The president was especially angry that child prostitution had become common in the Philippines and as she rode through the city, Cory could see children darting in and out of busy traffic islands selling single cigarettes, mouth mints and newspapers while wives, older women and younger children sifted through the cities' garbage salvaging bits and pieces to sell or trade or even feed their families.[18]

And in the countryside, the poverty was equally staggering. In her speeches, Cory announced that farmland settlement density in the Philippines (640 persons per square kilometer) was higher than in Indonesia and nearly twice as high as in Thailand. Cory was struggling against incredible odds: While 52 percent of all Filipinos lived in poverty, Indonesia fared better with 39 percent, Thailand with 31 percent and Malaysia with 28 percent.[19] The farmer's plight was worsened by low productivity. Philippine farm incomes averaged only $500 per hectare (2.41 acres) compared to $2,300 in China, $4,000 in Taiwan and $5,400 in South Korea.[20]

Having no land on which to raise their own food, inadequate farming skills and with foodstuffs generally expensive or in short supply, more than thirty million Filipinos were undernourished. Cory knew that most of her people lived on rice, dried fish and salt. She had learned that this poverty diet effects the unborn and the newborn, leaving millions of Filipino children with permanent physical and mental handicaps.

As Cory and her government struggled to improve the nation's infrastructure, millions of Filipinos had no running water or electricity. In the absence of toilets and sewers, waste and trash were left in the streets or tossed into the esteros (canals). Cory's advisors estimated that 38 of the 95 kilometers of waterways in Metro Manila were clogged and poisoned by waste. As the president warned, disease and death feed on such squalor. As a result, the infant mortality rate in the Philippines was 48 deaths per thousand[21] and 7 out of every 1,000 Filipinos had tuberculosis (that was roughly 380,000 people). In the developed nations the disease had been almost eliminated.[22]

President Aquino was aware of the impoverished and desperate condition of her people. "Poverty," Cory said at that time, "being a widespread and long-term problem, its eradication will require long-term solutions. But the sufferings that poverty inflicts—malnutrition, disease, pain, particularly on children—are always immediate, even as the wounds it leaves behind become permanent afflictions: mental retardation, weakness and an abiding mistrust for the order of things."[23]

Regularly during her short three years in office, Cory had spoken on behalf of the poor and struggled to create and fund programs that would alleviate their suffering. Still, there was a growing number of critics who suspected that the president and her cabinet were dragging their feet.

Sister Christine Tan

One of Cory's newest critics was her friend, Sister Christine Tan. Tan, who left the comforts of her wealthy Filipino family to serve the poor in Manila, had supported the president during the People Power revolution. Cory had appointed Tan as a delegate to the Constitutional Convention. The two women had shared a common hope for their nation, especially to end poverty and to decrease the suffering of the poor. But as the months and then the years of President Aquino's administration passed by without much accomplished, Christine Tan began to lose hope that Cory could or would do anything substantial to help the poor.

Sister Tan lives in the Leveriza area of Malate, a barrio of Manila not far from Cory's official residence. Tan and a handful of nuns from the Order of the Good Shepherd lived in a slum area housing at least 25,000 people. She and her sisters lived as their people lived, in a small house of wood and tin cramped together with thousands of little houses made of wood and tin.

No one knew better than Christine Tan the dark and desperate side of Cory's story. After eighty-eight years of America's presence and after three years of President Aquino's government, the Philippines remains one of the poorest nations in the world. Of a total population now over 56 million, 30 million Filipinos live in absolute poverty without enough income to satisfy even the most basic needs.

Sister Tan illustrated the plight of the nation's poor with a very practical example.

"There was only one toilet in our neighborhood," she explained, "one toilet for more than 25,000 people." Then Tan and her sisters moved into their own little shack with a wood floor, rough plank walls and corrugated tin roof.

"Now we have 72 toilets for 25,000 people," Sister Tan said proudly, "which we built together. Any time we go to inspect one of our public toilets, it is spotless—even cleaner than the tourist hotels nearby. That's a cultural revolution," she explained, "not cleanliness, but tenacity and determination, sharing and responsibility.

"We are about four sisters," Christine Tan continued. "We live in a slum area with more than 25,000 people who have been living in these conditions for about ten years. Having nothing, they have to forage like animals. Our idea of living is to pray well and then to really help our people arrive at some kind of human dignity. Besides that, of course, we try to build ourselves towards true nationhood, not just being a good person. We have to build our own country. My order is the Good Shepherd. I'm the superior of my little group. I don't know if my superiors are happy with me, but they allow it.

"Cory and her government try to help the poor," Christine Tan went on. "But they do not try hard enough. Neither Cory nor her advisors were ever really hungry. Our people have no concept of 'the next meal.' They have never thought of storage or savings. Day after day they just struggle to survive. If you have never experienced that kind of hunger, it is difficult to understand the urgency of helping the poor."

It was difficult for Sister Tan to criticize Cory. They had been friends for a long time. But as Tan explained, the people of Leveriza were dying of hunger "while administration officials talk and promise but accomplish almost nothing."

"Since Cory was elected president," Christine Tan recalled, "I had been her loyal but sometimes critical friend. To tell the truth, I had almost given up on her. The poor seemed poorer every day and Cory's eloquent words began to have an empty ring about them."

Tan was about to give up altogether on Cory and her government, when the president asked Christine Tan to make a visit to the palace.

"I told Cory that it would be better for her to talk to the poor, to hear firsthand about the squatter's life," Sister Tan remembered. "And without hesitating, Cory agreed."

Sister Tan described that moment when she and five of her friends, representing all the poor of Leveriza, were escorted into the palace.

"Cory and members of her cabinet showed our people great respect. They treated them like visiting dignitaries," Tan recalled. "After a greeting, Cory asked those very poor people to talk about their lives in Leveriza."

Haltingly at first and then with growing confidence, a handful of the nation's poor began to describe what it meant to be hungry, homeless and sick without medical aid and to be victims without justice or protection.

"They were eloquent," Sister Tan recalled, "and the president and her advisors listened, really listened to what they were saying. Cory was even taking notes."

When Christine Tan said good-bye to Cory that day, the sister realized two things.

"First, my old friend, Cory, is still the same humble person that she was before EDSA. She still pays attention to what's happening within her, and second, Cory seems to be doing the best she can. When we parted, Cory said to me, 'Let us always be friends, but go on criticizing.'"

Cory's Critics

In spite of the criticisms leveled against President Aquino and her government, every public poll proved that the people still liked and trusted Cory. Few doubted her integrity or her motives. But three different complaints against her were being heard with growing regularity: the president was "too inexperienced" to administer such a vast bureaucracy; she was "too weak" to deal with the graft and corruption in government and in business, with the military or the insurgents; and she sought advice "from the wrong people."

"Cory told us she was just a housewife," one wag remembered. "We should have believed her."

"She was never even a stewardess," a taxi driver explained, "and we asked her to fly the 747."

The State of the Nation

On July 25 Cory stood before a joint session of the Philippine Congress to deliver her third State of the Nation address. Accustomed to rave reviews, this time Cory's speech met with some skepticism and even disbelief. As could be expected, pro-Cory congressional leaders called the address "upbeat, realistic and inspiring." Her critics called Cory's address "misleading and self-contradictory."

There was "upbeat" and "inspiring" news about "democracy and the economy." Cory's government had survived the serious August 28 coup. The Constitution and the Congress were in place. National elections had been held as promised. Democracy was working "despite the difficulties." And the economy seemed to be recovering.

After a 5.7 percent growth of the GNP in 1987, during the first quarter of 1988 the GNP had risen to 7.6 percent. Unemployment had dropped from 11.1 percent in 1986 to 9.5 percent in 1987. Some 1.6 million jobs had been created in 1987, over 1 million of them by the private sector.

There were "realistic" words of warning about the nation's debt. "Our external debt burden must be drastically reduced," Cory warned. "We cannot indefinitely give more than 40 percent of the budget for total debt service." She found the estimated $12 billion in debt payments over the next five years "intolerable for a country whose basic needs are as acute as ours."

But to her critics much of the president's speech seemed "misleading" and "self-contradictory." Cory announced that "This may be remembered as the year the insurgency was broken." She listed the military accomplishments against the NPA, including the capture of 5 members of the CPP central committee, 8 regional leaders, 19 staff officers and 397 NPA regular soldiers. "7,000 regulars and tens of thousands of mass activists had surrendered . . . and another 2,000 had been killed in battle . . . ."

But even as Cory addressed the nation, intelligence reports were leaked with a different kind of score card. According to a top-secret quarterly review by the AFP, government forces had won just one of the 14 major battles with the NPA that year. The rightwing vigilante groups organized to protect people from the insurgents had become an equal menace. And vigilantes and guerrillas alike seemed to have no end of cash for the purchase of weapons and supplies, including surface-to-air missiles, a serious concern to Defense Secretary Fidel Ramos.

The reputation of the military had undergone another trial when nine members of the Armed Forces of the Philippines, including the still-at-large rebel Gringo Honasan, had been charged with the assassination of trade union leader Rolando Olalia. Again, critics wondered if they could trust the armed forces to defeat the insurgents, let alone control their own renegade forces.

In her State of the Nation speech, Cory called for the disbanding of the vigilante groups that had formed to assist the army in protecting the civilian populations and for new unarmed Civilian Volunteer Organizations to help secure the towns and villages.

One critic replied, "Weren't the old vigilante groups also supposed to be unarmed and trained? The change of title hardly attacks the root problems, namely the numerous grave offenses against life that have been inflicted by these illegally armed and undisciplined groups."[24]

The Bishops' conference of the Philippines had just suggested that since the military option wasn't working the president should call for another round of negotiations with the insurgents, but Cory rejected their suggestion, restating her position: "Until the NPA and their friends comes to trust their doctrines to the ballot box rather than the *armalite* [machine gun], government has no choice except to defend our people with the gun."

On one issue, no one seemed to fault the president. In her address she reminded them that history would judge the government's achievements "by our success in making a better future for all Filipinos. It is in the fields and barrios, in the slums of our cities, that we will ultimately be judged . . . . That agenda," she announced, "is straightforward: education, jobs, alleviation of poverty and an economy that can sustain these goals."[25]

During the wet, humid months of summer, criticism mounted against the president and her government. Cory was blamed for everything: graft, corruption, the failure of the presidential commission to retrieve the Marcos billions, the ongoing war against the insurgents, the apparent growing wealth and power of certain members of her family, the long, slow negotiations over the American bases. Even the garbage piling up in the streets of Manila seemed to be Cory's fault.

The Anniversary of Ninoy's Assassination

On the fifth anniversary of her husband's death, 21 August 1988, the president spoke at a memorial mass at the Santo Domingo Church. She stood where Ninoy's body was viewed just after his assassination. For that one moment, her critics were silent. Even they must have realized the price that Ninoy's widow was paying to be their president. She hadn't asked for the job. She hadn't wanted it. And now, as Ninoy had predicted, the person who succeeded Marcos was caught up in the throes of a terrible if not impossible task.

Cory paused, took a deep breath and then began to share a story that revealed much about the source of Ninoy's strength and her own, as well.

"On this day," she said, "I wish to honor not just my husband, Ninoy, but his beloved friend who showed him the way."

Cory described this mysterious friend as someone Ninoy "knew from childhood." Unfortunately, distance had grown between Ninoy and his friend "with every increase of Ninoy's fame, power and responsibility." It was during Ninoy's imprisonment that "their friendship began to flower."

Cory told how Ninoy's friend had been "a regular visitor to Ninoy's lonely cell." She explained how "neither guards nor high walls could keep him out, once Ninoy had let him in." "That friend," Cory said quietly, "came day after day, night after night, more faithful than any other."

When Ninoy's captors, seeking to break his defiance, threw him into a box, "unknown to them, his friend had slipped in with him. And there, in the utmost solitude and utter darkness of despair, Ninoy saw more vividly than in the full light of his days of freedom the true face of his friend and Savior."

"'He stood me face to face with myself,' Ninoy later wrote, 'and forced me to look at my emptiness and nothingness, and then helped me to discover Him who has never really left my side: but because pride shielded my eyes, and lust for earthly and temporal power, honor and joys drugged my mind, I failed to notice Him.'

"In that moment of recognition," Cory reminded them, "friendship turned to the love that never left Ninoy. Together they embarked upon that long journey which ended on this day of the week, five years ago. He would face even more dangers and difficulties, and suffering," she said, "but this time Ninoy had strength beyond his own. He was not alone!"

"Ninoy liked to quote St. Paul's letter to the Corinthians," Cory recalled, "to describe his new self-assurance: 'For the sake of Christ, I am content with weakness, insults, hardships, persecutions and calamities, for when I am weak, then I am strong.'"

Later in her speech that day, Cory said:

. . . when a bullet strikes you in the back of the head, the tendency is for the head to jerk back. So, the last thing that Ninoy saw, before his face slammed on the tarmac and the blood began to form in a pool around his head, was the sky, and the face of his Friend who had come to take him home.

I know his Friend watches now over every Filipino awaiting the moment of recognition on his or her part of the larger duties to God, country and fellowman that will finally rescue us from the prison of greed and ambition.

I am certain He walks in our hills and hinterlands, offering love and faith to the rebels, so that one day the destructive courage of their wrong convictions may turn into the constructive energy and commitment without which we cannot restore this nation.

He walks with the poor and meek, seeking to comfort their spirits and give them the strength to stand for their rights and struggle on to the life of abundance on this earth that is meant to be their inheritance.

He marches with our soldiers, giving them courage in the fight and faith in their cause, assuring victory and protection to the righteous, merciful and just.

He walks with our wealthy and powerful, seeking to temper pride with humility, lest it presage their fall, and riches with generosity; and to instill a sense of responsibility for the country and people that create their wealth.

Our unity is being tested by those who seek to further reduce it, who seek to undo the progress we have painfully made, and set this nation back again upon the downward course from which you and I had rescued it.

Every step we have taken toward progress has been challenged, particularly at this time of the year, by those determined to see this nation fail of its destiny.

You and I shall not let it. We will take this nation as far toward recovery and progress as God, duty and the people's support will let me. I shall not relent. I shall not rest, for there are too many miles to go to even think of sleeping. Nothing and no one will deflect me from this task. For my mandate is with this nation; not with its enemies. My covenant is with the Constitution. Our contract is with God. Our pledge was to Ninoy.

After her brief remarks, Cory and her daughter, Kris, were driven to the Ninoy Aquino International Airport. No one knew that she was coming. When she appeared, crowds of photographers anxious to get in range jostled with her security guards. The president struggled through the crowd to stand before the marble marker announcing her husband's assassination. She spoke a few quiet words, bowed her head in prayer and then hurried toward her van.

On the completion of President Aquino's 1,000 days in office, she delivered her own report card to the nation.

"Judgment will be rendered on me," Cory began, "and on how well or badly the government has done. But equally, judgment must be rendered on the rest of us who pledged with me to serve our country . . . ."

Then Cory proceeded to list the accomplishments of her brief administration. They included the return of democracy to the Philippines along with a new Constitution, a new Congress and free elections. Cory reported that 39 civil cases had been filed against Marcos and 314 of his cronies to regain the nation's stolen treasury.

The president reviewed her attempts to create a lasting peace and blamed the insurgents and the military rebels for "all but destroying the faith and confidence of a world in our country, and in undoing a great deal of what had been achieved from early reforms."

President Aquino listed proof "of the strength of the economy." More than $8 billion dollars had been paid to foreign creditors in interest and principal against the national debt. In spite of "uncertainty and hardship" Cory had pushed ahead with reforms in agriculture and public works. More than 100,000 families had received land grants. The government had built 4,411 kilometers of new roads, 896 ports, 35,028 wells. More than 75,000 hectares of land had been irrigated with 15,352 kilometers of access roads. Nearly 19,000 hectares of mountain watershed had been reforested.

The president announced that the quality of the nation's life had been raised. Some 175,000 new jobs had been created. The average Filipino's income had been increased by 25 percent. More than 53,000 new classrooms had been constructed. Some 9,000,000 children under the age of one had been immunized. The inflation rate had been drastically lowered while the gross national product increased from a negative 4 percent in 1986 to a positive 6.8 percent in 1988.

Cory announced her goals: an annual growth rate of 6.5 percent; one million new jobs a year; adequate international reserves; reducing poverty incidence to 45 percent of Filipino families.

"I look back on the past 1,000 days," she said, "and see much that we Filipinos can be proud of. I see also, in hindsight, how much more might have been accomplished without the struggle for mastery that followed the Revolution.

"Aside from God," the president concluded, "my greatest trust is in the people who never failed me and brought us through the many trials of the past 1,000 days.

"God gave us the gift of freedom," Cory exclaimed, "the rest we must work for—keeping our freedom and making progress in the economy . . . ."

President Aquino's speech evaluating "The First 1,000 Days," was greeted by mixed reviews. Few praised the president. Many criticized her angrily. At the same time an Ateneo University poll revealed that Cory's popularity with the people had reached a high of 70 percent.

After delivering her 24-page speech to the nation, Cory walked across the palace grounds to her office in the Guest House. A small crowd of people watched from behind a yellow rope. Someone on the edge of the crowd shouted, "Thank you, Cory." The president paused, turned and waved to the young Filipino who had spoken. For all that Cory had suffered, for all that she had done, they were words she seldom heard.

EPILOGUE
"Goodbye, My Friend, Chino . . ."
(1,000 Days)

I am determined to make a success of this government. I am not
doing it for Cory Aquino but for the people who are hoping and
praying. I am doing it for democracy. If I fail, it might be said that
democracy itself does not have a chance to survive here.

President Corazon C. Aquino

Everywhere, a greater joy is preceded by a greater suffering . . . .

Senator Benigno Aquino, Jr.

President Aquino welcomed her old friend, Joaquin "Chino"
Roces to the Hall of Heroes in Malacañang. A military honor guard
snapped to attention. Members of the press stood nearby. An impressive sampling of the nation's leaders were assembled at a luncheon in the presidential palace to honor this distinguished
publisher and faithful public servant. Cory's special guests stood to
their feet applauding enthusiastically as the old man took his place
on the dais before them.

Chino Roces was being honored for a lifetime of service to the
Philippines, but he was also receiving a token of the president's gratitude for his long-term friendship with the Aquino family. Don Chino
had been godfather to the political careers of both Ninoy and Cory
Aquino. It was publisher Roces who hired a teenaged Ninoy Aquino
to be a copy boy and then war correspondent. It was Roces who
convinced Cory to run for the presidency and Roces who organized
the "Cory Aquino for President" campaign and then secured one
million signatures to support her candidacy.

As he sat before the luncheon guests, it was obvious to everyone
that Chino Roces was facing death. During the last few months it

had become apparent that Roces would lose his painful battle against cancer. For that reason, President Aquino wanted to eulogize her friend and benefactor before he died. This was to be a happy occasion. Excitement charged the air as Cory awarded her friend the Legion of Honor for his service to the Philippines. After speaking eloquent words praising Roces, Cory Aquino stepped away from the microphone so that the honoree could make his short acceptance speech. In the embarrassing moments that followed, Roces shocked everyone with his stinging rebuke of Cory and her administration.

The distinguished publisher and public servant spoke quietly, looking directly at the president and members of her cabinet. He minced no words in telling Cory that her government had come to be characterized by "self-aggrandizement and service to vested interests, relatives and friends." He warned her that "We cannot afford a government of thieves unless we can tolerate a nation of highwaymen."

Roces went on to scold the administration for failing to live up to its promises of a "new moral order" after EDSA. Speaking of the promise of the People Power Revolution, Chino prophesied that "the great expectations we raised in them [the people] will be the measure of their scorn and retribution.

"The work is not finished," he said. "All people with power and influence must heed the warning . . . . If we fail the people, we, the friends of democracy, shall have a worse time of it than the clear enemies of the people."

After the ceremony, Cory remained silent about Roces's rebuke. His words had hurt her deeply. And following Roces's example, the media and opposition political forces published long and serious lists of their own complaints against Cory and her government.

Various columnists condemned the new military bases agreement that Cory's foreign minister, Raul Manglapus, was negotiating between Washington, D.C. and Manila. To allow America's nuclear strike force to continue its presence on Philippine soil was judged by her critics as a betrayal of the new Constitution and of the national sovereignty and safety of the Philippines.

Opposition politicians found evidence of "dictatorship" in the new political party that had formed to support Cory and her government and they judged her postponement of the barangay elections (because the insurgents threatened a peaceful poll) to be just another political ploy.

Friends and foes alike accused Cory of kowtowing to the military and of giving too much civilian power to former generals, especially to her Minister of Defense Fidel Ramos. They accused Cory's military and national police forces of human rights abuses comparable to the insurgents in their violence and frequency.

The Catholic human rights organization, Task Force Detainees, claimed that 11,300 Filipinos had been arrested or detained on national-security grounds (i.e., for political reasons) since Cory's inauguration in 1986. They claimed that "507 people were summarily executed, 149 abducted, and 159 killed in massacres during Cory's less than 1,000 days in office."[1]

In a University of the Philippines study released in August, Cory's administration was accused of having "a lack of political will and a failure to enforce regulations." The study found "a tendency to avoid confronting the issues and instead to blame the Marcos period for continuing irregularities."

The President's CARP land reform program was roundly criticized for its alleged failures as were the massive public works and population control program that Cory had promised.

The president was critiqued most harshly for not coming down harder on graft and corruption in the Philippines. The Philippine Chamber of Commerce and Industry estimated that 50 billion pesos, about $2.5 billion (or one third of the nation's budget) was being lost to corruption and inefficiency.

"Filipinos take for granted that payoffs and personal influence are parts of their lives," a reporter wrote, "in a society that is structured less around laws and institutions than friendships and family ties."

Cory had proven her own integrity. She had appointed men and women into office who were risking their lives to do an honest job. And though graft and corruption had plagued Philippine governments in the past, Cory was blamed for not eliminating it altogether during her two and one half years in office.

Members of the president's own government were being accused of corruption and inefficiency. Her Presidential Commission on Good Government, charged to find and recover what Ferdinand and Imelda had stolen, was being accused of "ineptness, incompetence and corruption" by Cory's solicitor general. Even Cardinal Sin had joined with those who were pressuring Cory to act more firmly against corruption and graft wherever she found it.

And though he couldn't find any evidence that Cory herself was corrupt, her old defense minister, Juan Ponce Enrile, made charges (largely unsubstantiated) about graft and corruption in Cory's family.

During those weeks following Chino Roces's attack on Cory and her government, a flurry of charges and countercharges rocked the country. But in spite of the flaws they uncovered in her administration, the critics found it difficult to fault their president's integrity or her deep personal faith in God.

Nevertheless, Cory had reestablished a democracy. After years of press censorship, journalists, columnists, editors, reporters, television newsmen and women, muckrakers and sensation seekers were free to ply their trade again. And during that long, hot summer and fall of 1988, it became painfully evident that the president's honeymoon with the press and opposition politicians was truly over.

Then, just weeks after chiding the administration for its failures, Chino Roces, 75, died of complications from his cancer. For months the nation's most famous publisher had been ill and failing, but his death still shocked and saddened the president and the nation. Roces had served as a kind of national conscience, asking the right questions just when they needed to be asked. The last question that Roces asked his family before he died was "Do you think our country will be all right?"[2]

On October 6, at least a thousand mourners carrying flags and yellow banners gathered at the Mount Carmel Church for Chino Roces's requiem mass and at the North Cemetery in Quezon City where they would bury him. Across the Philippines flags flew at half staff. Among the hundreds of floral arrangements displayed at the publisher's five-day wake were tributes from the president, from senators and congressmen, Supreme Court justices and cabinet members, and from such diverse sources as the communist National Democratic Front, the rightwing rebel colonel, Gringo Honasan, who was still at large, from Nur Misuari and the Moro National Liberation Front and even Ferdinand and Imelda Marcos, whom Roces had helped force from power.

The Requiem Mass for Chino Roces was being broadcast live on radio and television across the Philippines. The whole nation watched or listened as President Aquino began her eulogy for her old friend. It took serious courage for Cory to speak so openly and so honestly that day.

It was the first time that President Aquino had replied officially to Roces's stinging rebuke at the Legion of Honor award ceremony. "It hurt when he said it," she admitted, "but it had to be said and he was one with the moral authority to say it . . . I see now that it was his legacy to me and to us all."

And though Roces's "testy" remarks had "unleashed a wave of recriminations" Cory expressed her gratitude that there also followed a profitable time "of self-examination on the part of many."

The president remembered how Roces had paved the way for Ninoy's political career by assigning him to cover the Korean war. The publisher had made Ninoy "a national figure and smoothed his political ascent." Cory explained how Ninoy would always be conscious of Chino's help throughout his career, not as a debt to be repaid but as a great expectation on the old man's part that he could not disappoint.

"Don Chino believed," Cory affirmed, "that leadership by personal example . . . would pull this country back from the brink and set it on the right path again."

"Two years after the victory [at EDSA]," Cory continued, "Chino came back to remind us, especially me, that the work was not finished."

The president called on the people to heed Don Chino's call, "given the affection and the enormous debt we owe the old man for our freedom and for that piece of wisdom that he left us.

"Everyone whom the revolution has put in a position of power and influence whether in the public or private sector should heed his warning, for Chino was seldom wrong."

Cory ended her eulogy with a final farewell:

"Good-bye, my friend Chino," she said. "With God's help and with the help of the people I will not disappoint you."

The people present at that Requiem Mass were deeply moved by their president's honest, courageous words. Following her brief, poignant eulogy, Cory stood beside Chino Roces' widow at the front of the church. The president's eyes were closed. Her head was bowed in prayer.

Whatever her critics say about Cory, they know that there is no one at this moment in the nation's history who could replace her. Before his death, Ninoy warned that no one could clean up the mess that Marcos left in the Philippines. Cory is trying. "Where I succeed," she herself has said, "I will give God all the glory. And where I fail, I know I will have done my best."

NOTES

Introduction

1. For an intriguing eye-witness account of Ninoy's last hours, see "Aquino's Final Journey," by Ken Kashiwahara, *New York Times Magazine*, 16 October 1983, p. 41ff.
2. Ninoy Aquino, *Letters: Prison and Exile*, produced by the Aquino family in cooperation with the La Ignaciana Apostolic Center, Metro Manila, October, 1983, p. 8.
3. In letters from his prison cell, Senator Aquino himself called his spiritual experience in prison a "conversion." See *Letters: Prison and Exile*, p. 3.
4. Aquino, *Letters: Prison and Exile*, p. 7-8.
5. From an interview with Betty Go Belmonte at the Manila Hotel, 3 October 1988.
6. Aquino, Ninoy, *Letters: Prison and Exile*, p. 15
7. Charles Colson, *Kingdoms in Conflict* (Grand Rapids, MI: Zondervan Publishing, 1987), p. 315.
8. Ralph H. Elliot, "The Aquinos' Witness: 'Not by Might, nor Power,'" *The Christian Century*, 15 October 1986, p. 379.
9. Ibid.
10. Beth Spring, "Slain Philippine Leader Aquino Is a Christian Martyr, Says Colson," *Christianity Today*, 7 October 1983, p. 55.

Chapter 1

1. Teodoro A. Agoncillo, *A Short History of the Philippines* (Quezon City: National Book Store Press, 1975), p. 191.
2. Bananal, Eduardo, Op. Cit., p. 24.
3. Betty Go Belmonte, "President Cory's Early Years," *Fookien Times Philippines Yearbook, 1985–1986*, p. 31.
4. Belmonte, Ibid., p. 32.
5. Lucy Komisar, *Corazon Aquino: The Story of a Revolution* (New York: George Braziller, 1987), p. 13.
6. Nick Joaquin, *The Aquinos of Tarlac* (Manila: Cacho Hermanos, 1983), p. 157. I am especially grateful for the information offered by this biography of three Aquino generations.
7. Agoncillo, p. 232.
8. Ibid., p. 225.
9. Ibid., p. 229.

Chapter 2

1. Ninoy Aquino, *Letters: Prison and Exile*, p. 11.
2. Luzviminda Francisco, "The Philippine-American War," in *The Philippines Reader: A History of Colonialism, Neocolonialism, Dictatorship and Resistance*, Edited by Daniel B. Schirmer and Stephen Rosskamm Shalom, Ken Incorporated, 1987, pp. 16–19.
3. Nick Joaquin, p. 164.
4. Ibid., p. 179.
5. Ibid., pp. 181–182.
6. *Manila Chronicle*, 30 December 1947, p. 28, continued on p. 5.
7. Joaquin, Ibid.
8. Belmonte, p. 33.
9. Quoting a 1987 brochure describing the Notre Dame School and its curriculum.
10. Joaquin, p. 194.
11. Ibid., p. 196.
12. Alfonso P. Policarpio, Jr., *Ninoy: The Willing Martyr* (Manila: Isaiah Books, 1986), p. 33.
13. Joaquin, p. 210.
14. Joaquin, p. 216.
15. "Class '53 Reunion," *Philadelphia Daily Express*, 23 September 1986, p. 5.
16. Belmonte, p. 34.
17. Ibid.
18. Ibid.

Chapter 3

1. Joaquin, p. 250.
2. Go Belmonte, p. 34.
3. Neni Sta. Romana Cruz, "Life with Ninoy," *Ninoy Aquino: The Man, The Legend*, ed. Asuncion David Maramba (Manila: Cacho Hermanos, 1984), p. 56.
4. Joaquin, pp. 221–224.
5. Ibid., p. 229.
6. Ibid., p. 234.
7. Cruz, Ibid., p. 55.
8. Ibid.
9. Joaquin, p. 251.
10. Bell Trade Relations Act, cited by Teodoro Agoncillo, *A Short History of the Philippines* (Quezon City: National Book Store Press, 1985–1986), p. 254.
11. Joaquin, p. 240.
12. Agoncillo, p. 268.
13. Joaquin, p. 248.
14. Komisar, p. 15.

Chapter 4

1. Benedict Kerkvliet, *The Huk Rebellion: A Study of Peasant Revolt in the Philippines* (Quezon City: New Day Publishers, 1979), p. 239.
2. Corazon C. Aquino, "My Life with Ninoy," *Fookien Times Philippines Yearbook, 1985–1986*, p. 36.
3. Joaquin, p. 252.

4. Aquino, "My Life with Ninoy," pp. 36–37.
5. Joaquin, p. 256.
6. Ibid.
7. Ibid.
8. Alfonso P. Policarpio, *Ninoy: The Willing Martyr* (Quezon City: Isaiah Books, 1986), p. 52.
9. Policarpio, p. 52.
10. Joaquin, p. 258.
11. Aquino, "My Life with Ninoy," p. 37.
12. Joaquin, p. 258.
13. Aquino, "My Life with Ninoy," p. 37.
14. Joaquin, p. 260.
15. Joaquin, p. 261.
16. Joaquin, p. 276.
17. In an article by Joe Conason, staff writer for the *Village Voice*, reprinted in a booklet in the Malacañang Library, "President Corazon Aquino: As the Press Sees Her," p. 10.
18. Joaquin, pp. 278–279.
19. Aquino, "My Life with Ninoy," p. 37.
20. Ibid.
21. Joaquin, p. 293.

Chapter 5

1. Sterling Seagrave, The Marcos Dynasty (New York: Harper and Row, 1988), p. 205.
2. Benigno S. Aquino, Jr., "A Garrison State in the Make," a speech delivered in the Senate 5 February 1968 and published in *A Garrison State in the Make and Other Speeches* (Benigno S. Aquino, Jr. Foundation, 1985, Makati, Metro Manila), p. 11.
3. Seagrave, p. 205.
4. Raymond Bonner, *Waltzing with a Dictator* (New York: Times Books, 1988), p. 119.
5. Aquino, "Jabidah! Special Forces of Evil," *A Garrison State in the Make and other Speeches*, p. 43.
6. Aquino, "MrM—and Pilate, Too!" *A Garrison State . . . and Other Speeches*, p. 61.
7. Corazon Aquino, "My Life with Ninoy," *Fookien Times Philippines Yearbook, 1985–1986*, p. 37.
8. Ibid.
9. Aquino, "A Carrot and a Stick for Mr. Marcos," *A Garrison State . . . and Other Speeches*, p. 91.
10. Aquino, "The Bridge of San Juanico: Mr. Marcos's Folly," Ibid., p. 117.
11. Aquino, "The New Partnership, The New (Im)morality?" delivered in the Senate 8 August 1968, *A Garrison State . . . and Other Speeches*, p. 129.
12. Seagrave, p. 194
13. Aquino, "I Humbly Report," *A Garrison State . . . and Other Speeches*, pp. 211–212.
14. Seagrave, p. 190.
15. Raymond Bonner, Op.Cit., p. 72.
16. Ninoy Aquino, "A Pantheon for Imelda," delivered to the Senate, 10 February 1969, in *A Garrison State . . .*, pp. 215ff.

17. Ninoy Aquino, in Nick Joaquin's essay "Before the Blow: Ninoy's Senate Years," from *A Garrison State in the Make and Other Speeches*, Ibid., p. 366.
18. Bonner, Op.Cit., p. 76.
19. Ninoy Aquino, "Black Friday, January 30," a Senate speech in *A Garrison State in the Make and Other Speeches*, Ibid., p. 248.
20. *Philippine Free Press*, 8 July 1972, p. 46, quoted in Wurfel, David, *Filipino Politics*, Corneal University Press, 1988, p. 110.
21. Ninoy Aquino, "The (ln) Famous NBI Raid, or Marcos Power vs. Quintero," a Senate speech in *A Garrison State . . .* , p. 343.

Chapter 6

1. Aquino "Operation Sagittarius," delivered in the Senate, 13 September 1972, *A Garrison State . . . and Other Speeches*, p. 345ff.
2. Alfonso P. Policarpio, *Ninoy: The Willing Martyr* (Quezon City: Isaiah Books, 1986) p. 124.
3. Ibid.
4. Ibid., p. 126.
5. Ninoy Aquino, *Letters: Prison and Exile*, p. 2.
6. Ibid., pp. 7–8.
7. Aquino, "I Have Chosen to Follow My Conscience," a speech to the Military Commission No.2, 27 August 1973, Fort Bonifacio, in *Letters: Prison and Exile*, p. 21.
8. Policarpio, p. 134.
9. Bonner, pp. 230–231.
10. Bonner, p. 230.
11. Policarpio, p. 165.
12. Cory Aquino, in a speech at Mt. Saint Vincent College in Riverdale, New York, 21 September 1986, and in the videotape presentation of that event.

Chapter 7

1. Corazon Aquino, "My Life with Ninoy," p. 37.
2. Alfonso Policarpio, p. 169.
3. Quoted in *Ninoy Aquino: The Willing Martyr*, p. 169.
4. Quoted in *Ninoy Aquino: The Willing Martyr*, p. 173.
5. Policarpio, p. 171–172.
6. Interview with Ballsy Aquino in 1985–1986 *Fookien Times Philippines Yearbook*, p. 37b.
7. Cory Aquino, "My Life with Ninoy," p. 37.
8. Komisar, p. 47.
9. Cory Aquino, "My Life with Ninoy," p. 37.
10. Miguela Gonzalez Yap, *The Making of Cory* (Quezon City: New Day Publishers, 1987), p. 61.
11. Aquino, *Letters: Prison and Exile*, pp. 59–60.
12. Bonner, p. 311.
13. Aquino, *Letters: Prison and Exile*, pp. 48–53.
14. Ibid., p. 56.
15. Ralph H. Elliot, "The Aquino Witness: 'Not by Might, nor Power,'" *Christian Century*, 15 October 1986, p. 379.

16. Beth Spring, "Slain Philippine Leader Aquino is a Christian Martyr, Says Colson," *Christianity Today*, 7 October 1983, p. 55.
17. Cory Aquino, "My Life with Ninoy," p. 37.
18. Aquino, *Letters: Prison and Exile*, p. 53.
19. Cory Aquino, "My Life with Ninoy," p. 37.
20. Ibid.
21. Policarpio, p. 187.
22. Ibid.
23. Cory Aquino, "My Life with Ninoy," p. 37.
24. Policarpio, p. 188.
25. Ibid., p. 189.
26. Policarpio, p. 189.

Chapter 8

1. Nick Joaquin, "The Year of Mourning Ends for Cory Aquino," *Mr. & Ms. Magazine*, Manila, 17 August 1984.
2. Doña Aurora Aquino, in *People Power: An Eyewitness History, The Philippine Revolution of 1986*, ed. Monina Allarey Mercado (New York: Writers and Readers Publishing, Inc. in association with Tenth Avenue Editions, Inc., 1986), pp. 12–13.
3. Seagrave, *The Marcos Dynasty*, p. 386.
4. From Foreign Broadcast Information Service (FBIS), 24 August 1983, quoting RPN Television Network, August 23, in David Wurfel, *Filipino Politics: Development and Decay* (Ithica, New York: Cornell University Press, 1988), p. 276.
5. *People Power*, p. 14.
6. Ibid., p. 15.
7. Isabelo T. Crisostomo, *Cory: Profile of a President* (Quezon City: J. Kriz Publishing, 1986), p. 39, quoting from *The Manila Times*, 21 March 1986, p. 13.
8. Ibid., p. 34.
9. "Cory: Vox Populi, Vox Dei," Fookien Times Philippines Yearbook 1985–1986, p. 37h.
10. Crisostomo, p. 42.
11. Komisar, pp. 57–58.
12. See "The Complete Text: Reports of The Fact-Finding Board On The Assassination of Senator Benigno S. Aquino Jr," (Metro Manila: Mr. & Ms. Publishing Company, 1984). For a summary of the data see Crisostomo, *Profile of a President*, p. 109.
13. See Crisostomo, p. 133ff.
14. Komisar, p. 61.
15. Bonner, p. 390ff.
16. Crisostomo, p. 134.
17. Komisar, pp. 71–72.
18. Crisostomo, p. 119.

Chapter 9

1. Bonner, p. 397.
2. Ibid., p. 400.
3. Komisar, p. 79.
4. See Rolando E. Villacorte, *The Real Hero of Edsa*, an unpublished manuscript, p. 23.

5. In *Bayan Ko!*, by Project 28 Days, Kowloon, Hong Kong, 1986, p. 47.
6. Komisar, p. 85.
7. Ibid., pp. 90–91.
8. Villacorte, pp. 23–24.
9. Komisar, p. 90.
10. Cory Aquino, in a speech in Washington, D.C., 16 September 1986. See quotes in Villacorte, p. 1.
11. Komisar, p. 89.
12. Ibid., p. 70.
13. *Bayan Ko!*, p. 48.
14. Wurfel, p. 297.
15. Komisar, p. 88.
16. Wurfel, p. 299.
17. Seagrave, p. 404.
18. Crisostomo, p. 185.
19. Bonner, p. 430.
20. Ibid., p. 421.
21. Ibid.
22. Komisar, p. 98–99.
23. For a full text of the Bishops' letter dated 13 February 1986, see *People Power*, pp. 77–78. See also Felix Bautista, *Cardinal Sin and the Miracle of Asia* (Manila: Vera-Reyes, 1987), p. 175ff.
24. Crisostomo, p. 194.
25. Ibid., p. 195.
26. *Bayan Ko!*, p. 95.
27. Excerpt from Cory Aquino's speech in Washington, D.C., 16 September 1986.

Chapter 10

1. Cecilio T. Arillo, *Breakaway: The Inside Story of the Four-Day Revolution in the Philippines* (Quezon City: CTA Associates, 1986), p. 29.
2. Ibid. p. 56.
3. Darrell W. Johnson, *Jesus' Gospel of the Kingdom*, (Manila: the Union Church of Manila, 1986), p. 55.
4. Richard L. Schwenk, *Onward, Christians: Protestants in the Philippine Revolution* (Quezon City: New Day Publishers, 1986), p. 9–10.
5. Ibid., p. 13–14.
6. Ibid.
7. Doña Aurora Aquino, *People Power*.
8. Crisostomo, p. 226.
9. Arillo, p. 107–108.
10. Aquino, *People Power*, p. 236.
11. Ibid., p. 235.
12. Ibid., p. 245.
13. Darrell W. Johnson, Op.Cit., p. 55.

Chapter 11

1. *Time* Magazine, 10 March 1986, p. 16–20.
2. Ibid. p. 19.
3. Ibid.

4. "Welcome Home, My Soldiers," a speech by President Corazon Aquino. delivered 22 March 1986, at the commencement exercises of the Philippine Military Academy in Baguio, reprinted in *Fookien Times Philippines Yearbook, 1985–1986*, p. 27.

5. Ibid.

6. Miguela Gonzalez Yap, p. 200–201.

7. *Far Eastern Economic Review,* 10 April 1986, p. 36.

8. James Clad, "Power of the Pen," *Far Eastern Economic Review,* 3 April 1986, p. 12–13.

9. Komisar, p. 130.

10. *Manila Bulletin,* 20 April 1986, p. 1.

11. James Clad "A Stitch in Time," *Far Eastern Economic Review,* 8 May 1986, p. 12.

12. "Aquino, rebels hold dialogue," *Manila Bulletin,* 24 May 1986, p. 1.

13. "Aquino calls for people support," *Manila Bulletin,* 19 May 1986.

14. "Doña Aurora on Cory," *Manila Bulletin,* 20 June 1986.

15. Ibid.

16. Crisostomo, p. 262.

17. Jose Galang, "A room with a coup," *Far Eastern Economic Review,* 17 July 1986, p. 14.

18. "Aquino replies to critics," *Manila Bulletin,* 6 July 1986, p. 1.

19. "Cardinal Sin airs new call for reconciliation," *Manila Bulletin,* 22 August 1986.

20. President Corazon C. Aquino's speech at Sto. Domingo Church Mass, 21 August 1986, issued by the Malacañang Press Center.

21. "Aquino's address before US Congress," *Manila Bulletin,* 20 September 1986.

22. Nayan Chanda, "Cheers, aid and doubts," *Far Eastern Economic Review,* 2 October 1986, p. 14.

23. Yap, p. 211–213.

24. Komisar, p. 185.

25. Remarks of President Corazon Aquino before members of the constitutional commission during the presentation of the draft Constitution, Hall of Heroes, Malacañang, 15 October 1986, p. 2., issued by the Press Office, Malacañang.

26. James Clad, "Rumors in a hothouse," *Far Eastern Economic Review,* 20 November 1986, p. 16.

27. Departure statement of President Aquino, Manila International Airport, 10 November 1986.

28. James Clad, "A jolt of no confidence," *Far Eastern Economic Review,* 27 November 1986, p. 13.

29. Opening Statement, President Cory Aquino's press conference, 14 November 1986, p. 2, distributed by the Press Office, Malacañang.

30. Yap, p. 214.

31. Speech by President Corazon Aquino at the National Prayer Breakfast, Philippine Plaza Hotel, 11 December 1986.

32. President Aquino's Christmas Message, 25 December 1986, released by the Press Office, Malacañang.

33. "Bloody Thursday," *Maclean's,* 2 February 1987, p. 55.

34. Remarks of President Corazon C. Aquino on the Mendiola Bridge Incident, 22 January 1987, released by the Press Office, Malacañang.

35. "Can Aquino Take Charge?" *Newsweek,* 9 February 1987, p. 40.

36. Remarks of President Aquino on the aborted "coup," 27 January 1987, p. 1, issued by the Press Office, Malacañang.

37. Speech by President Corazon C. Aquino at the installation of Mrs. Josephine C. Reyes as president of the Far Eastern University, Philippine International Convention Center, 29 January 1987.
38. Speech by President Corazon Aquino at the Philippines Business Conference, Philippine Plaza Hotel, 29 November 1986, released by the Press Office, Malacañang.
39. James Clad, "Vote for stability," *Far Eastern Economic Review*, 12 February 1987, p. 10.
40. Speech by President Corazon C. Aquino at the Seminar on Troop Formation of Mid-Level Commanders, Camp Aguinaldo, Quezon City, 11 February 1987, released by the Press Office, Malacañang.
41. Yap, p. 127.
42. Remarks of President Corazon Aquino at Flag-raising Ceremony, Camp Aguinaldo, Quezon City, 25 February 1987, released by the Press Office, Malacañang.
43. "Cory leads prayer rally," *Manila Bulletin*, 8 February 1987.

Chapter 12

1. Speech of President Corazon C. Aquino at the 90th anniversary of the Armed Forces of the Philippines and the 1987 Philippine Military Academy graduating rites, Baguio City, 22 March 1987, released by the Press Office, Malacañang.
2. Speech of President Aquino at the testimonial luncheon tendered in her honor by the PMA Alumni Association, Inc., Baguio City, 22 March 1987, released by the Press Office, Malacañang.
3. James Clad, "The Soldiers of God," *Far Eastern Economic Review*, 12 March 1987, p. 30.
4. A Message from Cory Aquino, released 29 May 1987 by the Press Office, Malacañang.
5. James Clad, "Peace talk with Moros stalled," *Far Eastern Economic Review*, 7 May 1987, p. 28–29.
6. James Clad, "Taking poll positions," *Far Eastern Economic Review*, 2 April 1987, p. 28.
7. President Aquino's statement to a group of observers, 13 May 1987, released by Press Office, Malacañang.
8. Speech of President Corazon C. Aquino at the cornerstone-laying rites for the Our Lady of Peace Shrine, Epifanio De Los Santos, Ortigas Avenues, 31 May 1987, released by the Press Office, Malacañang.
9. "Constitution" speech by Cory Aquino, 18 February 1988, p. 2., released by Press Office, Malacañang.
10. "Cory's paper chase," *Far Eastern Economic Review*, 13 August 1987, p. 16.
11. Dorothy Friesen, *Critical Choices* (Grand Rapids: Zondervan, 1988) p. 31. Dorothy Friesen is founder and current director of SYNAPSES, a Chicago-based organization which links domestic and international issues of justice and spirituality. She was co-director of the Mennonite Central Committee service programs in the Philippines from 1977–1979. She has written a fascinating and disturbing account of Philippine society and the role of Christians in the revolution. She contends that the Aquino revolution did not deal with the substantive issues of military and land reform and international economic dependency—issues that are producing the present crisis in the Philippines.

12. "Agrarian Reform," President Corazon Aquino's speech remembering introduction of the CARP decree on its first anniversary, 22 July 1988, released by the Press Office, Malacañang.

13. Extemporaneous remarks of President Aquino during her induction into the international Women's Forum Hall of Fame, 6 August 1987, Hall of Heroes, released by the Press Office, Malacañang.

14. "A ghost of August past," *Far Eastern Review*, 3 September 1987, p. 36.

15. "The Coup that Failed," *Time* magazine, 7 September 1987, p. 25.

16. "When the Cheering Stopped," *Time* magazine, 4 September 1987, p. 40.

17. *Manila Bulletin*, 9 October 1987, p. 1.

18. Satellite Telecast, Sunday, 18 October 1987, 4:15 P.M., released by Press Office, Malacañang.

19. Deedee M. Siytangco, "Cory confides Christmas wishes," *Manila Bulletin*, 25 December 1987.

20. "Cory airs poll plea," *Manila Bulletin*, 30 December 1987.

Chapter 13

1. James Clad, "A people's levy," *Far Eastern Economic Review*, 11 February 1988, p. 34–35.

2. President Corazon C. Aquino, "National Security Situation," an address to governors and mayors, 4 March 1988, released by the Press Office, Malacañang.

3. James Clad, "Intensifying the struggle," *Far Eastern Economic Review*, 4 August 1988, p. 18.

4. "China Vows non-support of RP Reds," *Manila Bulletin*, 16 April 1988, p. 1.

5. President Aquino's Labor Day Address, 1 May 1988, released by the Press Office, Malacañang.

6. "Sin urges prayers for CARP," *Manila Bulletin*, 11 June 1988.

7. Statement of President Corazon C. Aquino on the Land Reform Council meeting, State Dining Room, Malacañang, 22 January 1988, released by the Press Office, Malacañang.

8. "Sin urges prayers for CARP," *Manila Bulletin*, 11 June 1988.

9. President Aquino's Vatican Speech, Malacañang Press Center, Press Release No. 3, 18 June 1988.

10. "Europe Visit Hailed by Rod L. Villa, Jr.," *Manila Bulletin*, 18 June 1988.

11. Ibid.

12. "Gimme Shelter!" *Manila Standard*, Thursday, 27 October 1988, p. 10ff.

13. Richard Vokey, "A Squatter's Life in Manila," *Newsweek* magazine, 26 September 1988, p. 18.

14. James Clad, "Procreation problems," *Far Eastern Economic Review*, 11 June 1987, p. 22.

15. Jamil Maidan Flores, "The Cresting Wave," *Philippine Panorama*, 25 September 1988, p. 24.

16. "Blessed is Cory, Wretched the Poor," editorial in *Philippines Dispatch*, 14–21 June 1988, p. 5.

17. "Why So Many Are Poor?" Op. Cit.

18. Sheila S. Coronel, "Child Labor: A Necessary Evil," *Focus*, A *Manila Chronicle* magazine, 23 October 1988, p. 13.

19. James Clad, "Poor Get Poorer," *Far Eastern Economic Review*, 18 August 1988.

20. *The Manila Chronicle*, Business Section, Sunday, 6 November 1988, p. 16.

21. Clad, "Poor Get Poorer," p. 34.

22. President Corazon Aquino, Anti-TB speech, 18 August 1987, released by the Press Office, Malacañang.
23. President Corazon Aquino's CEDP speech, 15 February 1988, released by the Press Office, Malacañang.
24. "Cory had nothing new to say," *Manila Bulletin*, United Nations: Institute on Church and Social Issues, 30 July 1988, p. 4.
25. Corazon C. Aquino, State of the Nation Address, 25 July 1988, released by the Press Office, Malacañang.

Epilogue

1. See Luis V. Teodoro "The Sound of Silence," *Manila Chronicle*, 21 November 1988.
2. *Manila Chronicle*, 6 October 1988.

BIBLIOGRAPHY

Special Resources

Joaquin, Nick, *The Aquinos of Tarlac: An Essay on History As Three Generations,* Metro Manila, Cacho Hermanos, 1983. (The primary source for Ninoy's early years and for the Aquino family history.)

Belmonte, Betty Go, Editor, *The Fookien Times Philippines Yearbook, 1985–86, & 1986–1987, & 1987–1988,* Metro Manila, Star Publishing. (The primary source for Cory's early years and for interviews with Cory and her family.)

Subject: Cory Aquino

Aquino, President Corazon C., *Democracy by the Ways of Democracy: Speeches of President Aquino during Her Official Visit to the U.S.A., September, 1986,* Manila, Presidential Press Office, Malacañang.

Aquino, President Corazon C., *Speeches of President Corazon C. Aquino, April–October, 1987,* Manila, Presidential Press Office, Malacañang.

Buss, Claude A., *Cory Aquino and the People of the Philippines,* Palo Alto, Stanford University, 1987.

Constantino, Renato, *The Aquino Watch,* Quezon City, Karrel, 1987.

Crisostomo, Isabelo T., *Cory: Profile of a President,* Quezon City, J. Kris Publishing, 1987.

Dauz, Florentino, *The Cory Alternative,* Manila, published by Dauz, 1986.

Komisar, Lucy, *Corazon Aquino: The History of a Revolution,* New York, Braziller, 1986.

Mamot, Patricio R., *The Aquino Administration's Baptism of Fire,* Quezon City, National Bookstore, 1987.

Munoz, Alfredo N., *The Philippine Dilemma: Exit Marcos, Enter Aquino,* Mooncrest Publishers, Los Angeles, 1986.

Yap, Miguela Gonzalez, *The Making of Cory,* Quezon City, New Day Publishers, 1987.

Subject: Ninoy Aquino

Aquino, Benigno "Ninoy" S. Aquino, Jr., *A Garrison State in the Make and Other Speeches,* Makati, Metro Manila, Benigno S. Aquino, Jr. Foundation, 1985.

Aquino, Ninoy, *Letters-Prison and Exile,* printed by the Aquino Family in cooperation with the La Ignacian Apolstolic Center, Manila, 1983.

Climaco, Gregorio, *Letters in Exile,* Manila, Leader's Press, 1986.

Colson, Charles, and Vaughn, Ellen Santilli, *Kingdoms in Conflict,* Grand Rapids-New York, Zondervan Publishing House and William Morrow, 1987.

Hill, Gerald N. and Kathleen Thompson, *Aquino Assassination: The True Story and Analysis of the Assassination of Philippine Senator Benigno S. Aquino, Jr.*, Hilltop Publishing Co., 1984.

Maramba, David Asuncion, *Ninoy Aquino: The Man, The Legend*, Mandaluyong, Metro Manila, Cacho Hermanos, Inc., 1984.

Policarpio, Alfonso P. Jr., *Ninoy: The Willing Martyr*, Quezon City, Isaiah Books, 1986.

————, *Reports Of the Fact Finding Board on the Assassination of Senator Benigno S. Aquino, Jr.*, Metro Manila, Mr. & Mrs. Publishing Co., 1984.

Subject: Ferdinand and Imelda Marcos

Bonner, Raymond, *Waltzing with a Dictator*, New York, New York Times Books, 1987.

Canoy, Reuben R., *The Counterfeit Revolution: The Philippines from Martial Law to the Aquino Assassination*, Quezon City, Philipino Editions, 1987.

Ellison, Katherine, *Imelda: The Steel Butterfly of the Philippines*, New York, McGraw-Hill Book Company, 1988.

Marcos, Ferdinand, *The Democratic Revolution in the Philippines*, New York, Prentice-Hall, 1979.

McDougald, Charles C., *The Marcos File*, San Francisco Publishers, 1987.

Pedrosa, Carmen Navarro, *The Rise and Fall of Imelda Marcos*, Manila, Bookmark, 1987.

Pomeroy, William J., *An American Made Tragedy: Neo-Colonialism and Dictatorship In The Philippines*, New York, International Publishers, 1974.

Rosca, Ninotchka, *Endgame: The Fall of Marcos*, New York, Franklin Watts, 1987.

Seagrave, Sterling, *The Marcos Dynasty*, New York, Harper and Row Publishers, 1988.

Subject: Jaime Cardinal Sin

Bautista, Felix B., *Cardinal Sin and the Miracle of Asia*, Manila, Vera-Reyes, 1987.

Villegas, Rev. Fr. Soc, *Who Is Cardinal Sin?*, (a book of essays on Jaime Cardinal Sin by his friends and co-workers), distributed by the Office of the Archbishop of Manila.

Subject: The Revolution

Arillo, Cecilio T., *Breakaway: The Inside Story of the Four Day Revolution in the Philippines*, Manila, CTA & Associates, 1986.

Baron, Cynthia and Suazo, Melba M., *Nine Letters: The Story of the 1986 Filipino Revolution*, Baron, 1986.

Benton, James, "The Snap Revolution" in *A Granta Special*, Cambridge, England, Granta Publications, 1986.

Bulosan, Carlos, *The Power of the People*, Quezon City, National Bookstore, 1986.

Byington, Kaa, *Bantay Nq Bayan: When Filipinos Staked Their Lives for the Ballot, Stories From The Namfrel Crusade: 1984–86*, Quezon City, Bookmark, 1988.

Carino, Feliciano, *Transformation of Church and Society: People Power*, Metro Manila, National Council of Churches in the Philippines, 1986.

Chapman, William, *Inside The Philippine Revolution: The New People's Army and Its Struggle for Power*, Quezon City, Ken Inc., 1986.

Elwood, Douglas J., *Toward a Theology of People Power: Reflections on the Philippine February Phenomenon*, New Day, 1988.

Forest, Jim and Nancy, *Four Days in February*, Marshall-Pickering, 1988.

Friesen, Dorothy, *Critical Choices: 17 Years with the Filipino People, A Background on the Revolution*, Grand Rapids, Eerdmans, 1988 (from typed manuscript before publication).

Johnson, Bryan, *The Four Days of Courage: The Untold Story of the People Who Brought Marcos Down*, The Free Press, 1987.

Johnson, Darrell W., *Jesus' Gospel of the Kingdom: Good News in Times of Turmoil* (Sermons Preached During A Revolution), Metro Manila, Union Church of Manila, 1986.

Maramba, Asuncion David, ed., *On The Scene: The Philippine Press Coverage of the 1986 Revolution*, Solar, 1987.

Martinez, Manuel F., *Aquino vs. Marcos: The Grand Collision*, 1986.

Mercado, Monina Allarey, *People Power: An Eyewitness History: The Philippine Revolution of 1986*, Writer's and Reader's Publishing, 1986.

Moyer, Robin, et al., *Bayan Ko: Images of the Philippine Revolt*, Project 28 Days, 1986.

San Juan, E., *Crisis In The Philippines: The Making of a Revolution*, Bergin and Garvey, 1986.

Schwenk, Richard L., *Onward, Christians: Protestants In The Philippine Revolution*, New Day, 1986.

Villote, Fr. Ruben J., *People Power: Church-State, Citizen Priest*, Syneraide, 1986.

Villacorte, Roland E., *The Real Hero of EDSA*, (Unpublished manuscript), written in 1988.

Subject: Philippine History and Government

Agoncillo, Teodoro, *A Short History of the Philippines*, New York, Mentor, 1975.

Aquino, Gaudencio V., *Philippine Legends*, Quezon City, National Bookstore, 1972.

Bananal, Eduardo, *Presidents of the Philippines*, Quezon City, National Bookstore, 1986.

Bello, Walden, et. al., *Development Debacle: The World Bank in the Philippines*, Institute for Food and Development Policy, San Francisco, 1982.

Beltran, Benigno P., *The Christology of the Inarticulate: An Inquiry into the Filipino Understanding of Jesus Christ*, Manila, Divine Word, 1987.

Canles, Mamerto, et. al., *Land, Poverty and Politics in the Philippines*, The Burning Bush, Claretians, 1898.

Halstead, Murat, *The Story of the Philippines, Our New Possession (The Eldorado Of the Orient)*, Our Possessions Publishing Co, 1898.

Kerkvliet, Benedict J., *The Huk Rebellion: A Study of the Peasant Revolt in the Philippines*, Metro Manila, New Day, 1979.

Power, John H., et. al., *The Philippines & Taiwan: Industrialization and Trade Policies*, London, Oxford Press, 1971.

Schirmer, Daniel B. et. al., *The Philippines Reader: A History of Colonialism, Neocolonialism, Dictatorship and Resistance*, Quezon City, Ken, Inc. 1987.

Shalom, Stephen Rosskamm, *The United States and the Philippines: A Study of Neocolonialism*, Quezon City, New Day, 1986.

Wurfel, David, *Filipino Politics: Development and Decay*, Ithica, Cornell University Press, 1988.

Subject: Travel in the Philippines

Chesnoff, Richard Z., (with introductions by Ferdinand Marcos and Imelda Marcos). *Philippines*, New York, Harry Abrams, 1980.

Hoefer, Hans Johannes, *Philippines*, Singapore, APA Productions, 1987.

Peters, Jens, *Philippines: A Travel Survival Kit*, Victoria, Australia, Lonely Planet, 1987 Edition.